18

The Wealth Code 2.0

The Wealth Code 2.0

HOW THE RICH STAY RICH IN GOOD TIMES AND BAD

Jason Vanclef

WILEY

John Wiley & Sons, Inc.

Cover image: Key, © Sarah Lee / iStockphoto, gold background,
© Gyro Photography/amanaimagesRF / Getty Images.
Cover design: Leiva-Sposato.

Published by John Wiley & Sons, Inc., Hoboken, New Jersey.
The first edition of The Wealth Code was published by Createspace in 2009.
Published simultaneously in Canada.

For general information on our other products and services or for technical
support, please contact our Customer Care Department within the United States at
(800) 762-2974, outside the United States at (317) 572-3993, or fax (317) 572-4002.

Wiley publishes in a variety of print and electronic formats and by print-on-
demand. Some material included with standard print versions of this book may
not be included in e-books or in print-on-demand. If this book refers to media
such as a CD or DVD that is not included in the version you purchased, you may
download this material at http://booksupport.wiley.com. For more information
about Wiley products, visit www.wiley.com.

ISBN 978-1-118-48336-7 (Hardcover); ISBN 978-1-118-48390-9 (ebk);
ISBN 978-1-118-48387-9 (ebk); ISBN 978-1-118-48381-7 (ebk)

Printed in the United States of America
10 9 8 7 6 5 4 3 2 1

For Tami, Grant, and Cole. You inspire me every minute of the day to be a better man.

Jason/Dad

Contents

Contents

Preface

A frog placed in a pot of boiling water will jump out and save itself. If that same frog is placed in the pot with cold water and heat is slowly applied, it will boil itself to death.

Running a wealth management firm in Los Angeles, California, I meet hundreds of people each year and discuss their finances. Nothing cuts more to the core than people and their money. With each passing year, as I see hard working people who have had their retirement goals shattered time and time again by the stock markets. I question, "Is the stock market just a big pot of water with the heat slowly being turned on?"

If this book was written in a year like 1999 or 2006, most people would disregard it. "The stock markets are great," they would say. "It has made us a lot of money." In spite of the terrible correction between 2000 and 2002, the sense that all was right was the prevailing belief. By 2006 most people were nowhere near the account value they had before the market crash, yet their faith in the market was unshakable. The heat was being applied to the pot of water, but most people stayed the course.

The timing of the first edition of *The Wealth Code*, mid 2009 and after the horrendous loss of wealth suffered with the stock market crash between 2007 and 2009, was no accident. I felt people needed to be shaken up before they could be open to a different viewpoint on building and protecting their nest eggs.

My goal was to educate investors on how using financial building blocks other than just stocks and bonds could provide the potential for more consistent returns and cash flow for their retirements. These other building blocks include investments such as Oil/Gas, Equipment Leases, Collateralized Notes, Real Estate, and many more. Financial ideas common to the super wealthy but generally not thought of as being accessible to the regular investor in a 401(k) plan or in their personal savings.

"Representing ideas of wealth, not Wall Street," has been a common saying to my clients for years now.

The objective of this second edition is to further expand the ideas, applying lessons learned in the last three years since the first edition was published, and more importantly to give people a new perspective and more control over their finances. After experiencing 12 years in the current bear market which began in 2000, most people are beginning to realize that maybe the water pot is not the best place for their money, and the revolt against staying the course has begun.

JASON VANCLEF
December 2012

Acknowledgments

A few people are directly responsible for making this book a reality. First, Nancy and Herve Vanclef, mom and dad, who had a huge impact on editing this book and smoothing out the rough edges. Your contributions and ideas sorted out my 2 A.M. feverish writings and made them coherent. You were the perfect sounding board to bounce ideas off. To my brother Cristian who from afar has always demonstrated to me that genius is often found in overlooked places. R.D. Hutchinson, Sr., my grandfather, who was the inspiration for my entire career as a financial advisor.

I also want to recognize Mark Trewitt for his contributions on the topic of discounted Roth IRA conversions. As a financial adviser you represent the epitome of excellence and I'm proud to work with you in our quest to improve people's retirements and lives.

Lastly, I want to thank all my clients who have constantly inspired me to grow and adapt in this ever-changing economic landscape. This book is dedicated to you.

For referrals to advisers who practice the concepts in The Wealth Code, go to www.TheWealthCode.com.

Introduction

If what you thought to be true turned out NOT to be true, when would you want to know?

Imagine you are on a gurney and they are wheeling you into surgery. You were out hiking in the woods, got caught in a freak snowstorm, and ended up with frostbite on your left big toe. In order to save your left foot, they have to amputate the left big toe.

Under the intense lights, as the anesthesiologist is about to knock you out, you happen to look over and see the instruction sheet to the surgeons for this operation. Much to your horror, someone has mistakenly written incorrect instructions. They read, "Amputate the RIGHT big toe."

The doctors are just about to knock you out. Would you agree you are at a juncture in your life?

What do you do? Do you scream bloody murder or rationalize to yourself, *No, these doctors are smart; they would never cut off the wrong toe. They know what they are doing.* Do you go to sleep hoping for the best?

Hopefully, you choose the option to scream bloody murder. If you choose hope for the best and wake up after surgery with your right toe gone, it will only add insult to injury, since they still have to amputate the left big toe.

To relate to this story, think back to March of 2000. Most people's stock market investments had gone up almost 20 percent per year for five years in a row, and they felt their financial advisors were geniuses. Then they noticed their statements in April 2000, and again in May and June. The money they had was disappearing. Instead of most people screaming bloody murder, they rationalized to themselves that their advisors were smart, that they knew what they were doing. Most people crossed their fingers, went to sleep, and hoped for the best.

To their shock, many people awoke in October of 2002 with their portfolios down 50–80 percent. Not only had the doctors amputated the right big toe, but they had taken the whole leg, both arms, and an ear.

Look what happened after the 2008 market crash. The previous five years of market gains were wiped out, and the markets collapsed to 1997 levels. Once again, we went to sleep and awoke to find numerous body parts amputated. At this pace, we might as well start looking into bionics.

Why is it when it comes to money we tend to throw common sense out the window with complex rationalizations? With simple axioms such as buy and hold, or dollar cost average, or don't worry about the long-term, your portfolio will come back, we second-guess what should be done. These sound good, unless you're already nearing retirement.

Here's another story about wishful thinking and hoping for a different outcome.

One sunny day you are driving to the beach when all of a sudden your car makes a loud clunk. As you slow down to see what has happened, you notice your car shifting between gears erratically, and you suspect your clutch has bought the farm. Good thing for you it is a Tuesday and you are playing hooky from work. The bad thing is now it will be spent at the auto mechanic's versus on a beautiful, warm beach.

After the mechanic gives you a quote for one thousand dollars to repair your clutch, with a long sigh and acceptance of your dilemma you decide to grab a sandwich and a movie as your car is being fixed. The day off from work isn't completely wasted.

A few hours later you pick up your car and begrudgingly pay the thousand dollars. You jump in and start to drive off. Lo and behold, your car is still shifting erratically and making the same loud clunking sound!

What is the first thing you do? You turn around immediately, clunk your way back to the mechanic, and demand that he fix it or give you back your money.

After taking your car back, the mechanic looks at it again and then advises you to keep driving it for a while. It will fix itself over time. What is your reaction to this advice? *"You're nuts! My car can't fix itself. If I keep driving around like this, the damage will get worse, and I'll be out of pocket even more money."* At this point, you fire the mechanic and take your clunky car to another mechanic who can fix the clutch.

How many of us are driving broken portfolios, nest eggs that seem to be going nowhere? When you go to your financial advisor, what do they tell you? *"Don't worry; you are buy and hold. Keep driving that broken portfolio, and it will fix itself."*

How many broken cars fix themselves? The same goes for money. Wall Street wants you to believe that stocks always go up. They want you to stay in their fee generating investments for many more years, hoping for your portfolio to fix itself. Sometimes, your portfolio does seem like it is on the mend. The clunking sound goes away for a while. For instance, many people who lost big between 2000 and 2002 made back a lot of their losses from 2003 to 2007. But, like the broken clutch that really couldn't fix itself, although the clunking sound might go away for a bit, a bigger problem was brewing under the hood; something much worse. . . .

As you were driving down the financial freeway in 2008 not only did your clutch freeze up again, but now the whole transmission fell out and snapped the rear axle to boot. That thousand-dollar clutch seems cheap now.

Continue this pattern of forgetfulness. Others who got clobbered in 2008 had their painful memories wiped away by the Federal Reserve's printing press rally between 2009 and so far through 2012. Like 2007, the current situation today feels like something much worse is brewing under the hood, yet many have forgotten the pain they felt in 2008. All is right with the stock market in their opinion, even though as of mid-2012 the S&P 500 is still 15 percent below its 2007 as well as 2000 peaks.

Money is an odd creature. Some people can spend all day preoccupied with it, others spend their days avoiding the very thought of it, and most of us are somewhere in between. It ruins relationships, creates green-eyed monsters, and generally frustrates most everyone who tries to deal with it. Strangely, some of the brightest and best educated can become completely inept when it comes to protecting and growing their wealth.

The eternal question is, "What is the best way to grow my wealth?" The answers you receive tend to reflect the viewpoint of the person giving the advice: a Wall Street hot shot, a real estate guru, a gold bug, a lotto winner, or an entrepreneur.

As with anything that is important to us, we try to hire people who are better at a specific job than we are. When I get sick, I see a doctor. When I want to redo my front yard, I hire a landscape architect. And, of course, when I want to grow my wealth, I hire a qualified financial advisor.

The problem with wealth of course is that there is no Holy Grail for protecting and growing it. If you ask 10 financial advisors how to protect and grow your nest egg, you will probably get 10 different answers. Although the answers will be different, there generally is a common thread. It usually revolves around using Wall Street as the key to increasing and protecting your wealth.

In writing this book, I hope to show that Wall Street isn't the only key player in a financial portfolio. Rather a single all-star player placed on a team of all stars from other teams, and when working together as an all-star team, these players have a much better chance of winning the trophy. In our case as investors, this all-star team of many different asset classes gives us a better shot at potentially reaching our financial goals.

Contrary to popular belief, most people who invest only with Wall Street see their wealth decline far more often than increase. How often do you read about people who invested in the markets for 30 years, only to watch half of it disappear right before retirement due to declining stock markets? These stories are far too numerous to count.

Most who are reading this book are thinking, "Hog wash. The stock market is great for building long-term wealth." Really? I challenge the reader to think about their money in the stock market. When carefully analyzed and totaled, did the majority of the investment balance come from market gains alone, or did the act of saving and adding hard earned dollars each year cause the principal to increase? The answer to this question is very important.

I put one prospective client to this test. He went to his adviser of 14 years, from 1998 to the present, mid 2012. We requested his statements from day one. The easy part was that he did not have any contributions or withdrawals during that time period, which made it simple to analyze the results. He only reinvested his dividends during that entire time.

To his shock, his starting balance was $367,000 and his ending balance, after 14 years with this brokerage firm—a household name—managing his money, was $366,715. A total loss of $285. The real loss is significantly more when you factor in inflation and loss of purchasing power. Even using the government's version of the consumer price index, which I explain in Chapter five as being artificially low, his money would have had to grow to $513,800 just to maintain the equivalent purchasing power it had in 1998.

To be able to buy the same groceries, gas, insurance, medical, education, and so forth as in 1998, he would have needed that extra $146,000 in his account. Needless to say, his adviser and the brokerage firm managing his money the entire time did far better for their pocketbook than for his.

Ask yourself this question. Is your financial portfolio better for your pocket or for your adviser's? The honest answer to this is worth addressing.

A *Key Wealth Code Concept* is something I feel is vital for your understanding of our approach to building a strong financial portfolio. You will see these concepts highlighted in their own text boxes.

KEY WEALTH CODE CONCEPT

For most people, the majority of their wealth comes from tangible investments which are not in the stock market. Such tangible investments include real estate holdings, a business built from the ground up, a product they created and sold, oil and gas royalties, and so on. More often than not, the money they have in the stock market is the excess from these other more lucrative endeavors.

The title of this book, *The Wealth Code 2.0: How the Rich Stay Rich in Good Times and Bad,* is meant to elicit different questions, such as:

- What is conventional thinking in terms of finance and investing, and how is it working against my wealth building process?
- Are there other financial ideas and strategies of which I am not aware?
- Is there a code for wealth, a map that we can follow to provide a more secure road to or in retirement?

I believe these questions will be answered in the following chapters.

CHAPTER 1

Freeing Your Estate from Conventional Thinking

Here's an example of conventional thinking. Talking head after talking head preaches that you make extra payments and pay off your mortgage early. You'll save tens of thousands of dollars in interest and will own your home outright sooner.

What are you doing by paying extra into the home? You are creating a situation that makes the mortgage holder salivate. Each time you pay extra, you place more money in their hands for them to invest for THEIR wellbeing, and you also lower THEIR risk. Let me repeat this. As you put more equity into the home, the mortgage gets smaller, and there is more equity protecting the lien holder in case you can't make your mortgage payment for whatever reason. Death, disability, and divorce are common unforeseen reasons. If their risk is decreasing, what is happening to your risk? It is going up! You have the most to lose if you can't pay your mortgage, and they take your home to auction and only cover what is owed to them, the mortgage balance. Auctions are not meant to protect the seller; they are meant to protect the lien holders.

I had a physician client who had not made a payment to the bank in 28 months on a $1.6M mortgage due to health issues that kept him from working. His monthly payment was around $9,000 and again, he stopped paying it twenty-eight months prior. The amazing thing was the lender, instead of sending him foreclosure notices, was sending him get well cards. The primary reason was his

1

house that was located in Beverly Hills California was currently only worth around $1.4M, and the lender knew they would take a significant loss if they tried to foreclose.

Conversely, I saw another situation where a senior was not able to make her mortgage payments, and like clockwork the foreclosure process in her case was painfully expedient. The reason, as you can probably ascertain, was she had lots of equity in her house. She had dutifully paid down the mortgage balance over 20 years, as conventional financial wisdom commonly suggests. Because her financial situation deteriorated and she couldn't keep up with the payments, she was forced to sell her house in a fire sale before the lender repossessed it.

An Unconventional Approach

Here is what I call unconventional or uncommon knowledge. Instead of paying extra equity into your home, make the exact same payment into a side investment account—something that can potentially earn 5 to 6 percent each year and compound on itself, and is fairly liquid. Even something with surrender charges will work. In the same time you would have paid off your house, the side investment account will have grown to equal your remaining mortgage balance—in actuality, faster. At that point, you can take your side account, pay off your mortgage all at one time and own your home outright. I'll explain ways to help earn the 5 to 6 percent in Chapter 6, but for now, assume you can achieve those results.

There are many advantages to this financial strategy.

First, you have an emergency reserve of immediate cash. Is equity in your home more liquid than a side account? No way. Unless you have a line of credit already established and it hasn't been taken away, like so many have been since 2009, then your equity in your home is stuck.

Without a pre-existing line of credit, you could apply for a line of credit, refinance your mortgage, or sell your home to unlock the equity to pay for your emergency. Today, all three choices are exceptionally difficult and time consuming. In an emergency, you usually do not have the luxury of time.

Second, by not paying down your mortgage, you will retain more mortgage interest to deduct on your tax returns, which will give you greater tax rebates from Uncle Sam. If you really want to be aggressive with your saving, take the rebate generated from the interest deduction and deposit it in your side account. There is a limit to mortgage interest that is deductible, but most homeowners are not affected by the limit.

In Summary

The point of this example is this: An idea might sound good on the surface, but only until you dive in and begin to analyze the logic behind it do you get the right answer, which can be very different or even the exact opposite. Conventional thinking in finance has caused a lot of pain and hardship for people, and often it has been promoted by the groups that have a vested interest in staying the course.

CHAPTER 2

The Best Portfolios Are Mixtures of Many Different Asset Classes

"The only guarantee in finance is something will go wrong." This is the **Wealth Code Golden Rule** and a statement I like to make to every client who joins my firm or comes in for financial education. I tend to repeat it time and time again to reinforce the concept that everything has risk and at some point something will not go as planned.

Take a certificate of deposit at your local bank. FDIC insured, correct? It's comforting to know you have that guarantee as long as you stay below the protection limits. The sad part, when looking at the assets of the FDIC, or really the lack thereof, is that the FDIC really boils down to being a front for the Federal Reserve which will essentially cover any losses that are FDIC protected in case your bank goes belly up.

In 2005 you probably felt pretty good about the 5 percent the banks were paying on the typical one-year certificate of deposit (CD). You might have looked at your income needs and calculated that at 5 percent you would be doing okay. The problem of course is when that one year term ended and the new rate dropped to 2 percent; now you were in a pickle and the income you counted on took a hit. The previous rate was not guaranteed forever. The drop in the CD rate from 5 percent to 2 percent in 2006 and even lower to 1 percent in 2009 and possibly even lower in the foreseeable future really put a damper on your income and financial well-being.

The other likely outcome of CDs is losing to inflation. There's only been one decade where CDs have outperformed inflation and that was in the 1980s. Oh, the days of neon and hairspray.

The Real Meaning of Portfolio Diversification

Knowing that the only guarantee in finance is that something will go wrong can be a very powerful tool to have in your financial tool chest. Most people will say they understand it, yet when I look at their portfolios, which are comprised of only one or two asset classes, I would beg to differ.

Take for instance the word *diversification*. You may have been told that if you have lots of stocks, bonds, and mutual funds, you are diversified. In actuality, your portfolio has a lot of only one asset class-equities.

KEY WEALTH CODE CONCEPT

There are many asset classes to invest in, and I believe the best portfolios are mixtures of many different asset classes.

Basketball is a great way to demonstrate the concept of a True Asset Class diversified portfolio.

Does it seem a bit unfair that in the Olympics the USA basketball team has the best players from the NBA all working together? By cherry picking the superstars from each team—knowing their statistics, their abilities, and track records—and crafting them together to make a super team, Team USA fields the most competitive team available.

I was watching a game between team USA and team Argentina in the 2012 Summer Olympics; the final score was 126 to 97. Pretty close compared to other matches that team USA had already played. I noticed during the game that players would substitute in and out. At one point Kobe Bryant, the superstar from the LA Lakers, took a five-minute break. Lo and behold, the score became more and more imbalanced, even though one of the greatest players in the NBA was not on the court. Why? Because LeBron James,

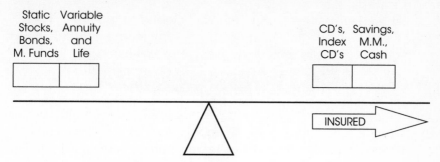

Figure 2.1   Typical Financial Portfolio

Kevin Durant, and others were still playing, and each was a superstar in his own right. I would argue that if Kobe Bryant had broken his leg in this game, LeBron and the rest of the guys still would have won and eventually still would have captured the gold medal.

If Kobe broke his leg during the regular season with the Lakers, it would have a devastating outcome for his team because Kobe is the all-star of his team. His team is not really diversified. But, on the Olympic team, he is one of many all-stars, and it would have been a minor setback for Team USA at best.

The difference in skill between the Lakers and the all-star Olympic team is the same as the difference between a portfolio that got crushed in 2008 and one that survived the storm and actually grew because of true diversification.

True diversification is the philosophy of a *Wealth Code* portfolio. It requires bringing many different asset classes together for the purpose of consistent wealth building.

Diversification is a word that means different things to different people. It is supposed to make people feel better about their investments and believe that they are doing the right thing. The problem is the viewpoint of the person promoting the idea. As previously discussed, most financial advisors view the world in two colors: stocks and bonds.

I will proceed to show you one prevalent view of diversification and then my own view. One common viewpoint of the financial world looks like the teeter-totter in Figure 2.1.

This example of diversification includes stocks, bonds, mutual funds, ETFs, variable annuities, and CDs, which I jokingly call Certificates of Depreciation or Disappointment. More on that later.

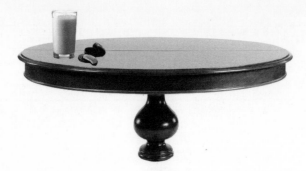

Figure 2.2   Undisturbed Table

Figure 2.3   Disturbed Table

If I were a carpenter and I had a business building one-legged dining room tables, it's easy to imagine that these tables would fall over due to instability at the slightest push, and my business wouldn't last very long (Figures 2.2 and 2.3). No one would be silly enough to buy a one-legged table because ultimately it would not do the job intended—provide a stable platform for eating.

Stocks, bonds, mutual funds, ETFs and variable annuities represent essentially one asset class, or one leg of a multi-leg financial table. The other legs are asset classes whose values are generally independent of the stock market. Examples include real estate, oil/gas programs, collateralized notes, equipment leases, rare coins, and fixed annuities. These are called non-market correlated investments.

KEY WEALTH CODE CONCEPT

The problem with Wall Street's single-leg viewpoint (Figure 2.4) is that no matter how many parts of this one leg you put together, you still have only one leg on your financial table. If that leg fails, your table will come crashing down.

Figure 2.4 Wall Street Single Leg Diversification

Wall Street can be compared to the carpenter building unstable one-legged tables, although this narrow approach is all that most groups offer the majority of investors. There are several reasons why the vast majority of investors invest all their hard-earned money in one-legged tables: It's all they know, it's all their advisors know, and these are the only opportunities offered as investments by most large firms holding their money.

In Summary

If you go to the grocery store very hungry and the store only has apples and oranges for sale, guess what? You are going to buy apples and oranges. You don't have any other choice since you choose to shop at a grocery store with limited options. That is Wall Street's version of "diversification," a one-legged table built of stocks, bonds, mutual funds, ETFs and variable annuities. Although variable annuities do represent another leg on the table, the foundation for variable annuities is still the stock market and thus is essentially the same leg.

CHAPTER

The Key to Protecting and Building Wealth in Good Times and Bad

We strive to build a quality portfolio for our clients using multiple investment ideas and offering a financial table with numerous legs. Just as the Olympic basketball team includes the best players from the NBA, we believe finding the consistent players in each asset class is imperative to long-term financial success.

Always remember **The Wealth Code Golden Rule:** that something will go wrong. Though in any given year one of the legs on a truly diversified financial table might fail, as long as you have many other legs on the table to provide support, you can better survive whatever financial storm comes your way. See Figure 3.1 and 3.2.

General Practitioner versus Specialist

Figure 3.3 shows all of the investments that are available on the planet. Everything can be grouped into these basic categories. Understanding every investment category is not the most important thing at this point. Understanding the concept of *The Wealth Code* from 20,000 feet is however, and I will keep it at that level for most of the book. A more complete discussion of each investment class is included in Appendix B for those whose curiosity is getting the better of them for any particular asset class.

When I published the first edition of this book, I had just turned 38. Some financial advisors would say I am too young to know anything.

Figure 3.1 **True Diversified Table**

Though fairly young and not having 20 years in the business, I knew one simple fact. I could never be the best at everything. There would always be somebody better. Knowing this provides clarity and vision.

If I can't be the best, who is?

Who has the track record, the years of experience, and the know-how to do the job they say they are going to do? What groups in each asset class have demonstrated that they are consistently the best or one of the best? These are the specialists whom I hire on behalf of my clients.

KEY WEALTH CODE CONCEPT

No particular financial adviser or firm can be the best at everything. If they say they can do it all with their own proprietary financial tools, RUN!

Figure 3.2 **True Diversified Table with Broken Leg**

Asset Class Diversification

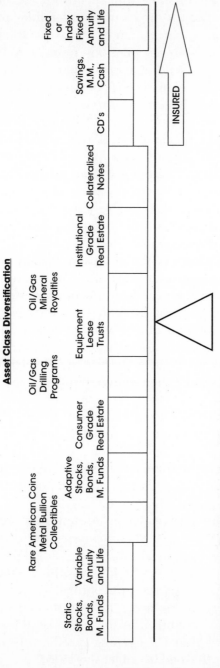

Figure 3.3   All Possible Investment Choices

13

My job as financial advisor is to be a general practitioner for my clients. I need to be someone who spends my time reading everything I can get my hands on, in many disciplines of finance. Not just stocks and bonds, but insurance, estate planning, income tax reduction, real estate, oil/gas, pensions, mortgages, rare coins, and so forth. Being well versed but always hungry for more. Never satisfied with what I have learned, but constantly trying to improve as well as question what I believe to be true.

Isn't that why the person with a BMW or Ford hires an experienced mechanic who specializes in BMWs or Fords? I don't believe any one person can call himself a financial advisor and try to be an expert at all these different asset categories. The stock picker, the real estate buyer, the developmental oil/gas driller, the coin collector: each requires considerable expertise. We choose to hire those who focus on one thing and one thing only, and we put them together as your Olympic team.

As an example, many of the groups we hire in the Institutional Grade Real Estate asset class have been in business longer than I've been alive. They have focused only on this asset class for their entire careers, and they don't deviate from their basic game plans. They are among the best of this asset class. Will they have down years? Absolutely. But they are persistent in their efforts to be successful and try to maintain a positive track record overall. The Lakers might not win all their games, but they consistently stick to their game plans.

We do not hire them to provide services for other legs of the financial table, as we don't hire a BMW mechanic to fix a Ford truck.

When looking for a financial advisor, ask them what legs of the financial table they work with, and more importantly will not work with, and why?

If they tell you a particular investment asset class is terrible, high risk, and will lose you all your money, ask them to give specific examples and experiences. No generalities. We find time and again that financial advisors who know nothing about a particular investment, or cannot represent a particular investment because their broker dealer (employer) forbids them from offering it, will automatically represent it as too high risk. Or they will claim that they are "conservative," meaning careful with the investments they recommend. "It's bad, terrible; stay away," they say. Then they promptly follow up with, "I have a great mutual fund, stock, bond, blah, blah, blah." Think about it. If someone were truly conservative in their approach, would they have allowed their clients to lose 30 to 40 percent or more of their wealth while holding stocks and bonds they have recommended?

In Summary

Up to this point, we have covered the concept of conventional thinking and how it is not always in your best interest, but possibly somebody else's. My view of most financial advisors is that most are very myopic in their ability to help people with their finances. Most do not promote the concept of true asset class diversification as a means to protect and grow an estate in the best and worst of times.

Chapter 4 introduces the concept of your wealth bucket and the process of building wealth. It covers why certain firms focus only on high net worth clients, as well as common *brokerisms*, a word I use to describe the excuses a financial advisor will use to never admit a mistake. Chapter 4 also discusses a simple secret of the wealthiest people in the world.

Chapter 5 describes the most common leaks in your wealth bucket, leaks from which countless dollars drain out of your pockets and into others' every year.

Chapter 6 delves much deeper into the concept of True Asset Class Diversification and gives a viewpoint on money as a financial table that even a third grader can grasp, yet few financial advisors ever will. This chapter also begins laying out a road map for making changes that will greatly improve the strength and stability of your financial table.

Chapter 7 explores fundamental concepts for the various legs on your table which need to be understood. They are like the glue that holds *The Wealth Code* table legs in place.

Chapter 8 describes a framework for you, the reader, to understand and craft a successful financial plan for yourself. You are not expected to be able to implement a complete financial plan on your own, considering most of the investments we'll introduce have to be purchased through a licensed financial advisor or broker, but nonetheless, you'll be able to put together the blueprint that will match your personal goals, and not the planner's pocket book. In this chapter, as well as Appendix A, there are case studies of hypothetical plans to fully immerse you in the *Wealth Code* methodology of portfolio design.

Chapter 9 includes a brief overview of my thoughts on where life insurance and annuities have a place in one's portfolio for both estate tax purposes and investment goals. It will also include the little secrets few insurance agents teach to prospective clients before they buy a particular type of annuity.

Appendix B covers all of the investment asset classes in detail, including the pros and cons of each one. There is no such thing as the perfect investment, something that returns double-digit growth every year, is guaranteed, and is completely liquid. All investments have their drawbacks. The idea is to find those investments whose pitfalls are not bad for your situation and to blend them together with many different financial tools to provide investment balance.

Not to be missed, Appendix C covers income tax reduction planning as one of the most successful and consistent investments you can make. My discussion revolves around converting an IRA to a Roth IRA at a fraction of the normal reportable income.

Appendix D covers the basics on real estate 1031 exchanges, which is a powerful tax advantage used by the super wealthy to transfer wealth from generation to generation.

I believe that, once finished with this book, you will have the tools to build a strong financial table for yourself and your family, and be better able to ride out the worst of any economic calamity that comes your way.

4

The Process of Wealth

Why do some people have a knack for making money? Part of the reason will always be that those people have some God-given talent, such as ambition and self-discipline. But for most who become wealthy, they have had great mentors and guides along the way. Why reinvent the wheel when you can get a head start from someone who has been there and done that?

The process of building wealth is the ability to accumulate and protect one's wealth. Understanding the fundamental steps will take you down the financial road toward your goals, versus causing you to take a detour. Basics such as consuming less than you produce and saving the difference is just one building block in a pyramid of concepts that serve to move you in the right direction.

I've always felt education is the most important block in one's foundation. The constant desire to improve your understanding of the world by reading what others have to say is crucial. More important than what you read on any given topic is just that you read. You are demonstrating this basic principle by reading this book. You might not agree with everything I say, but if you can pull out a few good ideas, then your time and money were worth it.

Clients always ask me for book recommendations, and I say if someone spent the time to write something and went through the effort to publish it, then there has to be a few good ideas in the book. Just read.

My goal in the following chapters is to define the process of building and preserving wealth as it relates to financial planning and investments in general. Too often, people get in a rut because they don't know what they don't know.

They are invested in mutual funds or exchange traded funds (ETFs) because that is all that has been presented to them or all that they know. They don't realize that there are many other opportunities that may be appropriate for their circumstances, which they should investigate and from which they could potentially prosper.

At my firm, education is priority number one. I am here to teach people who walk in the door as much or as little as they are willing to learn. I never charge for this service or request retainers. Education is always free. Why do I do this? I need to be paid, right? Of course, but from the client's perspective, most financial advisors work hurriedly to make the sale and then move on. Many people are disillusioned with the idea of working with a financial advisor because most have been burned by the process that Wall Street promotes: the quick sale.

An interesting question sums up most advisors out there. "Would you rather have Tiger Woods' golf clubs or Tiger Woods' golf swing?"

If I had his clubs and Tiger Woods had a three-foot long two-by-four piece of wood, Tiger Woods would still take my lunch money hands down.

It is his billion-dollar swing that wins all the money. A billion dollars is the Forbes estimate of what he has earned playing a game with a stick and a ball. Not too shabby.

When you see firms with high net worth minimums, it doesn't mean you are getting a better, more educated experience. It just means they don't want to waste time on small fries because they are more interested in selling golf clubs as fast as possible and moving on to the next prospect.

The critical part of financial planning should be education. You need to learn how to swing the club. In my opinion, groups that cloak their activities in secrecy and fast transaction times are the ones with the least to offer or are possibly scams, like the Madoff or Stanford Ponzi schemes—the "just trust us" attitude. Another fundamental block to building wealth should always be a healthy dose of skepticism.

I am not a follower of the cliché, "If it sounds too good to be true, it probably is," because many of the great investments out there do sound almost too good to be true. With a lot of due diligence and education, you realize they can indeed be good investments. They are just uncommon because few representatives are able to offer them. If you were to presume that few representatives offer them because they are bad investments, you would assume wrong. Many great, uncommon investments are highly conservative in their design and, with time, they may potentially generate great returns and tax benefits. They are uncommon because the commission schedule they pay to the representative is too low for most firms to want to offer them or the type of products they are do not fit the brokerage's business model of only stocks, bonds, mutual funds, and annuities.

Wealth Bucket 101

Let's begin with a visual concept we'll use for the rest of the book. I like to describe wealth using the metaphor of a large wooden bucket. It is a sturdy bucket with a good handle and steel ribbons encircling the tub. However, the bucket is made from wood and, because it is not indestructible, it is prone to springing leaks.

These leaks are the source of most of the frustration people experience with their money. The leaks occur because of higher taxes due to poor tax planning, excessive investment fees, insufficient estate planning and asset protection, and/or limited investment diversification and withdrawing too much money from a nest egg as currently designed.

Chapter 5 goes into great detail about the causes of leaks in one's wealth bucket.

In the introduction, we made it pretty clear that we believe in using many investment tools other than the stock market. Several leaks are directly related to Wall Street and the motivation to move money from our pockets into theirs.

Other leaks in the bucket are due to not understanding the process of building and preserving wealth. For instance, using cash to buy a liability represents a huge leak in the bucket. We are told to never have debt, to pay for everything with cash to be bulletproof. Yes, paying for everything with cash is stress free and a safe route to take. But it is not a very good route for building wealth, especially when purchasing an item that will depreciate over time.

An automobile is a perfect example of something that should not be paid for with cash.

Most people who have a large net worth realize the importance of using other people's money to add zeros to their bottom line.

What is a liability?

Anything you buy that takes money from your pocket.

A personal residence is a liability. Conventional thinking says a house is a great investment. Actually, it takes money out of your bucket every year for mortgage costs, property taxes, insurance, and repairs. The saying goes, better to buy than rent. Not necessarily. If you had bought a $584,000 median valued home in Los Angeles in 2006, that house as of 2009 would be worth about $319,000. In a mere two and a half years, the resale value would have dropped $265,000. Had you stayed in an apartment and paid rent of $2,500 per month, you would have spent only $75,000. In terms of net worth, you would be almost $190,000 ahead of the homebuyer.

Of course, there are numerous reasons to own your home, from personal enjoyment to pride of ownership, but financially speaking it is not always a black and white decision.

The opposite of a liability is, of course, an asset.

Assets are investments that put money in your pocket.

If people focused on using their wealth to buy assets, they would keep themselves out of a lot of financial trouble. Many who bought real estate between 2004 and 2007 bought a liability-type property, hoping it would appreciate. They now find themselves on the wrong side of a mortgage payment and upside down on the property. Buying for appreciation and not for positive cash flow has them in a financial bind.

Had they bought an asset property that generated positive cash flow each month, they wouldn't need to worry so much about the value of the property falling because they have time on their side. Worst case, they can buy time by collecting rent checks until the property eventually becomes more valuable.

Unlike the stock market, where time isn't necessarily the panacea for bad investments, we can agree that with enough time a property will eventually inflate upwards unless it has other really serious flaws.

Let's clarify that last thought on the difference between time with a stock and a piece of real estate.

If you pick a bad stock and that company goes under, you have nothing to show for your money other than a worthless stock certificate. If you make a bad investment in real estate, and are not forced to sell at any point, eventually the home price will appreciate above what you paid. It might take a long time but at least you have something real to hold on to. If you can collect some rents while you wait, even better.

Another example of a liability that people buy for cash is an automobile. We enjoy our cars, and we need them, unless we live in New York City or San Francisco, where there is great public transportation. At the end of the day, most cars lose value and end up costing money. They are a convenience, not an appreciating asset.

In summary, your wealth will grow as you buy investments that will appreciate over time and not depreciate. It is a key to the wealth-building process and to expanding your bucket of wealth.

Buy Assets to Pay For Liabilities!

Basically, how can I buy an asset that generates a positive cash flow to pay for a depreciating asset (a liability) that I desire?

For example, you see a beautiful Lexus in the window of a showroom. The cost is $50,000. This is your dream car, and you've got the money to pay for it in cash. Sounds like conventional thinking, doesn't it? But, you should ask yourself a question: "*Where can I put $50,000 to earn enough positive cash flow to make the monthly payments on a multi-year car purchase loan?*"

Applying the principle of using other people's money, you begin to search for multi-unit small apartment buildings around the country. You find an eight-unit building in a small city in Tennessee for $200,000, and after running the numbers, the net cash flow for this building with a $50,000 down payment is around $700 per month.

Sounds like a lot of work to buy your dream car, right? It is much easier to pull out the checkbook, whip out a check for $50,000, and sail down the road that afternoon with your hair flapping in the wind.

What have you accomplished with this quick purchase? As soon as you drove off the car lot, you lost $10,000 from your bucket of wealth due to depreciation on the car now being "Used." After a few years, the car might only be worth $25,000 from continued depreciation. Another $15,000 is lost from your bucket of wealth.

The person who spent time and effort to buy the little building in Tennessee now has $700 per month in cash flow from their eight-unit building to cover the car payment on a six-year loan for the Lexus.

The apartment rents probably won't cover all the expenses of the car for the first year or so, but the beauty of an apartment building is you can raise the rents year after year. Maybe by the third year, your net cash flow from the property is $1,000 per month, and you are now able to cover the expenses of the car, with some extra to pay for gas. By the time the six years are up and your Lexus is paid off, the little building you bought in Tennessee is likely worth the same as you paid for it, if not more, and you still have at least the $12,000 in positive cash flow from rent coming in each year. The value of the Lexus, on the other hand, is much lower than its original cost. Note the comparisons that follow.

Net result after six years:

Impulse buy of the Lexus with cash:

Car	Year 6 estimated value: $10,000
Cash Flow	Negative each year for gas, insurance, and repairs
Lost wealth from the bucket	At least the $50,000 purchase price

Buy the Asset (eight-unit apartment building) to pay for the liability (Lexus):

Car	Year 6 estimated value: $10,000
Cash flow	Positive by at least $12,000 per year
Wealth preserved	$50,000 down payment
Wealth gained	Potential Equity build up in property
Tax Benefits	Mortgage and depreciation deductions against income. More money in your pocket!

The added benefit of taking the road less traveled to purchase the dream car is that after the six years, you could use the positive cash flow received from the apartment building to buy another dream car and renew the hair flapping and smiles of the open road.

What does the person who bought the car outright have to show for it after six years? A beat up Lexus worth about $10,000 and lost wealth and opportunity, at the cost of tens of thousands of dollars.

So much for conventional thinking!

KEY WEALTH CODE CONCEPT

Do not pay cash for large value-depreciating liabilities such as automobiles.

Fortune 400 Secret

What do the four hundred wealthiest people in the world know about wealth building? That it doesn't come from the stock market. If you look at the composition of the Fortune 400, their wealth has come from tangible investments: real estate, oil/gas, timber, building a business, or the good old American non-tangible way: they inherited it. Only one guy on the list truly made it from the stock market: Warren Buffet.

Now, I know some would argue that there are a few hedge fund managers who made their money from the stock market, but I would counter that they made their money from the fees they charged their clients within the business of a hedge fund. Your response might be, well, of course, they had great returns in the stock market for their clients and received due compensation.

Hedge funds are the biggest rich person scam going. The allure is the exclusivity, almost country club feel, for investors with high account minimums, and the positive spin with which they promote performance fees. Performance fees are the fees paid for those returns a hedge fund makes over and above a common market benchmark. Typically, the hedge fund takes 20–25 percent of the excess profits. The nature of these fees is that they are measured quarterly, thus making them a sucker's bet for the client and the ultimate Vegas casino for the manager.

The manager is basically swinging for the fences each quarter, and if he or she hits it out of the park one time from sheer luck, the excess above the benchmark is usually enough for the manager to retire many lifetimes over. For example, between August and September 2006, Amaranth Advisors effectively lost 65 percent of their clients' money in one month, yet the lead manager for the fund had hit homeruns the previous quarters and made almost $100M for himself that year. Not bad for causing so much harm to his clients. Another example would be T. Boone Pickens, the famous oil/gas hedge fund manager. T. Boone made more than $1 billion of income in 2007 and lost 97 percent of his clients' money in 2008.

When a fund manager comes to our office to tout their excellent performance, I ask two simple questions:

- What is your 10-year average?
- How much leverage do you use?

The reason for the first question is history. Don't show me one, three, or even five years of performance. Show me at least 10 years. That way, I know they will have seen some bad years, and I can gauge their ability to protect the principal. The second question tells me the real returns of the group. For instance, if the answer to question one is 10 percent and question two is 3:1 leverage, all we need to do is divide the 10 percent by three to equal a real return minus leverage, or 3.33 percent. There are numerous other investments that can earn 3 percent without as much risk.

For the portion of money I do place in the stock market, I believe in using non-margin money managers. Money managers who trade without using leverage. Without the crutch of leverage in the good times, they really have to perform well. In the bad times, the benefit of not using leverage is more apparent. These accounts tend to have much lower volatility or price swings, and fewer of our clients are biting their nails down to the bone.

 COMMON SENSE CONCEPT

Less leverage equals less volatility in an investment.

Brokerisms

Part of the process of wealth building is understanding when you are hearing a lot of baloney, and more importantly, being realistic with your finances. Being able to make changes by addressing investments that are underperforming will serve you well. Wall Street is artful at changing perceptions to make their mistakes look like opportunities so that you will remain invested with them for as long as possible. You may have heard the running joke, "What do you call the advisor who keeps his clients in accounts, even though they have lost 20–50 percent? Vice President!"

Every year millions are spent on marketing campaigns using mumbo jumbo and celebrity voice-overs to grab your attention and grab your money. Part of the campaign is to change perceptions of reality. I'm sure most of you have heard the common brokerisms, or excuses, used to never admit a mistake and give them an opportunity to sell you something else.

"Don't worry, you're a long-term investor; you're buy and hold!"

If you had held stocks between 1881 and 1921 before you made any money, would 40 years count as long term? What about 1929 to 1954, or another famous bear market, 1965 to 1982? I take a very basic view of bear markets. If the stock market revisits a point on the journey, then the current sideway bear market started at the first point. For instance, in early March 2009, we touched levels on the S&P500 not seen since 1997. Thus, for most people, their money had gone sideways for 12 years.

Most would argue that the current bear market started in 2000. Again, I take a simple approach to money. If I had a hundred dollars in 1997, and in 2009 I still have only one hundred dollars, then my money hasn't grown one penny, and that is a bear market for me. There will always be scientific methodologies to identify when an official recession or bear market began, but again, for most people, they just care that their investments are worth more than in the past.

"It's cheaper at this price; we should dollar cost average!"

Imagine you are on the *Titanic* and you're sailing on the Atlantic at night. Suddenly, the ship rocks violently and lists to the starboard. You ask the captain what happened, and the captain answers, "*Don't be afraid; this is a strong ship. Instead of panicking and selling like other people, why don't you take advantage of the cheap prices for a cabin suite, spend more money on better accommodations, and ride it out?*"

Do you want to listen to that captain or to Captain B who says, "*I will admit that I don't know what has happened. To be safe, let's jump in a lifeboat, paddle a thousand yards away and watch from a distance. If the Titanic is okay and she starts to right herself and sail away, we will have to paddle hard to get back onboard, maybe spend some time and money, but at least we will know the ship is not going to sink.*"

Which captain would you rather listen to? I'd pick Captain B.

Dollar cost averaging is one of the biggest spin jobs on the planet. It's a way not to have to admit someone has made a mistake by keeping you in a stock as it goes down, but a way to turn the mistake into a positive and get you to buy more and even earn another commission.

You must ask your adviser, "If you are so sure the stock is cheap now, why didn't you know when it was more expensive and get me out?" Citigroup may have looked cheap when it hit fifteen dollars a share in October 2008, but if you ponied up more cash and doubled down—as in dollar cost averaging—you probably felt sick to your stomach when it dropped another 93 percent and hit $0.97 a mere five months later.

Successful traders have a general rule. Never throw good money after bad. Now I'm not implying everyone should be a stock trader, but if you are in a stock position and that position goes down 8 percent, I would suggest a move back to cash and re-evaluate. If you lose 8 percent, you have to make 8.7 percent to get back to even. If you lose 30 percent, you have to earn 42.9 percent. If you lose 50 percent, you have to earn 100 percent. If the old saying is true that the markets always average 10 percent, losing 8 percent means you'll wait less than a year to make it back. That sounds better than waiting four to ten years to make back losses.

Percentage Lost	Percentage Needed to Get Back to Even
10	11.2
20	25
30	42.9
40	67
50	100
60	150
70	234

Remember, you can always go back into a stock position. An analogy I use is the one about the forest and the trees. The idea is to pull back from the trees to see the forest, go to cash, and clear your head. Then if you see the forest is burning, you'll know to go and invest in fire extinguishers.

"Look how much money I made you last year!"

This one is great. When the markets go up, everyone thumps their chest to proclaim their brilliance. At the beginning of 2007, numerous clients came in declaring their advisors made them 10 percent in 2006 and were brilliant. My typical response was, *"How much did you pay them? And were they so brilliant as to underperform the S&P500 which averaged 15.86 percent?"*
The funny thing, in 2008, generally the opposite was heard.

"It's not my fault; everyone lost money in 2008!"

We hire mechanics to fix our cars and keep them running. If the car breaks and the mechanic can't or won't fix it, we fire him. How many people stay with their financial advisors as their losses mount and their net worth drops?

In Summary

Warren Buffet has two important rules:

Rule #1—Don't lose money

Rule #2—Don't forget Rule #1.
   - Consistency is far more important than hitting home runs. Lots of singles and doubles will always win more games than the occasional home run followed by 20 strikeouts.
   - Wealth building has always been about having time on your side and allowing the inflationary effects of our government's actions to increase your nest egg.
   - Buy assets to pay for liabilities.
   - Tangible assets can protect you in good times and bad, as long as you follow the simple "L" rules. Keep your debt low and long, keep your cash flow high, and keep a reasonable emergency account in the bank for the rainy days.

"L" Rules said another way:

Low Debt
Long-term Debt
Lots of positive cash flow
Lots of cash in the bank

Following these simple rules has put more millions in more millionaires' pockets than any other concept. We've all read about the guy who leveraged himself 100 percent, bet the farm, and won the lotto on an investment. Some people have come out smelling like a rose even though they took humongous risks, but the majority of us aren't so lucky. We will be burned far more often than we are willing to admit, and our story probably won't make the headlines.

CHAPTER

Leaks in the Bucket

Imagine you're in the desert. Your car has broken down, and you need to fill the radiator with water. Your family is getting hot sitting in the car but, fortunately, you see a gas station just a short walk away. You grab your handy bucket out of the trunk and head out to fill it with water.

After finding the water hose, you start to fill your bucket. Soon, you notice the water level in the bucket isn't rising, although the water is flowing into the bucket. You then notice that your toes are starting to squish inside your shoes and that there are several small leaks in your bucket and the water is draining out as fast as it is pouring in.

Everyone has a bucket that represents his or her financial net worth. Everything you own—your income, liabilities, taxes, and investments—makes up your financial bucket. The benefit of a leak-proof financial bucket is to hold and preserve your wealth and hopefully to allow it to expand and grow.

It is an important goal of any financial plan to plug potential leaks. But leaks happen, and leaks prevent the bucket from serving its purpose. These leaks vary in size, but the result is the same. They prevent you from filling up your financial bucket efficiently. You could have three financial quarts poured in while one quart is leaking out. Or in too many instances, people's financial buckets are more like three quarts in and four quarts out. Most people are going backward.

Common leaks in one's financial bucket are caused by a variety of factors including limited investment asset-class diversification and taking on the wrong types of risk; by inflation, hidden investment fees, and taxes; withdrawing too much income from a portfolio, and poor estate planning and asset protection. The biggest leak of all is usually the result of not following plain old common sense and letting emotion and irrationality overtake logic and reason.

These leaks threaten to drain your financial bucket over time, forcing you to either save more, work harder or for a longer period of time, or risk running out of money. All are choices that are never fun and make retirement planning more difficult.

Not Following Common Sense

"It is the obvious which is so difficult to see most of the time."

Isaac Asimov

"Common sense is not so common."

Voltaire

Almost all of the leaks in one's bucket can be attributed to a divergence from common sense. Cognitive dissonance can be a killer in financial portfolios. That is, being unwilling to keep an open mind in light of contrary evidence which suggests a better pathway or approach to investing. This stubbornness is the rust that creates the holes in your bucket.

A perfect example of this is when emotions are high, as they are during an extended stock market decline. Clients will come in and frequently state they need to sell some investments to raise cash. Granted, raising cash for something like a margin call is one thing, a forced need of immediate cash, but usually these clients want to sell because they are afraid everything is going down. Most of the investments I favor are not in the stock market and are generally not affected when the markets go down. That being said, the client usually wants the security of selling some winning positions to ease the pain of their losing positions.

This is a classic example of something I call "firing the wrong investment."

I clarify this concept to my clients using a simple story.

Imagine you are the owner of a construction site and you have two types of workers. Little skinny workers who sit around all day and stir up problems with gossip, and big strong workers who work from dawn to dusk and never complain about anything. You pay both types of workers the same amount.

If you are in a budget crunch, who are you going to fire first?

The lazy skinny workers, right?

That is common sense.

Yet, say you have a stock which is losing money and causing you heart palpitations. Selling your winning stock or investment to make yourself feel better is the same as firing the big strong worker when there's a budget crunch. Such action will only compound your problems on the construction site.

The same applies to one's investments. The losing positions are losing money for a reason, and keeping them while getting rid of winning ones is only going to cause bigger and bigger holes in your retirement bucket.

Getting rid of the losing positions and clearing your head are the right choices for preserving and reinforcing your wealth.

Limited Investment Diversification

Most financial programs, magazines, newspapers, blogs, and the like say that to be diversified you need many types of stocks, bonds, and mutual funds. Some even add annuities to the mix.

Most advisors offer only these asset classes due to their training, licensing, and limited exposure. Many follow plans that are very linear. A leads to B leads to C, and so on. Also, the majority of financial advisors were trained by the big wire houses and believe these investments are the only games in town. If you look in the yellow pages for financial advisors and brokerage firms, you will notice they are all basically the same.

My background is in science. My undergraduate degree is in Biochemistry, and it taught me to think in terms of how the body protects itself from harm, as well as how to look at problems from a different perspective. I think of it as cause and effect. What are the causes we are dealing with today, and what effects are most likely to result?

May I suggest a homework assignment? Ask your advisor a simple question. "What is going on today and how is my portfolio designed to withstand any problems on the horizon?" Sit back and critique the answer. If it is unresponsive or sounds similar to the sound bites you hear on CNBC, maybe it is time to find another advisor, one who spends more time reading about what's going on in the economy and the world as it relates to finance, and who would manage your portfolio accordingly. Financial advisers are paid for this very purpose, aren't they? They must have a deep knowledge of what is going on in finance today!

Here's an example of how the body protects itself and how we apply this cause and effect concept to finance. If a guy goes outside in only his boxers and falls asleep in a lawn chair on a sunny day, we know what will probably be the outcome. One, his neighbors will probably call the cops, and two, he'll have a painful sunburn. It won't make sitting on the cold concrete in jail very comfortable.

What has happened to him? He has damaged his skin all the way down to the DNA. The four base pairs of DNA are Adenine, Guanine, Cytosine, and Thymine. These are the building blocks of the DNA double helix. The problem with a sunburn, or more accurately UV exposure, is that it causes the Thymine base pairs to bond together forming what is called a T-T dimer. Long story short, parts that are not supposed to stick together are now sticking together.

The amazing thing about the body is that it has the means to repair itself. Little guys go in and fix the T-T dimer, unstick it so to speak, and we're back in business. If the little guys that go in to fix the problem don't do the job, our bodies have backup systems to make sure the problem is taken care of.

To relate to this story, there are no backup systems when most financial advisors believe that stocks, bonds, mutual funds, and annuities are the only investments a person needs. In 2008, it didn't matter what you owned; almost everything was drastically impacted in the second worst year in the history of the stock market.

Clients of all ages were coming in with every type of portfolio imaginable: all stocks, all mutual funds, all bonds, all variable annuities, and every mix in between. They all got hammered. A 92-year-old man came in to my office with a portfolio of muni-bond funds. "Well diversified and ultra conservative," his advisor had told him. The gentleman asked for my opinion. I told him, "*If you were well diversified, per your advisor, why then did your portfolio drop from $1,100,000 to $764,000? A drop of more than 30 percent.*" His answer, "*I'm not really diversified, am I?*"

Bonds are to Wall Street what CDs are to a bank—the conservative choice and the only choice they have to offer you.

The problem again is the point of view of the person defining something as conservative.

I was flying back to Los Angeles a few years back, and sitting next to me was a pilot returning home. She was not piloting this flight, mind you, just catching a ride home as a fellow passenger. Going from Las Vegas to Los Angeles, we flew over the desert on takeoff. The dry winds really create havoc for most planes, causing a lot of turbulence. I made an interesting observation. My knuckles were dead white, hers a nice mellow shade of pink. In fact, she was sipping a cup of tea, not even appearing to think twice about the rough turbulence we were experiencing. I said to her, *"No big deal, huh?"* Her response, *"A walk in the park. If it gets bad, I'll let you know."* Though somewhat comforting, I still had the feeling of pending doom.

Her definition of "turbulence" was very different from mine. I feel most financial advisors' definitions of risk are very different from the average investor's. Most advisors promote their version of conservative, which they say are bonds, variable annuities, or index mutual funds, and when the markets lose 40 percent and the bonds only lose 15 percent, then that is a conservative investment.

My definition of a conservative investment is not something that ONLY loses 15 to 20 percent!

In 2012, something I've run across often is the notion that bonds are the only true conservative investment. Most advisors have been in the business less than 30 years and their perspective on bonds reflects the fact that they have only seen a bond bull market.

Understanding the basic relationship bonds have to interest rates is imperative. Basically when interest rates fall, bonds increase in value and vice versa. See Figure 5.1.

Interest Rate

Bond Value

Figure 5.1   Interest Rates versus Bond Values

Many shrewd investors are still puzzled by this relationship between interest rates and bond values. The basic idea is, if you are trying to sell a bond you own, does another investor see your bond as appealing or not.

To cement this fundamental principle, let's use an example.

Assume you paid $100,000 for a bond paying 5 percent interest. If the current market interest rates are 5 percent, then you should have no problem selling the bond for around the same value. That is, your bond is paying the going rate.

$100,000 at 5 percent = $5,000 interest paid. $5,000 is what a potential buyer would expect to receive in interest for a current $100,000 bond, so you can sell for pretty much the same value you paid.

If interest rates go down, say to 3 percent, then for another investor, your bond, which is paying 5 percent, is more appealing. You will need to be compensated for the higher yield your bond pays, and thus you can more likely sell your bond for more than the $100,000 you originally paid.

$100,000 at 3 percent = $3,000 interest paid. Your bond is paying $5,000 so to be compensated your bond should sell for around $140,000.

$140,000 at 3 percent = $5,000 interest paid.

If interest rates go up, say to 10 percent, then for another investor, your bond, which is paying only 5 percent, is not very appealing. You will need to lower the value of what you will accept for selling the bond to make it comparable to the current going rate of 10 percent.

$100,000 at 10 percent = $10,000 interest paid. Your bond is paying only $5,000, so to attract a potential buyer; you will need to lower your value to around $50,000.

$50,000 at 10 percent = $5,000.

Based on whatever the current interest rate is your $100,000 bond value will have to be adjusted up or down to pay the same amount of interest another investor could get from buying anywhere else. Time to maturity as well as bond ratings are other crucial factors in a bond value, but for this book's simple discussion we'll stick to the basic idea. When interest rates go up, your bond's value goes down and vice versa.

Since early 1981, interest rates have essentially gone down and thus bonds have risen in value. To get a true picture of bonds and their risk, you need to look to the 1970s time frame to see how they performed.

Figure 5.2 shows a graph of the Franklin U.S. Government Bond Fund, FKUSX. Very few funds show their history going back 40 years.

You'll see that the fund has held its value and consistently paid a dividend since 1981. But, looking back further, you'll see the effects of rising interest rates and inflation in the 1970s. The fund went from around $10 per share to around $6—a loss of more than 40 percent. Even with the bond bull market from 1980 to the present in 2012, the fund has never made back those losses in principal, assuming you didn't ever reinvest your dividends.

As an aside, very few funds are still around after 40 years. Whenever a fund has a bad streak of returns, it is much easier to close the fund or absorb it into another fund and ta-da! No one can see the history of the poor performer tarnishing the image of the mutual fund family to which it belongs.

How would you feel losing 40 percent of the value of your "conservative" portfolio?

If you own a mutual bond fund and want some perspective on how it will react in the face of rising interest rates, take a look at your particular fund's chart and put the time period between October 1998 and January 2000. This was a period when treasury yields increased by more than 1 percent.

If for instance your fund dropped around 10 percent during that period, then you have a reference point. That is, for each 1 percent increase in treasury yields, your particular mutual bond fund could fall in value roughly 10 percent. Going forward, if Treasury yields return to normal levels of around 6 percent, which is 4 percent higher than current levels today, then your particular fund could easily drop 40 to 50 percent during that rise in yields.

Again, how's that for a "conservative" investment?

Inflation

When you read the papers and watch TV, you are bombarded with reports on how low inflation is, yet I see the indent at the bottom of the water bottle getting larger each year and the ice cream and shampoo containers getting smaller and smaller. I was curious about the cereal boxes. They looked the same. Same height, same width.

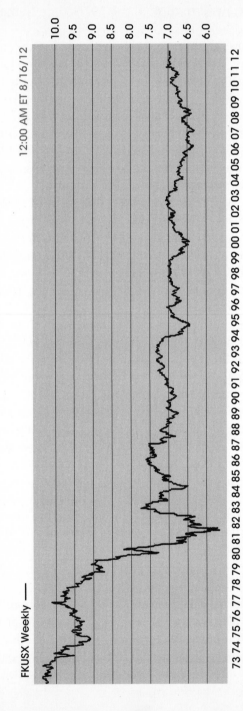

Figure 5.2 FKUSX 40-Year Chart

Then I noticed the depth of the box was getting progressively thinner. I see movie prices going through the roof and gas prices escalating. Most people have become accustomed to $4 a gallon for gas in 2012. The price in 2006 averaged $1.50 per gallon. That's an increase of more than 166 percent in just six years.

What would it cost to purchase the same amount of groceries in 2012 that cost one hundred dollars in 2000? It would cost $134 according to the Consumer Price Index for food and beverages.

If you don't have an extra $34 in investments, inflation will have eaten up a good portion of your food budget, and you will need to dig into other reserves just to buy the same things.

Food for thought (no pun intended): A hundred dollars invested in the S&P500, not adjusted for inflation and without dividend reinvestment—just net of investment performance between January 1, 2000 and January 1, 2012—would be worth $91.25. Far short of the $134 you would need to buy your groceries. You're really going to lose weight on this amount of money! An inflation diet, so to speak!

In "Hmmmmmm?", Investment Outlook, June 2008, bond expert Bill Gross added his voice to those claiming that the CPI (Consumer Price Index, the measure by which the U.S. government reports inflation) understates the actual rate of inflation. While Gross's analysis refers to factors such as hedonic adjustments and equivalent rental rates, the same gibberish that the Bureau of Labor Statistics (BLS) uses in producing its data, his argument adds up to this: The United States makes adjustments to its CPI that many other countries don't, and those adjustments don't reflect reality.

An example of one of the "adjustments" the BLS uses and Gross was referring to is called the hedonic adjustment. Introduced in 1994 by Alan Greenspan, he argued that if you buy a washing machine for $100 and it breaks, then, when you go and purchase the exact same washing machine the next year for $120, the extra $20 doesn't count in terms of the official inflation rate because you get at least $20 worth of enjoyment out of the new washing machine. HUH! If gasoline goes up 10 cents, we offset that with the enjoyment of clean air which is at least worth 10 cents. Only the government can think this stuff up.

Another viewpoint is displayed in the chart in Figure 5.3.

The chart shows an interesting phenomenon. Over different periods, inflation has been calculated in different ways. Using the

Different ways of measuring inflation

During the Reagan and Clinton administrations, the method of calculating rising prices was altered in ways that lowered the official inflation rate.
Below is a calculation of how the inflation rate would look today if it were meausred by the former methods.

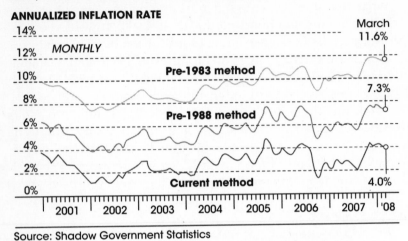

ANNUALIZED INFLATION RATE

March
11.6%

14%

12% *MONTHLY*

10%   **Pre-1983 method**

8%   7.3%

Pre-1988 method
6%

4%

2%

Current method   4.0%
0%

2001   2002   2003   2004   2005   2006   2007   '08

Source: Shadow Government Statistics

Figure 5.3 Different Inflation Calculations (2000—May 2008)

Source: Reprinted by permission from www.shadowstats.com

pre-1983 methodology, inflation for the first half of 2008 would be about 11.6 percent. Under the Reagan methodology, 1984 to 1998, inflation for 2008 would be 7.6 percent. Under the Clinton methodology, 1998 to present, inflation was a mere 4.1 percent.

Take a look at the official CPI values versus the pre-1983 version from 1980 to 2012 shown in Figure 5.4. The most glaring part of this is that we have basically been above 7 percent going back the last 20 years. That means our money is losing purchasing power at alarming rates. The next time they tell you about those tax free muni bonds at 3.5 percent, you'll realize even being tax free, you are still losing to inflation by more than 3 to 4 percent.

Why was the system to calculate inflation changed? Simple. The United States went from a creditor nation to a debtor nation. Pre-1983, other countries owed us money. We had a vested interest in showing actual inflation. When countries borrowed from us, we wanted to be paid back in true inflation-adjusted dollars. After Reagan, when we became a net debtor nation, our focus changed

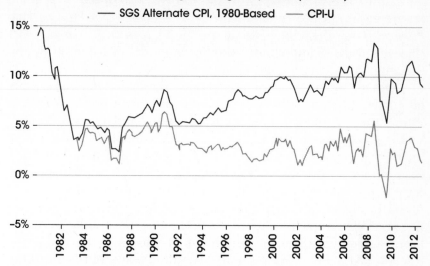

Figure 5.4 Different Inflation Calculations (1980 to July 2012)

Source: Reprinted by permission from www.shadowstats.com

to hide inflation. It was in our best interest since we owed money to other countries. Finally, 1998 under Clinton, with the unfunded liabilities of the United States growing exponentially, the calculation was changed again to hide the real inflation rate. With a lower rate, Social Security checks and Medicare reimbursement rates are lower, cost-of-living adjustments are lower, and the government can sell Treasury bonds at ridiculously low interest rates to the rest of the world and to the Federal Reserve to fund our deficits.

Whether you believe inflation is 4 percent or 12 percent, the point is it is very important to understand its effect on your retirement goals and to try to make sure you are not losing ground toward meeting those goals.

The other thing to keep in mind is the unchecked and prolific printing of U.S. dollars by the Federal Reserve. As consumers stop spending and try to increase their savings, this is counterproductive according to the Federal Reserve, and they are trying to re-inflate prices by running the printing presses at full steam ahead.

I find it fascinating to think about the history of the United States. We started as an agriculture-based economy, grew into an industrial-based economy, morphed into a consumer-service economy, and since early 2009, with the full frontal approach of quantitative easing by the Federal Reserve, descended to a *Printing Press Economy*. I say descended for a very good reason. When all asset classes and the economy are based on a model of printing money, the long-term outlook gets very gloomy.

Though we might experience price reductions on some capital goods due to a tightening of credit availability, don't be fooled. The United States is setting itself up for an inflationary debacle. When people start realizing all these newly printed dollars are eroding their purchasing power, they will stop saving and start converting their money at alarming rates into tangible goods, goods that will preserve their value against a falling dollar. This rapid consumption will make the velocity of money shoot through the roof and prices will skyrocket. The velocity of money is defined as the amount of time it takes someone to spend or turn over their money. In normal times, it might take six months to spend a certain amount of money. If the velocity is increasing, they might spend faster, converting dollars into tangible goods, and only take three months to spend the same equivalent amount of money. With the velocity increasing, prices rise quickly due to greater demand for limited supplies.

Case in point, look at the hyperinflationary time between 2006 and 2009 in Zimbabwe. After the world lost faith in the ability of Zimbabwe to pay back its debts and thus stopped buying its bonds, President Mugabe did what any country's leader in the modern world does today. He turned on the money printing press to pay for its needs. The problem of course is those newly printed bills erode the purchasing power of those printed before.

A roll of toilet paper cost $426 Zimbabwe dollars in 2006. By 2008 that same roll cost $250,000,000 and one year later it cost $100 trillion. That is $100,000,000,000,000,000.

Many people buy bonds with a set maturity with the belief that as long as they can hold out to the maturity date their money is safe. Though interest rates may rise and cause the value of the bond to go down, it doesn't matter because they can wait until the maturity date to get back the full face value of their bond.

Imagine if you had purchased a $100,000 Zimbabwe dollar bond back in 2006. It could buy a good amount of toilet paper in that year. That is, the $100,000 had a significant amount of purchasing power.

Let's say your bond matured in 2008. You are handed back your $100,000. What does it buy you in terms of purchasing power now? Not even the corner of a single sheet of toilet paper. Even though you still have your original $100,000, you have lost all the purchasing power of your original dollars. Said another way, you have lost your money. This is called the inflationary risk of bonds.

Other risks include interest rate risk, that is, rising rates will cause the bonds' value to drop and thus force you to take a loss if you need to liquidate the bonds before the maturity date. So much for being liquid!

What if the bond issuer has issued the bond with a call option? Your bond could be called at any time before maturity. If you had planned on holding it, you're out of luck. This is known as call risk.

My favorite risk to bonds that most people never think about is information risk. This is generally associated with municipal bonds. When you buy most any security, you are given a prospectus, the information to help you make an informed decision on that security *before* purchasing. When does the prospectus show up when making a purchase on a muni-bond? Generally months after the purchase. How can you know if you are buying a bankrupt municipality if you don't have the information to make that decision when you need it? You don't.

Another example of loss of purchasing power occurred when a lady who had all her money in certificates of deposit (CDs) came into my office for a consultation. She asked what the long-term effects of this investment strategy would be.

"Tell me something you like to do," I asked.

"I love the movies. I go twice a week," she replied.

"Great. If you keep all your money in CDs, over time you will have two choices," I told her. "Your first choice is to reduce the number of times you go to the movies."

"Never," she replied. "I love the movies; I will be going at least twice a week forever."

"Then," I warned her, "choice number two is to go broke."

Over time, her money would fall far short of her actual expenditures. Why? In her particular case, she takes out all of her interest from the CDs each year, so her principal is not growing. Without more principal to work with, as movie ticket prices—and everything else for that matter—go up, she will have to eat into the principal to maintain the same standard of living. Look at the price of movies over time. When I was a kid, they were $3. I'm sure some of you can recall the time when they were a quarter or even less. Recently, my wife and I went to the theatre and between the movie ticket price of $16.50 per ticket and one box of popcorn and parking, we were out more than $50. We're not in Kansas anymore, Toto.

Investment Fees

A man came into my office, curious about the fees he was paying in his portfolio. He even called his advisor that morning, and his advisor told him he was in no-load mutual funds and annuities and his cost was the 1 percent annual asset fee also known as a wrap fee.

His portfolio was about $250,000, so his annual fee was $2,500. His portfolio consisted of $100,000 sitting in a money market account, $100,000 in various no-load mutual funds, and $50,000 in a variable annuity.

Starting with his money market account, I asked him if he could guess the fees he was paying. "Fees, in a money market account? There are no fees!" he told me.

Going online and finding the prospectus for his particular money market account, on the sixth page, the fees of the money market fund were clearly spelled out: 0.5 percent management fees, 0.25 percent 12-b-1 fees (marketing expenses, someone has to pay for all those beautiful brochures), and 0.30 percent misc. All added together, the fees came to 1.05 percent. Below this number was a rebate of 0.05 percent bringing the total to 1 percent. I guess they did the rebate because they didn't want to seem like they were gouging the client on his savings!

On his $100,000 in the money market, he was paying $1,000 in fees annually, or a little over $83 per month.

Surprised, he pulled out the statements for his mutual funds. Using various resources on the web such as Personalfund.com, we broke down each of his funds.

Not only did they have management fees, but also transaction costs (these are the buying and selling commissions within the fund itself), 12-b-1 fees, and taxes for holding the fund. Taxes arising from the dividends received or reinvested if held within an after tax account. There are other invisible fees, such as soft dollar arrangements, and so on, which are usually buried in the transaction costs. Unfortunately, they don't report the transaction costs anywhere because in theory they don't know what they will be for the upcoming year. Isn't that convenient?

The typical fee for this man's mutual funds was 2 percent. Again, these were no-load mutual funds. All the "no-load" refers to is the upfront commission. It has nothing to do with the ongoing fees, which all funds charge. It is common for an advisor to sell Class-B shares that don't have an upfront fee but include higher ongoing fees. If you sell the fund before the surrender period runs out, the remainder of the commission due will be deducted from the proceeds.

For example:

Class A Fund has a 5 percent upfront commission and a 2 percent ongoing fee.

Class B Fund has a 0 percent upfront commission (typical No-Load) but has an ongoing fee of 3.25 percent.

Note that the advisor is making an extra 1.25 percent each year for the Class B Fund, and over the course of four years, will have been paid the same as if you had paid the upfront commission. At this point, ethical advisors will convert the B-Shares into A-Shares so that the client isn't paying the higher ongoing fee. The problem is that very few advisors actually convert the shares. Why do it and get paid less, right?

As a rule of rule of thumb, we don't recommend traditional buy and hold mutual funds. If you are going to buy something to hold for a long time, buy Class A shares. Yes, you will pay more upfront, but your ongoing fees will be less.

Finally, the gentleman had a variable annuity for $50,000. Right off the bat, he said his variable was earning 7 percent per year guaranteed.

Before I addressed his statement, I showed him that the variable annuity had similar mutual fund costs within the sub-accounts, but there was also an extra layer of fees for the insurance company who issued the annuity.

The fees included Mortality & Expense (M&E) fees of 1.25 percent. This fee is basically the cost of the death benefit, which in essence will reimburse you for the principal invested if you die still holding the annuity. Said another way, if the variable annuity loses money, you are paying for life insurance to pay back the principal lost if you die still holding the annuity. Great insurance, wouldn't you agree? You pay extra premiums to protect the insurance company from losing your hard-earned money.

Other fees include the bells and whistles for which these contracts are famous. An example was this man's statement about his annuity being guaranteed to grow at 7 percent. Now, I'm sure he is saying exactly what his advisor told him when selling him the annuity. The problem is that the advisor told only part of the story.

His contract was guaranteed to grow by 7 percent over a 10-year period. But not the way this man thought, which was that he could pull all the money out with the guaranteed growth at the end of the tenth year. That does not apply if the contract isn't annuitized. Basically, this 7 percent guaranteed number is only accessible if the man receives payments from the contract over his lifetime or for a minimum of 20 years. How is it possible the insurance group could guarantee a growth of 7 percent? They knew the only way the man would get this return was if he left the money with them for the 10 years plus an additional 20 years, for a total of 30 years. This was not what the man understood.

If he pulled out his money at the end of the tenth year, he would receive only what the contract was worth net of investment performance, fees, and withdrawals.

The total fees for this variable annuity averaged 4 percent or $2,000.

Fee tally on his $250,000 portfolio:

1 percent Advisor Wrap Fee	= $2,500
1 percent Money Market Fee	= $1,000
2 percent Mutual Funds	= $2,000
4 percent Variable Annuity	= $2,000
Total Fees	**$7,500 or $625 per month.**

Considering this man was living off his dividends, he was shocked to learn that he was paying approximately $625 out of his wallet each month into the pocket of this Wall Street company.

Why are fees such a big deal? Everyone deserves to make a living. We hire financial advisers for their expertise and knowledge. They are paid to do a job and deserve to be paid, as does your mechanic or doctor.

The problem is that fees can be a huge leak in the bucket if they are excessively high and continue for the life of the investment.

On a typical mutual fund held for 10 years, where fees average between 2 to 3 percent with all the hidden stuff added back in, it means you will pay approximately 20 to 30 percent out of your pocket to Wall Street just to cover fees. At the market bottom in March 2009, the stock market had essentially gone sideways for 12 years, yet most people's portfolios were nowhere close to the level they were in 1997 due to the fees paid. If you factor in the effects of inflation, the results are even more grim.

Since 2008 up to the present in 2012, most investor's portfolios have at best gone sideways. This is so even after the huge stock market moves and again when factoring in the fees paid since 1997. Recall the story in the beginning of the book of the potential client I met in 2012 who thought he had made a lot of money with his big-name brokerage house. After 14 years of professional management, his $367,000 investment resulted in a loss of $285! How much did the big brokerage house make in fees during that same 14 years? They probably made tens of thousands of dollars.

Take a look at your retirement funds. Have you ever wondered why you have so few choices in your 401(k), 403(b), 457, and so on? When the plan was first presented to your employer, often the choices in the plan were picked to provide the best return possible for the provider of the mutual funds. Wait, isn't that supposed to be the best possible return for the employee? Hardly. Most mutual funds underperform the S&P500 over time spans of five years or longer. If they truly were looking out for you, they would just have you invest in general index funds with low turnover and low expense ratios.

Who do you think worked so hard to get your money into the various retirement funds? Wall Street! Most people in the 1950s had pensions, and Wall Street couldn't get their greedy little hands on the money, so they fought the good fight, twisted a few arms in Congress to create IRA's and 401(k)s and finally won additional retirement choices for you to put in your pre-tax dollars from work. Now, they could charge their fees and all the while fill our heads with propaganda that the stock market was the only game in town. No wonder they have been fighting to privatize social security for 50 years. They would love to get their hands and fees on that giant trust account.

One more issue to consider is an eternal debate over fee-only advisors and commission-based advisors. Fee-only advisors are advisors who charge a fixed amount for designing a financial plan, say $5,000, and market themselves as an unbiased resource. We tend to think of fee-only advisors as a bit hypocritical. If you walk in and pay $5,000 for a comprehensive plan by a fee-only advisor, you obviously trust this person to guide you accurately.

Once you have this magical plan in your hands, the dilemma then becomes how do you implement the plan? Who can put all the pieces together and turn the plan into the pot of gold. Naturally, you want to trust the person who designed the plan and will probably end up back at his or her door to implement it, thus the hypocrisy of fee-only advisors. They take off their fee-only hat and put on their wrap-fee or commission hat to put the financial investments in place and earn a second round of compensation.

A wrap-fee is the fees an adviser charges based on the amount of money they are managing for a client. The fee is "wrapped" around the assets under management (AUM).

Let's take a look at commissionable investments, the direct placement programs (DPP) and private securities. On the surface the internal commissions paid to the advisor seem outrageous. Typically three to seven percent upfront. Many advisors point out this high upfront cost as being unthinkable and biased against the client. Actually, most of these products pay nothing ongoing, and the advisor is essentially being paid upfront to be the client's customer service provider for as long as they are in the investment. Most of these investments are designed to be long term, three to 10 years in length. Therefore, because of the time commitment element, a commissionable investment may better serve the client versus an ongoing AUM wrap-fee model. Commission-based investments don't have a recurring charge to the adviser for every year you are in it based on how big your account has grown. The commission is paid once, upfront.

Conversely, when assets are liquid as they are in the stock market, the AUM wrap-fee model is best. You only pay fees during the time you are in the investments. If you move the money somewhere else, the fees stop.

A key point to understand about most of the DPP programs is the commission is built into the original investment. Your distributions

Table 5.1   DPP Account Balance versus NAV

Year	Account Balance	7 percent Distribution Reinvested	Net Asset Value (NAV)
0	$100,000	$ 7,000	$ 90,000
1	$107,000	$ 7,490	$ 97,000
2	$114,490	$ 8,014	$104,490
3	$122,504	$ 8,575	$112,504
4	$131,079	$ 9,176	$121,079
5	$140,254	$ 9,818	$130,255
6	$150,071	$10,504	$140,073
7	$160,575		$150,577

are paid based on the initial contribution amount and not on the initial contribution minus the load (commissions and fees) of the DPP.

Before I show the difference between commissions paid and wrap fees paid to an adviser, it is important to understand how the true value of a DPP is calculated.

If a client invests $100,000 into a DPP, there are two values to consider: the account balance, which the distributions are based on, and the net asset value (NAV), the initial investment minus the upfront sales load. This is the true value of the real assets inside the investment, what was actually bought with the remaining money after the load is taken away.

In this hypothetical example assume the load is 10 percent, (7 percent commission plus 3 percent fees), the distribution is 7 percent, and the share price remains stable over a term of seven years. If a client was to reinvest their distributions their account would look like Table 5.1.

The goal of the DPPs is to eventually sell for the account balance value but I like to work with the assumption the investment will only be able to sell for the NAV. In this case, the client would have $150,577 at the end of the investment's seven-year term.

Now let's go back to the topic of actual fees paid between investments that are either commission oriented or wrap-fee based.

In a wrap-fee based account, your fees are deducted each year from your account balance.

Table 5.2   DPP versus Wrap Account Fee Comparison

Year	Product A NAV	7% Commission	Product B Value	1% Wrap Fee
0	$ 90,000	$7,000	$ 99,000	$1,000
1	$ 97,000	0	$104,870	$1,059
2	$104,490	0	$111,089	$1,122
3	$112,504	0	$117,677	$1,188
4	$121,079	0	$124,655	$1,259
5	$130,255	0	$132,047	$1,334
6	$140,073	0	$139,878	$1,427
7	$150,577		$149,669	
Total:		$7,000		$8,375

The best way to see the differences paid in fees is to look at the above example investment through the eyes of the adviser and his or her wallet.

Assume two hypothetical investments both last seven years and by either reinvestment of distributions or appreciation, the balance increases by 7 percent per year. The commission is 7 percent upfront for Product A and Product B has a wrap fee of 1 percent up front based on the account balance. Lastly assume the price per share for Product A stays level during the term of the investment (see Table 5.2).

At the end of the investment period, the client who is being billed annually at 1 percent by the wrap-fee adviser actually pays more in fees than the upfront cost of the commission based product. This is because the 1 percent is compounding based on the increasing account balance whereas the upfront single commission is based on the initial contribution.

I feel all clients should be in a mix of stock market investments as well as non-stock market investments depending of course on the results of your suitability analysis. Each comes with its own compensation model, either wrap-fee based (stock market) or commission based (non-stock market).

I believe that the best advisors are paid a combination of these types of compensation models and are upfront with the investor about it. It is the only way to effectively help people invest their money. By using a combination of payment models, an advisor can pick the ideas that make the most sense for the client instead of for the advisor's business model. As the investor, make an informed decision about the costs by asking lots of questions.

Income, Income, Income

How often have you heard that a reasonable withdrawal rate from a portfolio is around 4 percent? Study after study shows that pulling out more than this amount in a portfolio of stocks and bonds will likely erode the principal in the long run and risk your retirement nest egg.

I propose that stock portfolios, and now with rising interest rates for the foreseeable future, bond portfolios, *are not* designed for generating income and *should only* be used for growth purposes and liquidity needs.

Wall Street will always tell you that the markets average 10 percent. This is not true. The S&P500 from January 1871 to June 2012 has averaged 8.8 percent, with full dividend reinvestment. If you were taking out dividends for income, then the S&P500 returned a measly 4.14 percent. That's far short of the magic 10 percent number and represents over 140 years in the market. Not many of us have the potential to invest over THAT time horizon.

What most advisors don't know, won't tell you or frankly ignore is that there have been periods when the S&P500 averaged 0 percent. During the previous bear markets, 1881–1921, 1929–1954, and 1965–1982, these were extensive periods in history when you made nothing in the stock market.

The cover of *Business Week*, August 1979, said it best: "The Death of Equities." Why? Because the markets had gone up and down for the previous 14 years like a roller coaster and kept returning to where they began.

Here in mid-2012, the average investor is burned out on the emotionally driven volatility of the markets. We had a negative 26 percent start to 2009 swing completely around into a positive 26 percent finish due to the printing press of the Federal Reserve. A flash crash-laden 2010 followed by a violent rollercoaster in 2011, with an August to September crash that rivaled all crashes going back to 1932.

As quoted from the *New York Times* in September 2011.

> "The last few years have been the most volatile for all of recorded history."

The inherent problem with pulling income from volatile equity portfolios is the compounded effect in bad years.

Assume the markets go back and forth for several years in a row: 10 percent up and 10 percent down. Back and forth, back and forth as you see in Figure 5.5.

Typical side ways pattern in bear market.

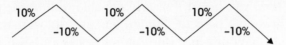

Figure 5.5   Sideways Market—No Fees or Withdrawals

Each year, you pull out the same amount of income from your account. How about the universal 4 percent that Wall Street recommends?

On top of the 4 percent you are taking for income, assume your fees are 1 percent a year.

The long-term effect is that the growth of your account is stunted in the good years and the losses are compounded in the bad years.

In the good years, you make 10 percent but then take out 4 percent for income and 1 percent for fees, leaving only 5 percent overall growth in the account.

In the bad years, you lose 10 percent, and with the 4 percent withdrawal for income and 1 percent fees, your overall portfolio has dropped 15 percent (see Figure 5.6). This path is unsustainable, and before long, you will run out of money.

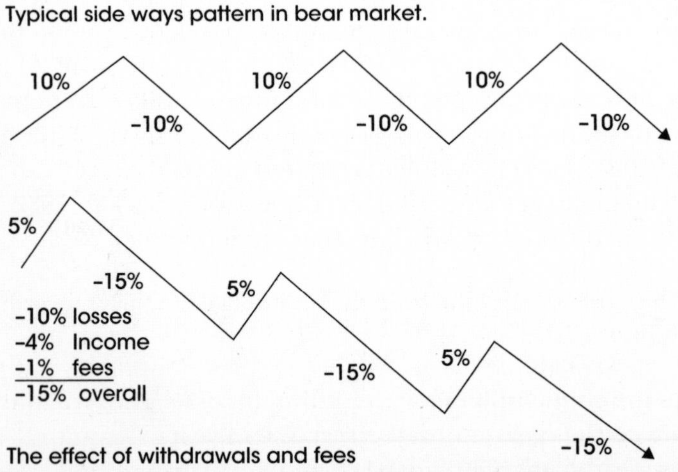

Typical side ways pattern in bear market.

10%   10%   10%
     -10%   -10%   -10%

5%
     -15%   5%
-10% losses
-4% Income
-1% fees
-15% overall
                    -15%   5%
                                  -15%

The effect of withdrawals and fees   -15%

Figure 5.6   Sideways Market Result with Withdrawals and Fees

There is another dilemma people face when only using equity portfolios for income needs. It is their flight or fight emotional response. When the market is going down, the flight or fight response kicks in, and people usually feel a lot of stress when pulling money out of their accounts. They don't want to compound the losses and thus will sacrifice their standard of living so as not to pull out too much from their accounts. Then in good years, they often will take out too much because they feel they are making up for a bad year, and thus, they diminish the long-term growth potential of their nest egg.

The result is the same: A lot of unnecessary stress because their money has been positioned in the wrong type of investments to meet their goals. The best investments for income purposes are the ones designed to provide the potential for income streams without causing market-driven wide swings in the principal balance.

Many of the investments we'll discuss in Chapter 6 and Appendix B are investments that are designed to generate cash flow, and, since the principal is not tied to the stock market, you don't necessarily see wild fluctuations in price. You may see your principal vary with changes in value of the underlying tangible asset, but they generally are not market or emotionally driven. When investments are not subject to wild fluctuations, people tend not to panic, and they allow their money to work over time. One of the biggest reasons most investments don't work out is due to the fear/greed cycle and irrationality of buy/sell decisions.

Buy high, sell low never pays!

Taxes

If a lawyer and an IRS agent were both drowning and you could only save one of them, would you go to lunch or read the paper?

I've always loved this joke as it demonstrates the attitude most people have in wanting to deal with either attorneys or the IRS agent who is potentially going to audit you or your business. The sad reality is, in order to build your wealth and most importantly keep it, you need to embrace both of these individuals.

Taxes are a giant leak in one's bucket. Everything from income to estate taxes is a drain on your wealth bucket each year and even after you kick the bucket. Uncle Sam is always looking for his take. There is nothing wrong with that, but to quote Arthur Godfrey,

"I'm proud of paying taxes; the only thing: I could be just as proud for half the money."

Pay the tax you are legally obligated to pay, just don't leave a tip!

Quoting the Honorable Learned Hand, U.S. Appeals Court Justice, 1914:

> "Over and over again Courts have said there is nothing sinister in so arranging one's affairs as to keep taxes as low as possible. Everybody does so, rich and poor, and all do right, for nobody owes any public duty to pay more than the law demands. Taxes are enforced exactions, not voluntary contributions. To demand more in the name of morals is mere cant."

He continued with the most astute observation I use when thinking about clients and their tax bills.

> "There are two systems of taxation in our country: one for the informed and one for the uninformed."

Most people depend so heavily on their CPA for tax advice that they forget this person is so bogged down with all the duties of just figuring out their tax bill that he or she doesn't usually spend a lot of time helping clients truly reduce their tax bills. That is a job for a tax attorney with help from a financial advisor. How many people reading this book can think of a sit-down with their advisor where they discussed tax strategies and were educated on possibilities?

Most financial advisors will never bring up the issue of income tax planning because of two primary reasons. First they are not paid a commission or fee for discussing taxes, so why bother? Second, they are not well informed in tax planning because they don't think of it as a worthy investment.

Investing in tax reduction education and planning is just as valid an investment as putting your money in a piece of real estate or a stock. The outcome of income tax planning is usually far more consistent than any other type of investment.

Would you put $15,000 into a stock if you had a very high degree of certainty this stock would grow to $45,000 over the next year? Most would probably say of course.

How many readers would pay a tax attorney $15,000 for the goal of achieving $60,000 in income tax savings? Far fewer in my experience. The thought of paying fees of $15,000 seems outrageous to most people, yet the result of this "investment" is the same. You will have an additional $45,000 in your pocket at the end of the year over and above the $15,000 fee the attorney charges.

Which pathway is more reliable? Does the IRS make you pay anticipated quarterly payments on the potential profit you will make if you buy a stock today? Of course not. Only if the stock goes up and you sell, thus triggering the gains, will you pay the tax.

The IRS does make you pay quarterly payments based on your previous year's income. So if they are so certain you'll make roughly the same amount the next year and force you to pay the tax in advance, investing in income tax education and planning generally is a far more consistent and reliable investment than any stock, piece of real estate, or other common investment one might make.

My reason for helping clients think outside the box is simple. Take care of the client, and they will take care of you. If I can show a client in conjunction with their CPA how to save $10,000 in taxes by using a simple C-Corp for their business and deducting some expenses they had been paying with after-tax dollars before, they now will have an extra $10,000 in their pocket for their enjoyment, not Uncle Sam's.

What might the client use the newfound $10,000 for? If they don't plan on spending it, maybe they hand it back to us for investment purposes. What goes around comes around.

On the topic of Certified Public Accountants (CPAs), Enrolled Agents, and so forth, these people are a vital part of your financial team, but please understand their general background. They are tax pros. Many times, clients will say, "*I have to consult with my CPA on whether this investment makes any sense.*" I encourage it but also jokingly say, "*After you consult with your tax person, you should consult with your mechanic and maybe even your doctor.*"

The reason I say this is that your mechanic and doctor probably know as much about these investments as your CPA does, so their opinions are probably just as valid. Your CPA may not understand these investments, and in turn give terrible advice because he or she has no idea what we're talking about. He or she may even automatically say that the investment is bad. If you think about their errors and omission insurance, it only covers tax issues, not investment advice. If a CPA is being cautious, it is in their best interest to recommend against these ideas because if something does happen in the future, they can come back and say they didn't recommend the investment and it is not their fault. The best CPAs will generally be upfront about this issue. They will say something like, "*The investment is outside my area of expertise. You should consult with other financial advisors to get an informed second opinion.*"

If you feel you need a second opinion on an investment portfolio or idea and are not sure who to ask, feel free contact me at 800-737-8552, or go to the book's web site at www.TheWealthCode.com. I'll be happy to give you my two cents worth.

COMMON SENSE CONCEPT

Always file extensions. This is not tax advice, it is just common sense. If you had to work on a 100 tax returns, how many mistakes would you make? The best way to assure yourself that your accountant is working with fresh batteries is to file an extension. Make a payment for the estimated taxes you will have and then relax, wait for late tax statements like K-1's to show up and then sit down with your accountant in June or July. Normally their desks are nice and clean, they are back from their vacations and rested. Isn't this the mental state you want for the person doing your taxes versus the overworked state of mind of one who is bogged down with dozens of returns due in a day or two? Another interesting belief commonly expressed by CPA's is that returns that are filed on extension are less often audited than returns filed by April 15. Do yourself a favor. Always file extensions and potentially lower your IRS audit chances as well as your CPA's potential for mistakes and stress level.

Taxes and investments go hand in hand. Many of the best investments have huge tax savings tied to them. For example, you have a small rental house, and in a given year you receive $10,000 in rental income. That same year on your tax return you deduct the depreciation of the house, for instance $10,000, against the rental income. In this situation, you have enjoyed $10,000 of rental income in your pocket and do not owe a dime in income taxes.

Compare that to the person who has $10,000 in CD interest income. If they were in the 30 percent tax bracket, they would only have $7,000 to enjoy after the $3,000 in taxes due.

Now, the person who was able to use depreciation to offset the rental income will have a lower cost basis for their rental property. But if they eventually sell the investment home and use an IRS Section 1031 tax-deferred exchange to get into another property of equal or greater value, no tax will be due. If that person eventually passes away, their estate will receive a step-up in the cost basis of the investment home, and the capital gains and recapture taxes that were due disappear. This is one way the rich get richer. They understand *The Wealth Code* on taxes and how to best preserve their nest eggs and pass them from generation to generation without the government taking half or more.

Poor Estate Planning

How is it possible for someone like Henry J. Kaiser, Jr., to die with an estate of $55,910,373 and only lose $1,030,415 in estate costs, while someone like Elvis Presley, who died with only $10,165,434 lost $7,374,635 or 73 percent to estate costs and taxes? The difference is estate planning, another huge leak in the bucket.

Most people do not realize the implications that death has on an estate. Usually something as simple as a living trust in the appropriate states, or wills in those states where those are more appropriate, would save countless hours of aggravation and money drained from an estate in probate court fees, attorney's fees, and so forth.

One reason people give for not having the proper estate plans in place is the initial cost. This is unfortunate and shortsighted.

One client with an estate more than $15M called me after sitting with a highly qualified estate tax attorney I had recommended. He told me he was outraged by the price the attorney would charge to implement a solid estate plan. In this case, the total cost was about $8,000. I reminded the client that he would be saving about $3M in estate taxes by using the plan. Still, the client was so focused on the "outrageous" $8,000 that he never implemented the plan.

Penny wise and pound foolish, as the saying goes. By focusing only on the cost, the client lost sight of the goal. Said another way, would you invest $8,000 in a mutual fund if it was assured of returning $3M in profits? Of course, this is a no brainer. Why then would it be unthinkable to spend $8,000 on attorneys' fees up front to get a big binder of paperwork that in the long run would save $3M in estate taxes?

A good exercise is to ask yourself two or three questions, depending on your situation.

If you are single:

- What happens financially if you are incapacitated tomorrow and cannot work?
- What happens to your loved ones financially if you die tomorrow?

If you are married:

- What happens financially if you or your spouse becomes incapacitated tomorrow and cannot work?
- What happens to your spouse financially and estate-tax wise if you die tomorrow?
- What happens to your children or beneficiaries in terms of taxes and financial well-being when the second spouse passes away?

Most people have never asked themselves these questions. It can be difficult to talk about such things as becoming incapacitated or dying. It's easier to push that topic to another day.

There is a saying that the only thing in life that is guaranteed is that tomorrow is not guaranteed!

People usually say death AND taxes are inevitable, but I'm not so sure about the taxes if proper estate and income tax planning is adopted.

Here's a sad reality. Dying with a large IRA can potentially cost 79 percent of the account in taxes.

Assume you have a $10M estate with $1M in an IRA. You die in 2012. Under the current tax laws, the estate pays the death taxes of 35 percent on the IRA balance, in this case $350,000. Then, if not properly designated, the beneficiary receiving the $1M IRA has to declare it for income tax purposes. In California with a state income tax of 9 percent and with the Federal top rate of 35 percent, you would lose 44 percent of the $1M, or $440,000.

Adding both taxes together, the $1M IRA has paid taxes of $350,000 and $440,000. For a total of $790,000 or 79 percent lost. Is this what you really intended to happen?

Please do not let this happen to your estate. There are several ways you can offset a lot of the taxes due by proper beneficiary designations and using allowable deductions. For instance, offset some of the taxable income by the amount of estate tax paid. If you have a large IRA and you have a large estate, please seek competent counsel on how to properly pass it to your spouse or next generation without Uncle Sam taking the lion's share. Why save for your whole life only to have the biggest beneficiary be the government because of being uninformed and having poor estate planning. Poor estate planning is a giant leak in the bucket.

Appendix C covers the concept of discounted Roth IRA conversions, the ability to convert large IRAs to a tax-free Roth IRA at a fraction of the reportable income conventionally assumed. This is a section of this book not to be missed if you have a large pre-tax retirement account such as an IRA or 401(k).

Poor Asset Protection

I read a story about an elderly lady who gave her grandson $16,000 for his 16th birthday. My first thought was wow, don't we all need a grandmother like that. What does the grandson do? He buys his first car of course. This is where this happy story gets ugly.

The grandson unfortunately causes an accident and hurts some people. They in turn hire a contingent-paid attorney (an attorney who gets paid only if there is a successful judgment), and sue. They don't sue the kid. They don't sue his parents as it is found out they really don't have any money. They sue the grandmother for making a negligent gift to a minor and the result is a judgment which cleans out her assets putting her in the poor house.

Your first thought should be, "How can that be true? That's not right."

You are correct, morally or even ethically it is not right, but when it comes to civil lawsuits, there is no right or wrong. It is what it is.

As with income or estate tax planning, asset protection is also a tool the wealthy understand well. They pay for competent advice while the vast majority of individuals and businesses remain woefully ill-informed. Many clients think that just because they have a revocable living trust they are protected from a lawsuit. This is not correct. A revocable living trust is your alter-ego with the same tax id number. It can be sued as easily as you can be.

An unexpected leak in your bucket is poor asset protection. Any day you are driving on the road, or conducting your business, is a day an accident can happen and you can have everything you have worked your entire life to save and invest taken from you.

How many people own a small rental property personally? That is, they have the title of the property in their names and not in a separate entity such as a Limited Liability Company (LLC) or Corporation. The day a tenant trips on a weed in the front yard is the day you get sued. Again, not that it is your fault that Mother Nature put a weed on the grass, but because you own the grass that weed grew on.

COMMON SENSE CONCEPT

The worse economically a country is doing and the more people are hurting financially, the more desperate they become. They begin looking for alternate ways to pay their bills or feed their family. It is human nature to do so. The problem is a lot of times it will drive people to frivolously sue as a fast means of padding their pocket book.

A common way of protecting your assets is to get a general liability umbrella policy. They are extremely cheap and in general a good thing to have. There is one problem though, and it revolves around the idea of low hanging fruit—something which is easily attained with minimal work.

If you are sued and the contingent-paid attorney does an asset discovery and finds your umbrella policy, he knows he *will* get paid. For instance if you have a $1M policy, that attorney knows he will get his roughly 35 percent contingent fee, or $350,000. If he knows he will get that, it is worth taking on the case and going for everything else you have. That is gravy on top of the $350,000 he knows he will get paid.

> **The key to asset protection is making it very difficult to be sued**
> **and more importantly to collect on any successful judgment.**

Said another way, I want my estate so well guarded by various entities (LLC's, Corporations, Foreign Trusts, etc.), that the opposing attorneys after their discovery of the assets and holdings of one's estate realize they will have very little opportunity to collect and thus very little opportunity to get paid. They will either not take the case or they will immediately try to settle for pennies on the dollar.

Either one of these outcomes is desirable for the person being sued. It puts him or her in the driver's seat instead of at the mercy of opposing council.

This is when an umbrella policy is a fantastic bargaining chip for a lawsuit because in general it will be the only thing the suing party can go after, and even then they will have to fight for it.

There are many great books and online resources for educating yourself on asset protection. Poor asset protection can be one of the most devastating leaks in the bucket because it can come out of nowhere and ruin your financial as well as emotional well-being.

Liquidity

Every day you hear the importance of liquidity with your money. A more complete description of this leak will be covered in Chapter 6, but, for now, a simple discussion will suffice.

While giving presentations at night to clients and potential clients, I used to ask for a show of hands. Who has had a $50,000 emergency that required pulling out money the very next day? This emergency does not include medical bills, which can be paid over time or a new car purchase on a whim, but something tragic, like your favorite uncle has been kidnapped and you need $50,000 in cash the next day to save him.

People always say they have tons of money in the bank for that "what if" emergency. The problem is that those "what if" emergencies rarely if ever happen and you are stuck with money sitting in the bank earning nothing. You are incurring opportunity costs. That money could be working harder for you, but since you keep a large chunk for that rare emergency, you rationalize it is ok to earn 1 percent because it is for peace of mind.

I have asked this emergency funds question to more than 10,000 people who attended my workshops over the years, and only six people ever raised their hands. Some people's emergencies were at the $30,000 level, and more at the $20,000 or $10,000 level, but rarely at the $50,000 amount. They just haven't experienced such emergencies.

Wall Street will always say that an investment that is liquid is usually considered a better investment than one that is not. I disagree. Liquidity to me means the investment is far more prone to emotional decisions, for instance, decisions made under duress or panic. An example would be when the markets are getting killed, people are always heard saying they sold at the bottom, right before the market turned up. When I wrote the first edition during March of 2009, the Dow Jones Industrial Average was at 6629 on March 7, 2009. In the papers and on TV, everyone was screaming about the average going to 3000 or 2500, the previous support levels dating back to 1984.

To quote my first edition book that was written on March 7, 2009, page 49.

> "The sad part is, we are probably at the bottom of the down-turn of the market. When people become so afraid and everyone is selling, that is usually the time to buy."

As it turned out, the bottom hit on March 9, 2009.

It was almost preordained that the masses were panic selling at the bottom. Again, all the talking heads were screaming about the market breaking the October 2002 low of 7200 and that the sky was falling with no end in sight. I saw dozens of prospective clients during this period and almost all had sold to cash very close to the eventual bottom at the recommendation of their advisors.

Illiquid investments provide a buffer from the irrational decisions we humans are prone to make. Since one can't sell even when all seems lost, the investments will usually have time and the potential to regain any lost value and become profitable.

A good example would be the drop in value owners experienced on their personal residences bought pre-1990, the last residential real estate market top before the 2006 real estate top. Most homes decreased in value from 1990 to 1994, but because it wasn't easy to sell a home due to the general illiquidity, owners ended up riding it out, and over time, the house became worth a lot more. An advantage of owning tangible investments, as long as you are not forced to sell in the bad times, is their ability to appreciate in value over time due to inflation.

The illiquidity of the home provided a buffer, making it difficult to sell at the bottom, say in 1994, preventing the owner from making a bad investment choice. Stocks don't have the luxury of being illiquid. They can be sold on a whim, when one's emotions are in control, which often leads to those who buy the tops, and those who sell the bottoms, taking terrible losses, in panic.

Let us re-address this enormous leak in the bucket, liquidity, in Chapter 6, after a more complete discussion of the different investment classes available to you and the general characteristics of each one.

COMMON SENSE CONCEPT

When you inventory your estate, from your liquid stocks and bonds to your illiquid real estate and other tangible assets, where have you made the most money in terms of appreciation?

Most will come to the realization their illiquid assets such as their home, business, art, bullion, and so on, have been their most profitable assets in the long run.

Summary: Leaks in the Bucket

We all have financial buckets that represent our net worth. Unfortunately, we also have numerous leaks in our buckets that drain off money each year and reduce the size of our nest eggs. Leaks include everything from excess taxes, estate planning, limited investment choices, and fees. Fortunately, once the leaks are identified, you can begin plugging them. As more and more of the leaks get plugged, you will find that your bucket will fill more quickly with even the slightest gains. Recognizing the problem is the hardest part, but that is the purpose for the solutions we present in the upcoming chapters.

CHAPTER

True Asset Class Diversification

I n the beginning, I introduced a chart of all the investment classes into which you can invest your hard earned money. I talked about why the Olympic basketball team could still win the gold medal even though one of its stars, Los Angeles Laker Kobe Bryant, was not on the court.

The goal of this chapter is to present a new common sense approach to portfolio diversification that is easy to understand but is usually not recommended by the Wall Street crowd.

The General Asset Classes

There are simple descriptions for each of the general asset classes (see Figure 6.1). These descriptions are meant to keep you reading by providing a basic understanding of each asset class, and building on your knowledge without bogging you down with nitty gritty details. My goal is to leave you with the big picture and a general comprehension of *The Wealth Code*. More detailed discussions of each investment class are provided in Appendix B, after the full concept and case examples are presented.

Static Stocks, Bonds, Mutual Funds

This category includes any stock, bond, mutual fund, or derivative that is held longer than one year. I call this the-hope-and-pray leg on the financial table. The vast majority of investors only know this

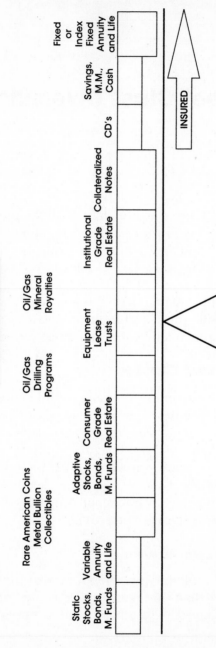

Asset Class Diversification

Static
Stocks,
Bonds,
M. Funds

Variable
Annuity
and Life

Rare American Coins
Metal Bullion
Collectibles

Adaptive
Stocks,
Bonds,
M. Funds

Consumer
Grade
Real Estate

Oil/Gas
Drilling
Programs

Equipment
Lease
Trusts

Oil/Gas
Mineral
Royalties

Institutional
Grade
Real Estate

Collateralized
Notes

CD's

Savings,
M.M.,
Cash

Fixed
or
Index
Fixed
Annuity
and Life

INSURED

Figure 6.1 All Possible Investments

asset class. This class tends to do well in bull markets. The problem since 2000, however, is that we have been in a bear market, a market that has trended mostly sideways or down. Historical comparisons to previous bear markets suggest we could be in this sideways pattern of ebbs and flows for years, if not for decades to come. A recent example is Japan. They have been in a bear market since 1989 to the present, 2012, with no resolution in sight.

Variable Annuities

These are essentially the same as static accounts, except they offer more bells and whistles such as death benefits and generally have more fees associated with them. Variable annuities can be liquidated quickly for the account balance minus any surrender fees and recent additions to these contracts are the various guaranteed income riders and withdrawal benefits. Guaranteed income riders can provide income streams over an investor's lifetime or guaranteed minimum withdrawal amounts.

Adaptive Managed Stocks and Bonds

This category includes investment managers who take an active role in changing the portfolio throughout the year to adapt to what is going on in the economy and world. The managers I tend to recommend essentially rebuild the portfolios from scratch every quarter or more often and do not have restrictions in terms of which types of equity classes they can use to build the overall portfolio. For instance, they can use bonds, stocks, or commodities. They have the ability to mix and match any of the three equity classes as they see fit. The main criteria for the advisors I hire is that they cannot use leverage. They work with all cash, which eliminates hedge funds.

Side note: How many times did your investment advisor change your portfolio in the year 2008? How many times did he or she even call you in 2008?

Consumer Grade Real Estate

In general, real estate valued at $5 million or less, including residential homes, apartment buildings, as well as small commercial properties, is considered Consumer Grade Real Estate.

Their prices tend to fluctuate far more than prices for large commercial properties because the buyers are generally less sophisticated than a group purchasing say a $100M property. More emotion is involved, which causes larger increases in good years but more significant drops in bad years.

One of the most popular investments I refer clients to is single family homes in various parts of the middle of the country where home values are generally much more reasonable compared to states such as California, Florida, or New York.

Families who would love to buy but do not have sufficient cash to buy the house outright, are forced to rent. Usually you cannot get a mortgage on these homes because the price of the house is below lending thresholds for mortgage minimums. Thus, people who do not wish to live in an apartment and do not have $60,000 or $70,000 cash in the bank are forced to rent and pay disproportionately high amounts. Typically the rents run about 15 percent of the gross value of the home. In California for instance, it is rare to pay rent above 4 to 6 percent of the value of the home.

Collectibles

What assets are considered collectibles? Anything that can be purchased and potentially demand higher prices in the future due to its rarity and popularity. Collectibles include everything from trading cards, stamps, books, and automobiles to the most popular types which are bottles of wine, fine art, and rare coins.

The most important thing to consider in whether to jump into the collectible investment game is the total net price you think you can command at the time of the sale. You then must calculate your compound annual growth rate based upon how long it takes you to sell. If the figure is substantially more than you expect to make from any of your other investments, it may be worth considering. Why must the return be significantly more than other investments such as real estate or stocks and bonds? The commissions paid are far higher than any other type of investment, typically in the 15 to 20 percent or more on both the buy and sell side. If you are going to pay a minimum of 30 percent round trip, then the collectible needs to appreciate by at least that to just break even.

The danger with valuations is that collectibles are subject, to a large degree, to the individual tastes and preferences of the populace at the time. What makes a Rembrandt or a Picasso worth $20M, $50M, or $100M? Simply the fact that others will pay such prices. Unlike an oil field or chain of taco restaurants, there is no underlying cash stream upon which the value is based. With the latter type of investment, it doesn't matter if the value of the real estate the restaurants sit on crashes—you can still rely upon the customers who are generating cash for you. There's also the issue of theft; you can't exactly throw a building into the back of a pickup truck and make a break for it like you can with a case of valuable wine.

A final danger is the simple fact of destruction. The highest price paid for a Ming porcelain vase to date is $21M in October 2011 at a Sotheby's auction. Another vase which was estimated to be worth $4M was sold at the knock-down price of $550,000 because the ill-informed owner had turned it into a cheap lamp. Imagine if the $21M vase was dropped on its way to the auction or fitted with GE light bulbs. Whoops.

For the above reasons, you may want to insist upon an additional margin of safety. A rare book set, normally trading at $2,000, may be compelling at $1,800. If you come across it for $900, however, you have left yourself ample room for attractive investment returns even if the item were to suffer a substantial shrinkage in value. Such opportunities are ephemeral, yet they do occur from time to time.

The main strength for collectibles as an investment is their tendencies to protect against inflation. The main weaknesses are of course the illiquidity, difficulty in determining value, and no cash flow to offset price fluctuations.

Rare American Coins and Bullion

Most investors focus on metal bullion but for my discussions, I prefer rare coins, which have a higher multiple against inflation. That is, for instance, if gold goes up 50 percent, rare coins in general might have a 100 percent appreciation.

As for investing in bullion such as gold and silver, there are many different routes you can take. It really depends on your level of trust/paranoia as to who has the gold or silver, will they be able to ship it to you, or do they even have it. Morgan Stanley paid $4.4M to settle a lawsuit in June 2007 which claimed Morgan Stanley charged millions in storage fees on gold held for clients which Morgan Stanley never actually possessed. In 2011 UBS was sued for the same situation but this time for charging storage fees on phantom silver. Needless to say, investors have good reason to question who is purchasing and storing their precious metals.

The easiest route to own precious metals is to use an exchange traded fund (ETF) such as SIVR, SGOL, or others. With these ETFs you never have the right to call them up and ask for the underlying precious metal. You do have the ease of these ETFs trading on a public exchange and the correlating ability to buy and sell quickly.

For those who wish to know with certainty that they COULD get their gold or silver, you can use an allocated custodian such as Bullionvault.com or Goldmoney.com. They store the precious metals for you in allocated accounts, which are individually audited and guaranteed to be in possession. With these types of bullion ownership you could request they send you your precious metals. Of course if all hell is breaking loose, good luck getting the delivery.

This brings up the last version of bullion ownership, having your gold, silver, platinum, or other metals physically in your possession under your pillow. My recommendation to most of my clients is a happy medium among the three types is the best route, but for most intents and purposes, the ETFs work just fine.

Oil/Gas Investments

These include everything from exploration and developmental to royalty programs.

Exploration Programs—New wells in uncharted areas. In general, these were the majority of the programs in the late 1980s, which everyone remembers lost all the money. They tend to have a very low success rate and as a general rule I do not recommend them to clients. I feel you might as well go to Vegas. At least you'll get free drinks for throwing your money down the drain, or a well in this example.

Developmental Programs—New or reconditioned wells in existing fields around existing producing wells. Think of an oil/gas field with wells already producing. These programs are all about putting more straws in the dirt. Common drilling success rates can be in the upper 90 percent range. A benefit to investing in these types of oil/gas programs is the tax advantage of the intangible drilling cost (IDC) deduction allowed by the IRS. Basically if you put $100 into a developmental drilling program, you can write off almost all of the $100 on your income tax return as a deduction that year. The nice part, this deduction is considered a self- employment loss and will offset all types of income: passive, ordinary, and capital gains, as well as significantly lowering the alternative minimum tax (AMT) floor. This is a huge advantage for those who are running into AMT problems at tax time.

Royalty Programs—Buying land with mineral rights and letting the developmental or exploratory drillers do all the hard work. For their hard work, the drillers generally get 75 percent of the production. Royalty owners sit back and collect 25 percent of the production coming from their lands. This is considered the most conservative form of direct ownership energy investing.

Equipment Leases

Investments in companies that specialize in purchasing and leasing equipment to other companies, generating cash flow, and later selling that equipment after the lease period expires. The biggest problem with this type of equipment leasing investment is predicting what the residual value of the equipment will be when they need to sell it. Other versions of these investments are based on lending money to big companies for equipment they are purchasing, with the equipment being collateral along with the full faith and credit of the company. The lender version of equipment leasing tends to be the prevalent trend with these types of investments as the biggest problem with the purchasing version, predicting the residual value, is taken out of the final equation. They simply supply money for a loan and are paid back the loan principal at the end.

Institutional Grade Real Estate

This is generally real estate valued at $5M or more, either single or portfolio properties, Tenant-in-Common, Delaware Statutory Trusts (DST), or Real Estate Investment Trusts (REITs). There are two types of REITs: stock exchange REITs and non-traded REITs. Non-traded REITs are *not* available on the stock market and thus fall into the illiquid category. I prefer these types of REITs simply because it allows me to evaluate the real estate and not be concerned with the stock market as a whole. REITs that trade on the stock market are classified as static mutual funds. Though they are real estate, since they trade on the markets, they tend to follow the markets in general and lose much of their non-correlation status. Did the real estate underlying the stock exchange REITs drop close to 85 percent as did the stock market REIT index did during the 2008 market collapse? Most likely not, but the emotionality of the rest of the equity market caused investors to oversell the REIT shares to far below book value prices. An example of how the stock exchange REITs had lost their correlation to the underlying asset they represent due to emotion and not fundamentals.

Collateralized Notes

These, in a nutshell, are pools of debt instruments and loans collateralized by real estate, company assets, or life insurance policies.

A mortgage pool is collateralized by real estate. These are usually first position deeds only, but under certain circumstances blended pools of first position and some subordinated loans are used to enhance overall return.

Business Development Corporations (BDCs) are investments of loans collateralized by a company and its assets. These loans are generally senior secured debt, the highest in the pecking order of a company. If a company goes out of business, as was the case of General Motors in June 2009, the investors in GM senior secured debt were paid back 100 percent, whereas the stock, bond, and preferred stock holders were almost all completely wiped out.

BDC investments basically allow an investor to act like a bank and loan money to a private company. These companies use the proceeds for any number of reasons such as growing the business, buying manufacturing plants, managing cash flow, and so forth. Many of the loans are structured with interest rates that vary with LIBOR and thus can potentially provide an inflation hedge for the BDC investment.

Normally BDCs were only available to investors with deep pockets such as pensions, college endowments, and ultra-wealthy families. But, with the global credit crunch the investment groups who sponsor these BDCs were in need of other investment capital infusions and opened themselves up to the general public by accepting smaller financial commitments.

Finally, life settlement notes are collateralized by large pools of life insurance policies which individuals have sold to an investment group. The return for the investment group as well as investors in the life settlement note is generated as the various life policies within the note pool pay out. That is, when an insured passes away, the life settlement note as the new beneficiary collects the death proceeds.

Certificates of Deposit

Bank instruments that are FDIC insured. This category includes a new investment vehicle called structured CDs. These CDs are tied to a stock market index, some with guarantees of principal via FDIC insurance.

Cash

Bank instruments that are FDIC insured as well as cash held in foreign denominations

Fixed Annuity

Either fixed or index fixed, these are similar in design to variable annuities from an insurance standpoint. They include the same types of annuitization features, income riders, and bonuses, yet they are not directly in the stock market as variable annuities are. Recently, the Securities and Exchange Commission (SEC) ruled that index fixed annuities, since they correspond to various market indexes, should be considered securities and must be sold by licensed individuals. The insurance industry fought back and got the ruling reversed. I feel index fixed annuities should be classified as a security because many insurance-only licensed agents have represented themselves as full-service advisors, discussing the stock market in general yet not having any of the required licenses or true breadth of knowledge the basic security licenses minimally require for them to pass. Oh, the power of lobbyists.

The last category that has not been discussed is life insurance as an investment. Life insurance has many purposes, and many different advisors use it depending on their viewpoint. Some only sell life insurance so that two years down the road they can sell the policy in the settlement market for a cash payout. Others use it for estate planning purposes, and others use it as a long-term retirement vehicle. These are a few of the uses for life insurance and all have their advantages and pitfalls. In Chapter 9, I will discuss my viewpoint of the various ideas I see coming across my desk. Insurance is a very important part of financial planning for some people, but it doesn't make sense for others. It depends on the client and his or her needs.

This has been just a brief overview of the different asset classes. After being introduced to the whole *Wealth Code* plan, you can continue your in-depth education of the various asset classes by reading Appendix B.

20,000-Foot Viewpoint on Money

The next sections are included to provide a different viewpoint on money; one that I think is simple to grasp yet powerful to know. Most people will tell you that finance is too complicated. I remember a fellow advisor who once told me that if they could make a children's book out of Einstein's theory of relativity, then teaching people about finance should be a walk in the park.

Let's start with the view at 20,000 feet and begin to look at money in terms of general groupings.

The investments on the left side of the following teeter-totter are generally emotional investments (see Figure 6.2). They trade, and their prices fluctuate based on fear and greed. The general public has the ultimate control. When they get greedy, the prices tend to jump quickly. Of course, when fear sets in, prices tend to drop even faster. Why? Fear is a more powerful emotion than greed.

The investments on the right side of the teeter-totter tend to be unemotional investments. A CD is a good example. You buy a CD, assume 4 percent interest for one year, and over the duration of that year you will earn 4 percent. There isn't a lot to worry about with a CD, unless of course the bank you have your money in goes belly up. Even though you are probably within the FDIC's limits, no matter what people say, it is still unnerving to be in a bank that becomes insolvent.

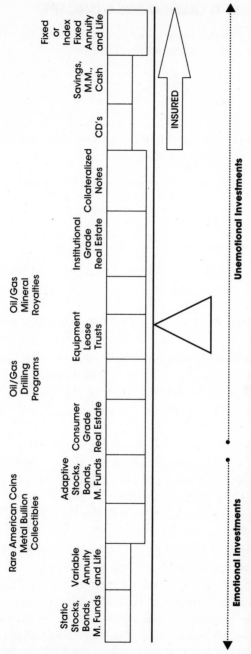

Figure 6.2 Emotional versus Unemotional Investments

KEY WEALTH CODE CONCEPT

In general, emotional investments are liquid and unemotional investments are illiquid.

Coming down to the 10,000-foot level, investments can generally be thought of in three categories:

High Return (HR)	Goal of 10% or more per year;
Liquid (L)	Access to all your money essentially within 30 days;
Capital Preservation (CP)	The reasonable assumption your money is protected and the balance won't fluctuate much if at all.

There is a fourth description that applies to fixed annuities or index fixed annuities, and that is:

Mid-Return(MR)—Goal of 3 to 5 percent per year.

Fixed annuities are meant for someone who has very specific goals. I don't necessarily feel they will keep up with inflation in the long run and thus are not part of the three main groupings. Annuities do serve a purpose, however, and will be discussed in Chapter 9.

With capital preservation, as always, assumptions must be made. The key word is *reasonable* assumptions. For instance, let's say a particular oil royalty program effectively pays 5 percent when oil is at $50 per barrel. At $80 per barrel, the distributions will effectively be around 8 percent and at $100 oil, the cash flow could be around 12 percent.

No two royalty programs are the same, and there is never a guarantee of distributions or return of principal.

With that being said, after some detailed due diligence on the group that is bringing out the royalty program, let's say you feel the above percentage payments will generally match those oil prices. The overall assumption that needs to follow is your own. If you personally think oil is going down to $5 then you would never want to get into this particular investment. Anytime the price of oil drops, you'll call your adviser in a panic and want to sell. On the flip side, if you believe oil is going to average $80 and will at least stay above $50 for the foreseeable future, then you believe your distributions should be 5 percent or more.

You would be going into the investment with eyes open and with assumptions that are reasonable. When the price of oil ebbs and flows, because you firmly believe oil in the long run is going up then you won't stress a whole lot about the inevitable fluctuations in your corresponding distributions. When people don't stress or panic, they tend to not make as many irrational buy/sell decisions with their investments and thus see greater returns overall. They tend to avoid the buy high and sell low dilemma we see all too often with investors.

KEY WEALTH CODE CONCEPT

Matching investments to your own perceptions and beliefs, and not your advisor's, generally leads to long-term success. The good investments are allowed the time to work and not be cut short in a panic sell.

KEY WEALTH CODE CONCEPT

The catch to all investments in general is that you can have *only* two of the three attributes per investment.

There is no such thing as an investment that meets all three goals: High Return, is Liquid, and offers Capital Preservation. If someone tells you about an investment with all three general descriptions, I have a great bridge from Brooklyn to sell you.

Goal: **High Return and Liquid (Figure 6.3)**
Trade off: **Capital Preservation**

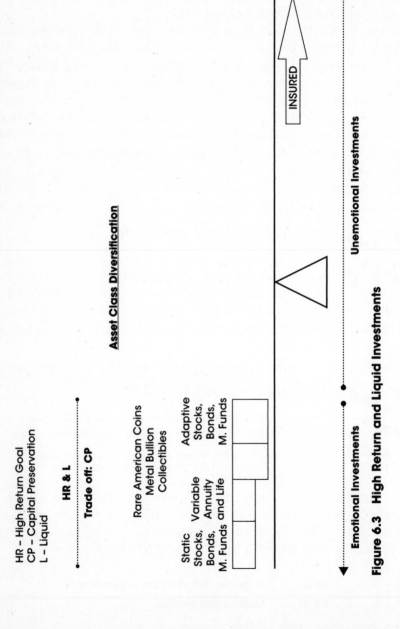

HR – High Return Goal
CP – Capital Preservation
L – Liquid

HR & L

Trade off: CP

Asset Class Diversification

Rare American Coins
Metal Bullion
Collectibles

Adaptive
Stocks,
Bonds,
M. Funds

Static
Stocks,
Bonds,
M. Funds and Life

Variable
Annuity
and Life

INSURED

Emotional Investments

Unemotional Investments

Figure 6.3 High Return and Liquid Investments

As a group, investments that fall into the emotional category tend to be described as High Return and Liquid (HR-L).

Stocks and bonds can be thought of as high return and liquid, as can bullion and rare coins. The tradeoff for these investments is you give up the preservation of your capital and take on increased volatility and risk of principal. Between October 2008 and March 2009, it's interesting to observe that there were more plus/negative 5 percent moves in the stock market during those five months than in the previous fifty years combined. It gives new meaning to volatility and high risk.

You might think, "My bonds are conservative and they preserve my capital." Do they? In January 2009, 30-year Treasury bonds sustained their biggest losses in U.S. history, around 12 percent. That's a loss of 12 percent in a single month. Does that sound like an investment that preserves one's capital?

Bonds perform well in an environment of falling interest rates, such as we have had between 1982 and 2012, but ask yourself a simple question: How much lower can interest rates go? How much longer can the Federal Reserve artificially keep interest rates contained? If history is any guide, these secular or long-term interest rate trends move in roughly 20-year cycles. We are long overdue for the trend to reverse, and, unfortunately when it does, it will not be pretty for fixed interest investments such as bonds and preferred stocks.

Variable annuities are in the HR-L category but with a few caveats. Yes, they can be liquid but for a price, a surrender fee. Variable annuities also can provide account protection in case the stock market tanks. This is generally accomplished via guaranteed withdrawal benefits and death benefits. In terms of guaranteed withdrawal benefits, to activate you generally have to get your initial money back over many years or even your lifetime and of course to get the death benefit, well, you have to die. How's that for a benefit.

Goal: **High Return and Capital Preservation (Figure 6.4)**

Trade off: **Liquidity**

The investments in the middle of the teeter-totter are as follows: consumer grade real estate, oil/gas, institutional grade real

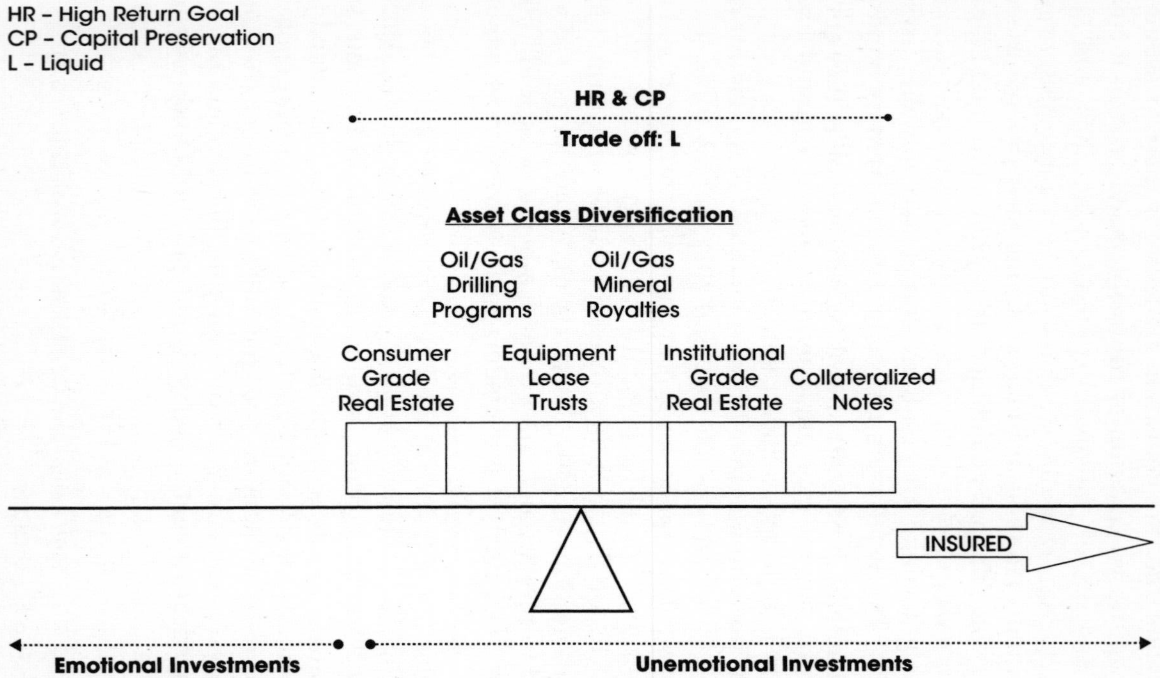

HR – High Return Goal
CP – Capital Preservation
L – Liquid

HR & CP

Trade off: L

Asset Class Diversification

| Consumer Grade Real Estate | | Oil/Gas Drilling Programs | Equipment Lease Trusts | Oil/Gas Mineral Royalties | Institutional Grade Real Estate | Collateralized Notes |

INSURED

Emotional Investments

Unemotional Investments

Figure 6.4   High Return and Capital Preservation

estate, equipment leases, and collateralized notes. These generally fall into the High Return and Capital Preservation (HR-CP) category, but the catch to these investments is that you give up liquidity.

The key to these investments is *time* and *collateral.* There is something backing the money that in general provides an inflation hedge. Look at the wealth of the very rich. The majority of it was built from tangible assets: real estate, oil/gas, timber, or from building a business.

When Enron went out of business, the stockholders lost everything. The bond holders lost everything. Who didn't lose? The real estate group that owned the Enron headquarters building. They lost a tenant and some rent for a while. But, as soon as they got new tenants, they were back in business.

If Fed Ex were to go out of business, the stock and bond holders would get nothing. The equipment leasing group that owns the plane Fed Ex is using would simply take back the plane, paint it brown, call it UPS, and re-lease it. Then they would sue Fed Ex for the difference in lost lease payments.

The key is that there is more than a promise and a stock certificate backing the investment.

Many will argue that stocks over time will provide the same inflation hedge. I disagree. As reported in a 2012 Study from DALBAR, Inc., a Boston based research firm:

> "From January 1, 1992 to December 31, 2011, the average equity mutual fund investor earned 3.49 percent annually: compared to inflation of 2.50 percent and the 7.81 percent that the S&P 500 index earned annually for that 20 year time period."

DALBAR studied the cash inflows and outflows of the market over these time periods which demonstrate the emotional buying and selling of the typical investor. Buying at the top (Greed) and selling at the bottom (Fear) dramatically affected the long-term performance results of their portfolios.

Table 6.1 shows the various holding periods and the results for the average investor.

Table 6.1 DALBAR 2012 Results

	20 Year	10 Year	5 Year	3 Year	1 Year
Average Investor Return	3.49%	2.39%	−2.21%	12.56%	−5.73%
S&P 500	7.81%	2.92%	−0.25%	14.11%	2.12%
Behavior Difference	−4.32%	−0.53%	−1.96%	−1.55%	−7.85%

Now that you've seen the results, perhaps you're wondering why investors have done so poorly in achieving returns in line with the most popular benchmark. Well, I believe the answer stems from one main issue: emotion.

Buy high and sell low. Wall Street preaches the opposite, but in practice, few people achieve great results in the markets. Few people have the patience to ride out the rough times. This results in the behavior difference between the S&P 500 index results and the results of the average mutual fund investor.

When the going gets tough, many people panic. They sell at the wrong times, miss rebounds, and buy at the emotional tops before the next correction, further compounding poor performance.

Yet, most people swear up, down and sideways that they are making money hand over fist. Over the years, as I've met literally thousands of prospective clients and discussed their investments, they tend to exaggerate dramatically the performance of their portfolio. They, almost subconsciously, do this to justify the years they have been in the markets. Yet, when the numbers are crunched, they generally have made little to nothing in terms of growth. The dollars in the accounts are mostly from good old hard savings.

A gentleman came in and said, "Morgan Stanley did a great job. I started with $300,000 12 years ago. I've pulled out over $200,000, and I still have $280,000 today. My advisor says I've averaged over 10 percent." It is easy to say something, and most investors lack the tools to double-check a statement made to them about their performance results.

My favorite side companion is my HP10bII calculator. It's a very simple financial calculator to use, and I strongly suggest anyone who wants to have a clearer picture of their finances pick one up and learn simple calculations like future value, interest earned, and so forth.

Handing it to the man, I had him punch in the appropriate numbers.

Starting principal: $300,000

Ending principal: $280,000

Time: 12 years

Payments received: $200,000 at $16,666 each year

Solve for the Interest earned: 5.14 percent

I asked him whether he likes watching his accounts go up and down, and he responded that he hated it. The stress drove him nuts. The realization that he had made basically what a CD would have paid over the same period of time eroded his belief in the stock market.

A doctor came in raving about the great performance of his mutual funds within his 401(k). "I started with $100,000, and today I have $200,000 in my accounts a mere five years later. Can you match that?" he asked. I then pointed out that his statements showed he had contributed another $100,000 over that five-year period, in addition to the $100,000 he started with. He looked sternly at me and said, "I'm too busy working to make any money!"

Goal: **Capital Preservation and Liquid (Figure 6.5)**

Trade off: **High Return**

Investments in the Capital Preservation-Liquid (CP-L) category are generally the banking and brokerage products: CDs, savings, cash, and money market accounts. These investments are generally for emergencies and short-term financial goals. I've described these investments to clients as short-term parking spots. If you park a car on a street and forget about it for a week, what happens? You get a ticket, or worse, your car gets towed.

The penalty you incur for keeping your money in these investment products is that you are losing to inflation. Your purchasing power on the dollars in these investments is going down, thus the

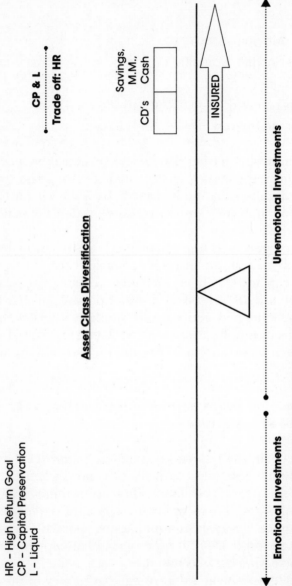

HR – High Return Goal
CP – Capital Preservation
L – Liquid

CP & L

Trade off: HR

Asset Class Diversification

Savings,
M.M.,
CD's   Cash

INSURED

Emotional Investments

Unemotional Investments

Figure 6.5 Capital Preservation and Liquid

joke, "Certificates of Depreciation." The only decade when CDs have outpaced inflation and taxes was the 1980s, and only by a smidgen.

In 1980, inflation spiked to more than 13.5 percent while a six-month CD paid on average 12.94 percent. The owners of these CDs actually lost 0.56 percent in purchasing power that year because of inflation. To put this in actual dollars, if you had put $10,000 into a CD, your statement at the end of the year would have shown a balance of $11,294. It looks pretty good. The problem is that $11,294 would only buy $9,951 worth of goods in terms of the previous year's dollars. Worse yet, if you were in the 20 percent tax bracket and 4 percent state tax bracket, now you would be down to $9,677. The inflation diet is having a powerful, negative impact on your savings.

Using the completed teeter-totter (see Figure 6.6), I want to give you a way to look at your money from a new perspective and show you how to build a solid financial table.

I feel the best portfolios are mixtures of these investment categories, having money in the HR-L bucket, as well as the HR-CP bucket and CP-L bucket. You never want just one or the other.

Liquidity, though often overstated in terms of necessity, is important for part of your money. High return is vital to keep up with the hidden tax called inflation, and preservation of your capital is the foundation for the other two.

In general, I believe moving people away from static stocks, bonds, and mutual funds, as well as from variable annuities down the teeter-totter is important for achieving the goals of most investors. Some of the money in the CP-L category can be moved a little bit up the teeter-totter because you can be too safe with your money and lose to inflation.

Sometimes, people will move from this category down the teeter-totter into the fixed annuity asset class (see Figure 6.7). Although moving from other categories into the fixed annuity asset class will not keep up with inflation in the long run, it is sometimes what is needed. There are times when it is appropriate to provide a high degree of protection and the tax deferred attributes of a fixed annuity, or the pension-like payouts that are possible under an annuity.

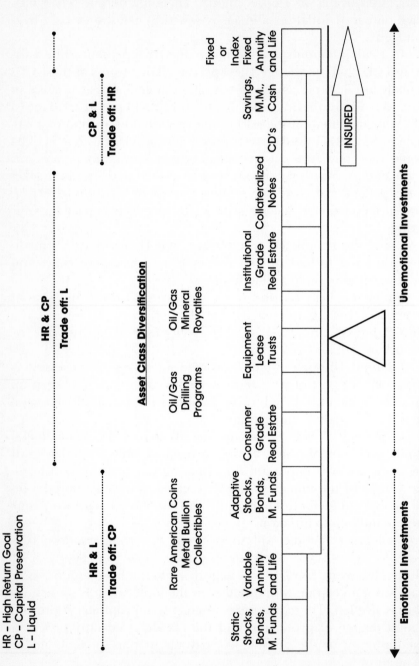

HR – High Return Goal
CP – Capital Preservation
L – Liquid

HR & CP
Trade off: L

CP & L
Trade off: HR

HR & CP
Trade off: L

HR & L
Trade off: CP

Asset Class Diversification

| Static Stocks, Bonds, M. Funds | Variable Annuity and Life | Rare American Coins Metal Bullion Collectibles | Adaptive Stocks, Bonds, M. Funds | Consumer Grade Real Estate | Oil/Gas Drilling Programs | Equipment Lease Trusts | Oil/Gas Mineral Royalties | Institutional Grade Real Estate | Collateralized Notes | CD's | Savings, M.M., Cash | Fixed or Index Fixed Annuity and Life |

INSURED

Emotional Investments ←→ Unemotional Investments

Figure 6.6 Complete Financial Teeter-Totter

84

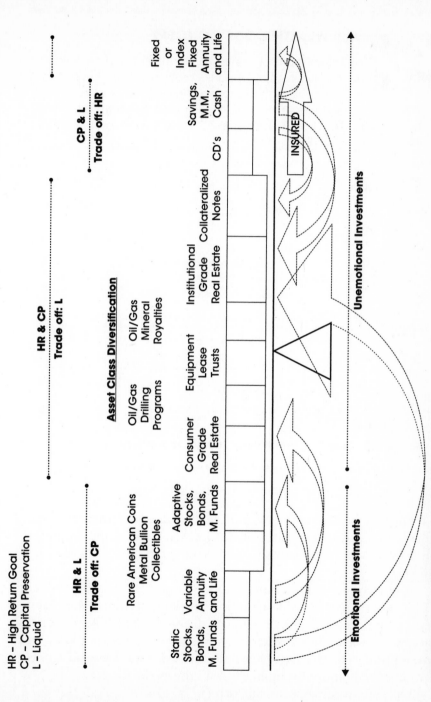

HR – High Return Goal
CP – Capital Preservation
L – Liquid

HR & L
Trade off: CP

HR & CP
Trade off: L

CP & L
Trade off: HR

Asset Class Diversification

Static
Stocks,
Bonds,
M. Funds

Variable
Annuity
and Life

Rare American Coins
Metal Bullion
Collectibles

Adaptive
Stocks,
Bonds,
M. Funds

Consumer
Grade
Real Estate

Oil/Gas
Drilling
Programs

Equipment
Lease
Trusts

Institutional
Grade
Real Estate

Oil/Gas
Mineral
Royalties

Collateralized
Notes

CD's

Savings,
M.M.,
Cash

Fixed
or
Index
Fixed
Annuity
and Life

INSURED

Emotional Investments

Unemotional Investments

Figure 6.7 Possible Portfolio Improvements

85

KEY WEALTH CODE CONCEPT

A rule of thumb I use for asset allocation once suitability has been established is one-third in the High Return-Liquid bucket (the emotional investments, not counting your personal residence) and two-thirds mixed **between** the other two categories: High Return-Capital Preservation and Capital Preservation-Liquid (Figure 6.8).

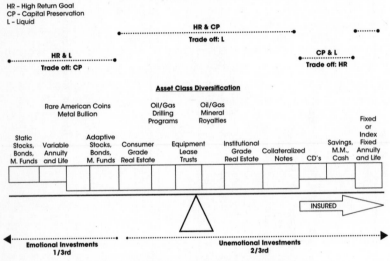

Figure 6.8 *Wealth Code* Rule of Thumb Allocations

Each person is different, and each situation ultimately determines the appropriate category into which their money is placed. Sit down with your advisor and find placements appropriate for you.

A guy comes in for a consultation. I notice he has 100 percent of his money (over a million) in his checking account. After listening to him and his lifestyle choices, I encouraged him to put his money into a higher insured deposit account, up to $50M, and wished him well. Most people would think this was lousy advice. He is losing to inflation; his money is not growing at all.

Yes, your arguments are all correct.

The man was a bit eccentric. The greatest pleasure he had in his life was going to an ATM, withdrawing twenty dollars, then leaving the ATM slip on the counter and watching from a distance as the next passerby who used the ATM would notice the slip and the large amount and then possibly look around to see who was Mr. or Ms. Big Bucks. He would do this five to ten times per day for the pure enjoyment of seeing the reaction on people's faces as they noticed the large dollar amount.

To each his own . . .

Liquidity Leak Reexamined

At this point, we have seen a new way to look at money. We understand there are many investment asset classes, and we have begun to categorize those classes by common characteristics such as high return, capital preservation, and liquidity. We know that all investments have tradeoffs and the best portfolios are mixtures of the investment asset classes that best match each individual personally. I tend to believe that mixtures of the three general categories provide the best protection in uncertain times.

When I discuss liquidity, it is very important to understand the pitfalls of emotion. In early 2009, a typical headline or business program lead would declare that the next shoe to drop would be commercial real estate. Bad loans and high leverage were the usual reasons. Because of all the publicity, commercial REITs on the stock market were utterly destroyed in the first eight weeks of 2009. Many were down more than 50 percent when the overall market was down 25 percent at that point.

Everyone was panicking because of what they heard about commercial real estate and were selling the stock market REITs as fast as they could. Did any of these people who were selling the REITs spend the time to find out how the actual buildings within the REIT were performing? Before they sold, did they find out who the tenants were, how long the leases were, what percentage of the leases was to expire soon, and how many tenants were leaving? Or did they just sell the shares because that was the only thing they knew to do emotionally?

I argue most did the latter.

Non-traded REITs are another form of investment in large commercial real estate. Many of these groups are in the exact same types of properties that the stock market REITs are in yet, since the shares cannot be sold on a whim, these investors are having far fewer sleepless nights than those holding stock market REITs.

Stock market REIT valuations are essentially controlled by the general public's fear and greed and generally uninformed opinion, whereas non-traded REITs are controlled by people who manage them as a business and know the status of their tenants, their leases, their occupancy, and so on.

If you want to sell your shares in a non-traded REIT, the originator of the shares will potentially redeem them at the market value of the actual buildings. The value is determined by the people who bought the buildings, know the leases, the tenants, and in fact know as much as possible about the buildings to determine the NAV, or Net Asset Value.

Yes, in non-traded REITs, there is a penalty for withdrawing your funds based on how long you've been invested with them. Yes, if necessary, the sponsor, the official name for the group who bought all the buildings, can even stop redemptions if they feel that investor withdrawals are taking out too much of the principal and will hurt the overall portfolio and fellow investors in the portfolio. This would result in investors being unable to sell their investment and withdraw the principal. They would most likely still be receiving their rent checks, just not have the ability to cash out of the investment. A similar situation is seen for any type of real estate if the economic times are not conducive for selling.

Like stock traded REITs, the sponsors can reduce the dividends if they feel it is in the best interest of the portfolio. There are many actions that both types of REITs share in common but there are other significant reasons that non-traded REITs are performing reasonably well now—such as access to cash infusions, low debt, and long-term debt—which distinguish them and will be explained in greater detail later.

Why do I like single-focused professionals controlling my money and not the general public? Carefully chosen professionals tend to be much less emotional in their decisions and make more consistent and informed choices. We hire them for a reason. They understand their investment class very well, and we are going to let them do their job without the interference of the less-informed general public, which tends to overreact to the latest headline.

Lately, the stock market REITs are following the trend of the general stock market. They are no longer acting as a non-correlated investment which is one of the main purposes of owning them: diversification. When the market goes up, they tend to go up. When the market goes down, they go down.

In early 2009, I'm sure that the managers of stock market REITs knew that we were in some of the best times in history to buy large commercial real estate, but they could not act on it due to limited access to credit and falling stock prices. The non-traded REITs, who were actively raising money, did not have that problem. They had access to cash from investor inflows and could gobble up deals not seen in 40 years. Thus, they were building their portfolios, making them even stronger amidst the chaos of 2008 and 2009.

There will be a more detailed discussion of the different REITs in Appendix B, but for this discussion, they serve to help distinguish the effects of liquidity on the performance of a portfolio. In general, I do not want the public determining the outcome of my investments. I prefer to hire groups who can make reasonably informed decisions about investments with my money and not make irrational decisions based on little knowledge of the facts.

This does not mean that there are no investors able to understand investments as well as seasoned professionals. As evidenced by the market turmoil of 2008 and the global credit crunch, many seasoned professionals on Wall Street obviously didn't anticipate—or care—what the outcomes of their reckless endeavors would be.

In general, however, someone who has spent a lifetime working in one profession, whether it is in real estate or underwater pearl diving, will have knowledge of the subject far superior to the general public. That is the person I want investing my money.

Finally, liquidity needs to be a piece of one's portfolio, but it comes with a price. It is appropriate to meet short-term goals, emergencies, the what ifs, as well as providing available funds for investment opportunities found in the future. Giving up either capital preservation or high return is the price paid for liquidity. Thus you are forced into either the stock market or CDs.

The next chapter will focus on understanding fundamental concepts of the legs on the financial table, and Chapter 8 will combine all previous chapters to provide a comprehensive understanding of building your own financial blue print.

Foundations for Your
Financial Table

Every investment has unique characteristics, some good and some bad. Like people, some are temperamental and easily influenced by the ebbs and flows of the general economy while others just go with the flow, no matter what is happening.

Matching Beliefs to Your Asset Choices

When selecting appropriate investment classes to build the various legs of your financial table, one of the most important questions to ask yourself is what is your temperament? Are you a gambler who likes the excitement of possibly doubling your money with the next roll of the dice, or do you seek stability, wanting nothing but consistency in your life?

Once suitability is established, many investments are worth considering, and sometimes having a mixture of the extremes and everything in between is the answer. The aggressively investing young hotshot looking to double his money may potentially benefit by looking at some consistently performing thoroughbreds, and the 95-year-old widow may benefit from looking at some potentially inflation busting quarter horses. The bottom line for any portfolio is balance, and from experience, I feel that the portfolios with the most legs or potential for "checks in the mail" are the most successful ones.

Let's say you have 20 different legs or sub-legs on your financial table. Maybe check number three drops one month, but checks numbers eight and number fourteen rise that same month. Overall, you are still in the ballpark of what your *Wealth Code* portfolio model estimated for income that particular month or year, even though some investments have not performed as well as hoped. This is not unlike some advisors methods for equity portfolio design—a blend of beta (or risk) across the investment choices to help smooth out the ride.

Always remember the **Wealth Code Golden Rule**. The only guarantee in finance is something will go wrong. Design your portfolio around the concept of planning for the worst and hoping for the best.

Most of us do not live in a bubble. We all exist in the same macro-economic environment and if the global economy enters another great depression, even the most well thought-out investments will most likely not work out as planned. The idea of having as many legs as possible is simply following the concept of true asset class diversification. Knowing we need many support legs to prop up our table from the legs which potentially end up breaking. More legs under the table potentially help us achieve our goals as best as possible and keep our overall financial table stable and hopefully rising.

In my opinion, the ultimate design of a portfolio will depend on the individual investor's beliefs and past experiences. If you have always made your money in real estate and feel it is the only investment class worth its weight in salt, then adding an equipment lease trust or mutual fund probably won't work for you. If you do not believe this investment will work, in the future you will tend to look for reasons why it is not working, and thus, the "bad" investment becomes a self-fulfilling prophecy. You're setting yourself up for disappointment by adding investments that don't match your beliefs.

On the flip side, using investments that match your beliefs will generally provide you with a sense of calm in tumultuous times. I've seen the most loyal stock holders sit back, cool as a cucumber, while their portfolios of stocks and bonds were crashing 40 to 50 percent. They absolutely believed in the longevity of their positions, and nothing could rattle them.

One's beliefs tend to be shaped by past experiences. A client came in for a consultation, and the first thing out of his mouth was the time he lost $5,000 in an oil/gas exploratory drilling program back in 1987. His previous advisor told him all these reasons for going into the position—tax benefits, huge returns, and so on—and what happened next? The single oil well project came in dry, and he got nothing but a $5,000 tax deduction. Since then, he has always told the story of why oil/gas investments are worthless and scams. I'm sure individuals like Rockefeller would disagree, but that's not the point. For this man, unless he was open to setting aside his opinion formed over the last 20 years, oil/gas investments would most likely not be a good fit.

Time and Real Assets

A key to the successful financial performance of real assets is time and inflation. Let's say you just inherited the Empire State Building from a long-lost family billionaire and were informed that the building had no debt on it, had net positive cash flow of a million a month, but was probably not as valuable as it was in 2007 and not a good time to sell. Would you feel compelled to sell? Would you feel anxious if you sat around collecting rents to the tune of a million a month? Probably not!

Over time, the beauty of real assets is that they tend to be worth more eventually. In the meantime, you're enjoying the income from rents.

The nice thing about rental rates is that they tend to follow inflation. If the rent would buy 100 loaves of bread today, then in 20 years, whatever the cost of 100 loaves of bread is, the rent will usually have adjusted at the same relative ratio.

Since large commercial real estate tends to be valued based on the income of the property, the value of the building generally goes up if the income has gone up.

If time is not on your side, you potentially put yourself in a position where you will need to fire sale the property.

Fire sales are never any fun for the seller, but the cash-ready buyer will have lots of fun. If your house is worth $500,000 today and would reasonably sell for that amount if listed and marketed properly with plenty of time, how much do you think it would sell for if you were forced to sell it in the next 24 hours for cash? That is, what price would lure someone to snap up your house with a cashier's check the next day? Would the quick sale price be $400,000 or $250,000? The answer usually falls in the 60 percent range of the fair market value of the house.

If I drive by and see a $100,000 house with a sign out front declaring fire sale, today only, the first person with $60,000 gets it, I will be running to my bank as fast as I can. Not being greedy, the day after I buy it, I list the house for $70,000 and will probably sell it rather quickly. Not bad for a day or two of work. 60 percent of fair market value is generally the quick sale value of a piece of real estate.

As an example of some of the real estate investments we work with, non-traded REITs generally have time on their side. They tend to follow the rules of low leverage, typically under 50 percent, and long-term debt, five or ten years or longer, with fixed interest rates. With cash coming in from investors and rents coming in from their properties, they have the other keys to success: cash flow and a piggy bank filled with emergency reserves. All of these factors give these REITs time. Time to wait around for the properties to eventually become more valuable.

Have we seen the share prices of the REITs fall in the last few years? Of course, as they are tied to the overall economy and almost all classes of real estate have fallen since 2006. That being said, as long as we can ride out the rough patch, collect some rent, time will help re-inflate the value of the properties to hopefully above the original share prices.

Again, anyone who has owned a home for more than 10 or 15 years knows that time on your side always helps the bottom line. This is a benefit of owning real assets (your home, other real estate, or tangible investments)—inflation works for you.

Direct Participation Programs

One way to put money into tangible assets is through investment programs called direct participation programs (DPPs). Most of the investments within the High Return-Capital Preservation (HR-CP) category are DPPs.

When you have a direct investment in tangible or real assets, such as real estate, leased equipment, and energy resources, you own a share of the actual assets of an operating company and may benefit from the assets' value, typically the income they produce.

The most common DPPs are business development corporations (BDCs), non-traded real estate investment trusts (REITs), equipment leasing corporations, and energy exploration and development limited partnerships.

Investing through a DPP gives you partial ownership of actual physical assets. For example, if you invest in a non-traded REIT, you're a part owner of the real estate holdings of the REIT. If you invest in an equipment leasing corporation, you're part owner of the actual equipment offered for lease by the corporation. If you invest in a business development corporation, you're part owner through common shares of the BDC, of the loans funding many publicly and privately traded companies. If you invest in an oil development corporation, you're part owner of the corporation's wells and the proceeds of oil sales.

The pooled investment structure of DPPs is sometimes described as a way to provide the average investor with opportunities previously available only to the wealthy. Because you invest as part of a group, you don't need the means to acquire a large percentage stake in the venture or fund your own start-up company to invest in new businesses.

In each case, the sponsors who offer DPPs pool your funds with the funds of other participating investors to make investments they have identified as appropriate to the program's investment goals. The sponsors are responsible for managing the assets of the program as long as it continues to operate and for devising an appropriate strategy for ending it (exit strategy).

The legal structures that provide the foundations for different types of direct investment programs vary. REITs are a special type of corporation. Equipment leasing businesses are structured as limited liability corporations (LLCs). Energy ventures are formed as limited partnerships. In practice, however, the investments behave as limited partnerships, regardless of their differing legal structures.

In brief, a limited partnership has a general partner, in this case the sponsor, who runs the business, and a number of limited partners who invest but aren't involved in the partnership's operation or liable for losses beyond their own investment.

Accreditation of Investors

While learning about the different legs on the financial table, you'll notice several disclosures I've included throughout the book.

> State suitability and accredited investor rules apply—not suitable for all investors.

As licensed security advisors, many of the investments I discuss in general terms are considered accredited investments. That is, the potential investor needs to meet certain net worth and income requirements to invest in these financial tools.

Working with an experienced advisor will help you understand which investments have what type of requirements and will be appropriate for your financial portfolio.

Accreditation rules generally apply to investments that have limited liquidity or liquidity requirements. The SEC wants to make sure a person has other means besides this particular investment. I fully stand behind the idea of balance and of using appropriate vehicles for an investor, but as discussed below, I question the motivation for the rules. No one should ever put all of their eggs in one basket. You need money in many different categories to be well diversified: some resources in the High Return-Liquid category, such as stocks, bonds, and mutual funds, and other money in the Capital Preservation-Liquid category, such as the bank. Access to cash is very important for a part of your money, but as previously mentioned, it is not necessarily the Holy Grail for building wealth.

Examples of investments with partial (State) accreditation standards include the typical Non-Traded REIT, Equipment Lease Trust, Business Development Corporation, Life Note, or Mortgage debenture. These financial tools will generally have a net worth requirement of $250,000 depending on the state where you live. Another way to qualify for these particular investments is to have a net worth of $70,000 and an annual income of at least $70,000. Net worth does not include a personal residence. The particular state where you live will set the accreditation rules, and discussing this with your advisor is imperative before building a successful investment blue print.

Most oil/gas and other private securities are full accreditation investments, meaning you typically need an investible net worth of

Table 7.1   Accreditation Standards

Non-Accredited Investments	Stocks, Bonds, Mutual Funds, Annuities, Consumer Grade Real Estate
State Accredited Investments: $70,000 Income and $70,000 Net Worth Or $250,000 Net Worth	Non-Traded REITs and BDCs, Life Notes and Mortgage Debentures, Equipment Leasing, some Oil and Gas
Full Accredited Investments: $1,000,000 Net Worth Or $200,000/$300,000 Income	Most Oil and Gas, Partnerships, and Private Securities

$1M. Investible net worth is calculated without the equity value of your personal residence.

The other way to qualify for full accreditation is to have an income of more than $200,000 for each of the last two years, or $300,000 if you are married.

Table 7.1 categorizes the basic investment accreditation standards.

Other rules apply for entities such as irrevocable trusts or Limited Liability Corporations (LLCs).

Though adamant about using appropriate tools for any given investor's financial table, I am personally torn by my beliefs of accreditation for investments. I'm torn because Wall Street is the primary driver on investment rules. You could argue that the SEC or Congress sets the rules, but I disagree. Politicians' pockets are lined with Wall Street cash, and Wall Street wants to promote the investments that make them the most money year in and year out. If a particular investment doesn't pay a commission that matches their criteria, then the investment will usually have accreditation standards placed on it and thus limit the ability of advisors to recommend certain ideas.

I'm the first to believe in balance and in using many concepts that are all suitable for a particular investor, but when the rules allow an 80-year old to buy as much high tech widget IPO stock as possible, yet limit their ability to add what I consider to be an extremely conservative collateralized note program with equity three times that of the notes and a strong track record over decades, I start to question the reasons for the accreditation limits.

Are they meant to protect the individual from less scrupulous advisors or to protect Wall Street from losing that money to investments that are not as lucrative for their advisors?

It is most important to note that the investments I am discussing are securities registered with the Securities and Exchange Commission (SEC). Any investment can be a private placement or an investment not registered with the SEC, but as a licensed advisor, I only represent registered securities. Registered securities must follow the rules for disclosure and come with prospectuses. For instance, a mutual fund is a registered security, and that is why when you purchase one, you receive in the mail that big legal document most people just throw out or use to jump start a nice winter fire. However, a prospectus is very important because it tells you the information you need to evaluate an investment properly. It includes and discloses the fees, risks, management, and conflicts of interest for that particular investment.

Due diligence is the key to protecting oneself from being caught by a guy like Madoff and his $50 billion Ponzi scheme. Having registered securities provides at least a semi-transparent view of the investment. Nothing is perfect, and I'm sure there are countless examples of registered securities falling through the cracks. A great example was mortgage securities that were pitched to investors as a great alternative to cash in the bank. When the credit crunch hit in August of 2007, these "Liquid" investments became completely "Illiquid." Yes, they came with prospectuses, but nowhere in the prospectus did they fully disclose the extent to which investments inside the fund could use toxic or esoteric mortgage pools and the risks they truly represented.

One client came to me asking for help with his daughter's marriage. He had placed all the funds needed for the wedding in a mortgage-backed security, which was sold to him by an advisor pitching it as a great alternative to cash earning 1 percent. "Don't worry; it is as safe as cash," the pitchman said. "Just as liquid, also. You can sell whenever you like, since these are on the stock market!" he was told before buying it. Well, when his daughter's wedding approached and he went to sell the security for the needed cash, to his surprise, he was told, "Sorry, no one is buying that security. You'll have to wait."

My answer to the gentleman was a little more complete, but not much. We discussed the secondary market for the security and that if he did want to sell, he would probably take an 80 percent or greater loss. I felt this was not the answer and advised against it. The man was stuck with a wedding he had to pay for with credit cards at 17 percent interest rates. The point is this: Just because a security is registered and has a prospectus does not guarantee that it is a good investment.

Commissions and Fees

All investments have fees and commissions. The particular kind of investment determines which is being paid. In general, when you are in the stock market, you are paying ongoing asset fees. With real assets, in general, you are paying commissions.

If you were to buy an investment rental property, say for $100,000, and you set aside $25,000 for the purchase, this would include the down payment (20 percent or $20,000) and all initial loan costs, inspections, appraisals, and miscellaneous purchasing expenses. In this example the other costs total $5,000.

Your net cash flow is the amount left after all ongoing expenses, such as property management, property taxes, mortgage payment, and so forth, have been paid. For this example, let's say it is $4,000.

To figure out your net cash flow percentage, simply divide the net income, $4,000, by the initial investment, $25,000.

The result is around 16 percent. That is the beauty of leverage and using other people's money.

All investments, one way or another, have ongoing expenses, whether in the stock market or in real assets.

With real assets, not all the money used for the purchase is going to buy the dirt/asset. In the previous example, only $20,000 is going into the ground, the down payment. The other $5,000 covers the miscellaneous expenses to acquire the property. You might call these the commissions earned by the various parties involved, such as the appraiser, the home inspector, and the mortgage consultant.

When purchasing securities that are part of the High Return-Capital Preservation category, not all of your money goes to buy the real asset. Commissions are paid to the various people or groups involved, including the real estate or real asset agents, the appraisers, the sponsor, and the financial advisors who recommended this investment to you. For example, if you invested $100, maybe only

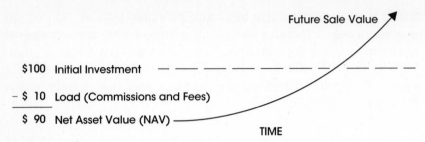

Figure 7.1   Time/Growth Overcoming Investment Fees

$90 goes into the ground/assets. Your statement, however, will reflect $100 as your balance, not $90, and if the dividend for a particular investment is 7 percent, you will see $7 of dividends paid to you that year.

The key to this category is time. The sponsor knows that it takes time for the real asset to appreciate to earn back the 10 percent or $10 paid as commissions to the various parties. They will need time for the actual ground/asset to gain value above the $100 you put in as your initial investment (see Figure 7.1). Once the property is stabilized, the rents/distributions from the real assets will cover the dividends, but the asset's appreciation is the only thing that will cover the original costs to get into the investment.

Of note and to revisit the leak in the bucket previously discussed, I believe the main reason the larger wire houses will not represent the majority of the investment classes in the High Return-Capital Preservation category is because of the one-time commission aspect. A mutual fund or variable annuity is much more profitable in the long run due to the internal ongoing fees that are paid by the investor each year, whether the investor is making money or not. This is compared to a single commission paid on a real asset security investment that might take years to go full cycle— to potentially return the principal and growth back to the investor not counting the dividends—and to free up the money to be re-invested somewhere else.

Only if the result is positive would most investors in the commission oriented investments reward the adviser by keeping the money with them, which then allows the financial advisor to make another commission. It is all about the Benjamins, they like to say.

Prioritization and Placement of Portfolio Investments

Something I hear time and time again from other advisers is "don't put a tax advantaged investment inside a tax deferred vehicle such as an IRA or 401(k)." The logic behind this is if an investment has tax advantages, they are being theoretically wasted inside the deferred vehicle and the client will not receive the benefits. Advisers will often regurgitate the inappropriateness of using an tax deferred annuity or tax advantaged piece of real estate inside an IRA or other retirement vehicle because, again, you are "double" tax deferred and potentially wasting the tax benefits. When I design a portfolio recommendation for a client, I prioritize the possible investment choices according to the client's resources and income needs. Resources are defined as how much pre-tax and after-tax money the client has available as part of their investable net worth.

The first thing I do is match the types of investments or legs on the table to the amount of investment dollars I'm working with. For example, $100,000 might be four investments while $1M could be as many as 20 different investments.

I consider each potential investment to be used in a portfolio by the following prioritization:

- What is the expected potential income and growth
- What is the expected liquidity and flexibility
- What are the tax advantages

If the client has all their money in retirement accounts, then tax advantages don't necessarily matter. Any income generated will be fully taxed.

If a client has a mixture of both types of money, then after the first two prioritizations are satisfied, then and only then do I consider the tax benefits and the ultimate placement of the investment. That is, should a particular investment go into a pre-tax account or an after-tax account.

Look at the three considerations for an investment. First and foremost, whether an investment is going into a pre-tax or after-tax account, the bottom line is whether it can potentially have a good return. That is priority number one. Who cares if something is double deferred by placing it into a retirement account. If that investment has the potential to bring home the bacon and is suitable for the client, use it.

I have heard many advisers say you should only put investments with loss potentials in after-tax accounts because if they lose, at least the client will be able to write off the loss. A quick reminder to the reader; ALL investments can lose your money. That fact alone negates this erroneous concept.

Second, once I believe an investment is suitable and has the potential to generate a return, then I consider the liquidity of that investment. This is priority number two. Liquidity will determine if a particular investment is better situated in a pre-tax retirement account or an after-tax account.

Many illiquid investments can work well inside a retirement account because the investor's goals usually don't require them to need access to the principal, just the potential income. Liquidity is not their concern so investments in the high return–capital preservation category are natural fits.

I try to maximize more liquid investments such as the adaptive managers in the stock market or the illiquid investments with shorter expected durations in the after-tax accounts. This is done for the simple reason of access to principal and tax consequences. If a client calls me up needing $50,000 for a new car, after-tax money is a far better resource to pull from than pre-tax dollars as the pre-tax dollars will most likely cause a larger tax consequence.

Finally, the third priority for an investment and where to position it, whether in a pre-tax or after-tax account, is the tax advantages. Does the investment come with perks such as depreciation, depletion, deferral, and so forth?

If all things are basically equal and I've picked two investments for a client's portfolio that I believe will have roughly the same potential return and the liquidity is comparable, I'll focus the investment with greater tax advantages in the after-tax pool of money. A Business Development Corporation which generally will not have any tax advantaged income will work better in an IRA than a non-traded REIT because the REIT should generally provide depreciation offsets on its distributions. If the client is pulling income from both investments, by using the REIT in the after-tax account, the total reportable income should be lower and thus lower the eventual tax bill.

In Summary

Becoming a competent carpenter requires a strong understanding of the basics of woodworking and craftsmanship. Something as simple as which types of glues work best with which types of woods is an example of understanding the basics.

The foundational concepts for *The Wealth Code* portfolio can be thought of as the glue for each investment leg on your financial table and are vital to beginning to build your portfolio's blue print as described in the next chapter.

Understanding the effects of inflation and time on tangible investments, how fees and commissions are paid, and access to private securities known as DPPs gives one a more diverse playing field to choose from when designing their custom portfolio.

Building a Strong Financial Table

Up to this point, I have covered the principles of *The Wealth Code*. The key to preserving and growing wealth is understanding that the world is a lot bigger than stocks and bonds and that the most successful portfolios are ones which include many asset classes, which work together like an Olympic basketball team.

The goal of this chapter is to provide a framework for you to control your own destiny, to build your own financial table. I want to take the mystery out of the planning process and give you a solid foundation for building a blueprint for your investments, one that matches your personality and risk tolerances. You can then hand this over to a competent advisor to implement and oversee, knowing the plan truly is in your best interest and not someone else's.

I describe most people I see at my firm as rafting down a river. The problem is that this particular river has a very large waterfall at the end. Most people drift down the middle somewhat aimlessly hoping for the best, and of course, we know where this drifting eventually takes them: to retirement and investment results that are far short of what they had envisioned. The key to navigating this river is to find the small offshoot, the side stream hidden by the brush, and to steer your raft to it and to the end, where you arrive at a nice sandy beach, a restful place where you can have a bountiful picnic with your family, without a care in the world. In order to spot the side stream, education is the key. Being able to recognize the alternative is 90 percent of the battle and takes five crucial steps.

Step One: Know Yourself

I will describe this step from the viewpoint of a financial advisor.

The first rule for any financial advisor is to know the client: his or her goals, background, income, future income needs, expenses, investments, estate planning, insurance and insurance requirements, taxes, college needs, family planning, past disappointments, and so forth.

Without understanding the client and putting down on paper all of the above, and reviewing it frequently, it is impossible to design a good plan. You can't make a bull's eye on an invisible dartboard.

Here is a list of common questions to help fill in the pieces of the puzzle:

General

Age?

Professions, current and past?

Income?

Changes in income anticipated?

Health concerns?

Marital Status?

Social Security/anticipated at different ages: 62, full benefit age, and 70?

Pensions?

Other anticipated income sources?

Retirement timeline?

Living trust/will/durable power of attorney/health directives?

Tax bracket?

Monthly living expenses?

Children?

Children's financial needs?

Grandchildren?

Health insurance?

Investment objectives?

Liquidity needs?

Risk tolerance?

Real Estate

For each of the properties you have, primary residence, secondary homes, investment properties, or partnerships, fill in the following questions:

Cost basis?

Cost of improvements?

Fair market value?

Mortgage balance(s) and type of mortgage(s)?

Reset date if adjustable mortgage?

Rental income?

Net rental income as a percent of the equity in the property?

Planning/willing to sell?

Do you want to pay off the mortgage or never pay off the mortgage and arbitrage the interest rate?

Who manages the property?

If you self-manage, do you like the terrible Ts (tenants, toilets, trash, termites, teenagers) that encompass management of the property?

Investments

Retirement accounts?

Active and contributing?

Which accounts are inactive or from an old employer?

Do you want to consolidate the old accounts?

After-tax accounts?

Real performance of investment accounts over one-, five-, and ten-year periods, taking into account contributions you've made?

Emergency money?

Life Insurance

What happens if you or your spouse dies? How will the other spouse/children be financially?

Estate tax planning and the use of insurance?

Charitable gifting and estate preservation?

Using leverage via loans when purchasing life insurance?

Estate Planning

Special needs of your family/self?

Goals to accomplish?

Gifting?

Reduction or estate freezing?

Guardians for underage children?

Irrevocable trusts?

Asset Protection (Lawsuit) Planning

Corporations, LLCs?

Foreign versus domestic domicile of companies?

Ownership versus control?

Irrevocable trusts?

Finally, a general understanding of the person's background, culture, beliefs, bad experiences, and good experiences will round out the information needed.

Step Two: Liquidity Time Lines

Crucial for designing an appropriate portfolio is understanding each client's needs for lump sum money or future income.

Examples would be:

Are you planning to buy more real estate/investments in the future, and will you need deposits or large sums of ready cash?

Education needs?

Health care needs?

Large purchase needs?

Retirement time lines?

Age of client?

It is important to have emergency money for those what-if needs, but as previously mentioned, very few large emergencies ever happen, and keeping money tied up in low returning, liquid savings accounts will end up costing small fortunes in missed opportunities and losses to inflation over time. Three to six months of liquid reserves is a typical safety net. If someone has a lot of cash flow, then safety reserves can be even lower.

Personally, I feel the best safety nets are lines of credit on real estate. If you have a line of credit worth $100,000 on your home or investment property, keep the balance at zero. If the what-if emergency does happen, write a check and pay for it. Then pay back the line of credit as soon as possible. At least you will be able to deduct the interest. In the meantime, while that what-if emergency is not happening, you don't have money sitting in a savings account earning 1 to 2 percent and losing purchasing power by the day.

Varying the timelines of the real asset investments is also a way to keep money available for whatever comes your way, either a better investment or other opportunities. By designing a portfolio with different maturation dates, money increasingly becomes liquid as time passes. This concept is the same as a CD ladder or bond ladder, but I like to do it with ownership of tangible assets.

No one knows what the world will look like three to six years from now. Designing a portfolio where 80 percent of the money will be essentially liquid within those time lines can provide the flexibility to shift and reallocate resources into more appropriate investment vehicles should circumstances call for it. For instance, by using the stock market and adaptive managers and/or bullion (liquid), consumer grade real estate (120 days or less), collateralized note programs (six months to five years liquid), REITS and BDCs (three to six years liquid), and possibly other ideas with shorter maturation dates, if the rest of the world stops buying United States Treasury bonds and demands higher yields for their risk and treasuries go to 15 percent yields, no problem. Pull your money out of the investments that will earn less than 15 percent and move them into treasuries. The ability to adapt is vital for long-term success.

Table 8.1 shows what a simple investment ladder might look like. It provides additional liquidity as time passes and more and more of the investments become effectively liquid. This is the same concept as a bond ladder where you buy bonds with different maturity dates to provide liquidity and an opportunity to increase yield.

A last discussion on liquidity time lines revolves around the use of retirement accounts such as IRAs, 401(k)s (or 201k if yours hasn't done well in the various stock market crashes), 403(b)s,

Table 8.1   Simple Investment Ladder

Investment:	Liquidity Timeline:
Stock Market and/or bullion	Liquid
Consumer Grade Real Estate	120 days or less
Collateralized Notes	6 month to five years
REITs	Three to six years

COMMON SENSE CONCEPT

Assume market interest rates were 15 percent and remember that bond values are inversely tied to interest rates. That is, as interest rates increase, the value of the bonds will drop (Figure 8.1).

How liquid are those muni bonds you own? What price would you get if you had an emergency and needed to sell them quickly?

For instance, the market value of a 20-year muni-bond paying 5 percent would have dropped by approximately 75 percent if interest rates had risen to 15 percent. If you purchased a bond worth $100,000, its market value would be approximately $25,000.

Does this bond provide the owner the ability to adapt to the current market place and inflation? Of course not. If there's any hope of getting the original principal back, the investor is forced to stay in

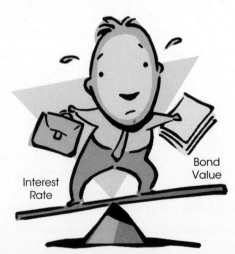

Figure 8.1   Interest Rates versus Bond Values

the bond until maturation, 20 years from purchase. In the meantime, you'll be stuck with 5 percent interest payments when the cost of goods and services is climbing 15 percent each year, effectively losing 10 percent in purchasing power. Finally, once the original principal is returned, how much has inflation destroyed the original purchasing power of those dollars?

Needless to say, in these inflationary times we are not fans of anything long term (10 years or greater) such as bonds, preferred stocks, or most debt instruments.

457s, profit sharing plans, and everything else that is treated as a tax-deferred retirement plan by the IRS.

If someone is 50 years old and has an IRA that he or she does not plan on touching for at least another 10 years, does this person really need a lot of liquidity within this IRA? The answer is most likely no. As long as there are plenty of resources outside the IRA that remain liquid and available in times of emergency, liquidity within the IRA becomes a detriment. It forces you to be either in the stock market or in the banks.

If you realize that time is on your side, that you will not be touching the money for a long time, then you have far less a need for liquidity and can focus your IRA or whatever retirement account you have on financial tools that fall into the High Return-Capital Preservation (HR-CP) category (see Figure 8.2). The drawback to this category is time, but if time is something you have, then you can manage your investments and benefit from a different strategy. The nice part of these investments, the tangible investments, is that they usually pay monthly dividends or distributions that can be reinvested during the years, and once you hit your magic age of 59½, you can turn on the potential income streams and leave the principal alone. Isn't that what retirement accounts should be designed to be, slow income payers?

Many clients never want to touch their IRAs or other tax-deferred retirement accounts until they are forced to at age 70½. The good news is the HR-CP investments generally pay more than 3.6 percent in dividends, which is roughly the starting required minimum distribution (RMD) percent at age 70½. In order to satisfy your RMD, just pay out some dividends for a portion of the year, and then turn the distributions off. Thus, you will not be over

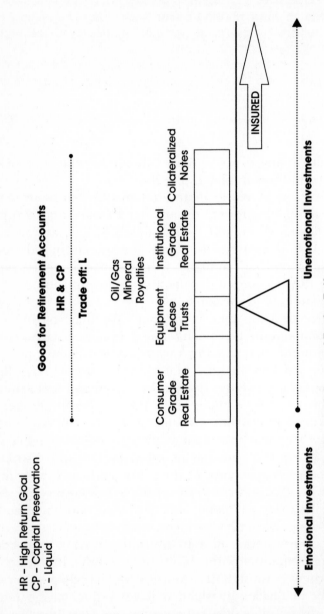

HR – High Return Goal
CP – Capital Preservation
L – Liquid

Good for Retirement Accounts

HR & CP

Trade off: L

Oil/Gas
Mineral
Royalties

Consumer   Equipment   Institutional
Grade   Lease   Grade   Collateralized
Real Estate   Trusts   Real Estate   Notes

INSURED

Emotional Investments   Unemotional Investments

Figure 8.2 Common Retirement Account Teeter Totter

withdrawing from your retirement account and paying unnecessary taxes on money not needed.

The one drawback to using tax-advantaged investments within an IRA or other tax deferred retirement account is that you do not get the tax depreciation or other deduction benefits. As previously described many advisers make rigid statements like, "Don't be double tax deferred in an IRA." That is, they are stating that using investments which can provide tax benefits if used outside of a retirement account are not good investments to be used inside a retirement account. Who cares! In a retirement account you just want total return and, if you believe a certain investment will deliver a solid return, then the HR-CP investment is a natural fit even within a tax-deferred, time-based account like an IRA.

Not to be missed if you currently own an IRA, 401(k) or other pre-tax retirement account, in Appendix C I'll show a little known yet powerful tax strategy which only works with the illiquid HR-CP investments in a Roth IRA conversion.

Step Three: Income Needs

Knowing how much income a person needs as a base amount is one of the first steps in creating a successful financial plan. We always recommend that clients have as many income streams as possible to help protect against the *black swan* event.

What is a black swan event? Something totally unpredictable and uncontrollable. For instance, you own an apartment building, and a giant meteor crashes into it, completely destroying the building and making the land radioactive. That is a far-fetched example, but imagining airplanes crashing into the Twin Towers and causing small buildings down the street to sustain massive damage is also far-fetched, and yet we saw it happen. The small grocery store owner could never have thought his little business would be wiped out in seconds.

The term *black swan event* comes from a concept. If you studied swans your whole life and every swan you looked at was white, you might conclude that all swans are white. You could spend your whole life looking at millions of white swans and confidently conclude that all swans are white. But one day someone shows you a *single* black swan, as they have in New Zealand, and your entire life's work and conclusion are wrong. Thus the black swan event.

Between 2002 and 2007 many advisors felt that the global credit crunch and stock market and real estate crashes *were* black swan events. These were opinions based on ignorance, or more likely,

*IGNORE*ance. Ignoring the obvious signs of excess between 2002 and 2007 and hoping the world could sustain such financial lunacy was common. The sad part is that many people had put their full faith in these financial advisors.

The global credit crunch and following stock market crash beginning in August 2007 and continuing into 2009 was not a black swan event. This was totally predictable as demonstrated by passage of the Bankruptcy Law of October 17, 2005. This law is proof that the lenders and credit card companies as well as Wall Street knew this tidal wave of foreclosures and defaults was coming, and they (the lenders) were designing laws which would give them better protection from people using a Chapter 7 bankruptcy filing and sending the debt and losses back to the irresponsible lending banks.

In 1993 and 1994 when real estate values dropped considerably from their previous highs in 1989, many people would mail their house keys back to the lender and walk away from their residences, which were worth less than the loans on them. The envelopes received by the lender would rattle, and thus were called "Jingle Mail." Yes, their credit was hurt for the next seven years, but walking away from the upside down home would give these people a chance to rebuild without the burden of the debt. Several clients of mine did have bankruptcies in the early 1990s, but since the debt burden was alleviated, they were eventually able to get loans again and build multimillion-dollar estates.

Now, in order to file a Chapter 7 bankruptcy, you need to earn less than the average income in the United States and take six months of credit counseling. For those who earn over the average income, you will only be able to file Chapter 11 bankruptcy, which effectively keeps the burden of the debt on your shoulders forever. I believe that without the ability to rebuild, a few of our clients who intelligently used bankruptcy to give themselves a second chance would never have been able to rebuild multimillion-dollar estates and become citizens who pay high taxes again.

Don't get me wrong. I'm all for personal responsibility and accountability in handling money. But what I saw in the real estate bubble between 2002 and 2006 with predatory lenders, shady appraisers, and real estate agents up-selling and overburdening people, getting them into homes they should never have owned in the first place, was a major cause of the global financial crisis which began in 2007. Most people are great at their jobs, but most will admit when it comes to mortgages and finance that is not their specialty, and they rely on lenders and agents to be honest and put the needs of the home purchaser above their own pocketbook. This was not the case, as evidenced by the record number of people being foreclosed on today.

In 2006, my wife and I were purchasing a property with great net cash flow. The loan we were promised was a 30-year fixed, 10-year interest only loan. This allowed us to repay the bank as little as possible while letting inflation eat away our loan. The point of the story is, the mortgage broker we used tried to pull the wool over our eyes for a much larger commission.

He stated the rates he could deliver for us, a quarter point below the rest of the field, were because he was hungry and willing to work for less commission.

I'm all for someone trying to earn my business by shaving their fees somewhat. Making 80 percent of something is better than 100 percent of nothing.

After no documents showed up for a week, I started calling this mortgage broker to confirm the terms of the loan. He so much as swore on his kid's life that the loan we would get was the one we asked for—the 30-year fixed, 10-year interest only. Four days before the close of escrow, he finally showed up with the documents. I took one look at the documents and they were not as promised. He brought us a 10-one ARM. That is, a loan fixed for 10 years and an adjustable interest rate afterwards. The other thing was, the loan papers were doctored to reflect an interest rate of 6 percent, but the payment buried deep in the documents reflected a different interest rate, that of 7.25 percent. He had intentionally typed the interest rate we were expecting on the front cover to mislead us into a 7.25 percent loan.

He looked me in the eye after I questioned him on the discrepancies and said, "Oh, there must have been last minute changes by the lender." He was counting on the fact that most people would never scrutinize the documents too closely, and I'm sure he knew we were under the gun to close escrow or lose our good faith deposit of $30,000.

I politely stood up and escorted him to the door saying, "I would rather lose $30,000 than pay you one dime for your dishonesty."

The point to this story is, if this shady mortgage broker was trying to pull a fast one on a financial advisor well versed in real estate and mortgages, what do you think he got away with in documents prepared for an average person, a potential first-time homebuyer who didn't understand mortgages and loans and relied on the broker to be honest and fair?

Era of the Printing Press Economy

Let's examine the idea of how the world economies in 2012 and for the foreseeable future are really just based on the printing presses of the Central Reserve banks—the banks which control the ability to print money. Why this is important is that your income needs have to be inflation adjusted.

As an aside, when I discuss the Central Reserve banks printing money, I am speaking in shorthand of course. It is more convenient to say, "printing money," than to say, "the Federal Reserve is crediting member bank accounts with increased balances electronically, which it does by means of a computer. If these balances are actually lent out and the borrowers prefer to use some of this money as cash, the Treasury will go ahead and print the cash."

The last time the U.S. deficit went down was September 1960. Many people believe that we had a surplus budget in fiscal 2000, but when looking at the official treasury debt to the penny, it still increased by $18 Billion. A pittance compared to the trillion dollar deficits we are running today, but an increase none the less.

Mainstream and Keynesian economists claim we can print ourselves rich. If we just keep printing money, we can solve the debt issues we are currently experiencing and build wealth and prosperity.

Piling up more debt to solve our debt issues is the solution to spur growth.

Think about a simple concept. If every man, woman, and child on the planet were given a million dollars, would we all be rich? Of course not. We would all have a million dollars but the next day the prices on all goods and services would adjust up by a similar ratio and thus our purchasing power would stay the same.

Increasing the money supply does not create wealth. Money is NOT wealth, it is just the means of exchanging real wealth. A loaf of bread, a piece of real estate, a bar of gold. That is wealth. It is limited in supply and you cannot just push a button and magically create more of it out of thin air, as is the case for printing money.

Many people falsely believe inflation is the rise and fall of prices. That is the effect of inflation but *not* the cause. The cause is an increase or decrease in the quantity or supply of money. Here is a simple example:

If I have 10 apples and there are 10 dollars in circulation chasing or rather wanting to buy those apples, then the price of the apples will be one dollar.

Ten dollars divided by 10 apples. The price will be $1 per apple.

If you have a robust economy with full employment and full manufacturing, for instance the 1950s, and you wanted to cool the economy from growing too fast, one solution would be to take dollars out of public circulation and try to slow spending. Incidentally, if fewer dollars are chasing a set amount or increasing amount of products, the prices will tend to fall.

Five dollars divided by 10 apples. The price per apple will fall to 50 cents. This is true deflation.

If the price of gas or groceries goes down, to you or me it would be a wonderful thing, but according to the government and the Federal Reserve, that is a disaster. This is because of how they report financial growth for the country, for instance gross domestic product. It is based largely on rising prices and not increasing actual real wealth and productivity.

Let's look at the other result of our apple example and the effects of increasing money supply.

During bad economic times, the Federal Reserve likes to print money and spur consumer spending. They add more money into circulation. For our example let's say there is now $20 chasing the same number of apples.

Twenty dollars divided by 10 apples. The result is prices go up to $2 per apple.

To add insult to injury, during bad economic times usually manufacturing and real productivity are dropping. Factories are being shut down and jobs are being lost. This will compound the negative effect of more money in circulation by taking away how many apples are being produced.

Twenty dollars divided by five apples. The result is apples now cost $4.

This is when inflation starts to kill real productivity because people are earning less and yet prices are rising faster and faster, taking away their ability to buy the goods and services they need. This results in a dramatic reduction in the standard of living.

Welcome to Zimbabwe!

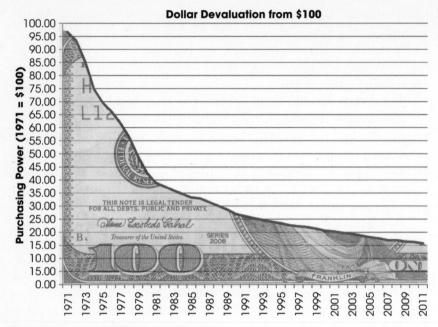

Figure 8.3   1971 Dollar Devaluation

Source: Bureau of Labor Statistics CPI

One of the most prosperous times for the United States was immediately after the Civil War, from 1866 to 1912 according to William Buckler of *The Privateer*. We had great increases in manufacturing, standard of living, and real wealth. An interesting point during this time was that our official debt did not increase by one penny.

A can of tuna which cost 5 cents in 1866, still cost just 5 cents in 1912. Purchasing power was consistent which gives people the confidence to manufacture and produce goods and services, to save more than they consume and build real wealth.

When purchasing power is eroded as it has been ever since the Federal Reserve was created in 1913, real wealth comes to a standstill. Since 1971, the U.S. dollar has lost approximately 84 percent of its purchasing power and *real* disposable incomes in the United States, and thus the standard of living, have been decreasing in lockstep (see Figure 8.3).

Real disposable income is the amount of disposable income adjusted for inflation rate (see Figure 8.4). Though the nominal value might go up, the real value has been falling for 30 years.

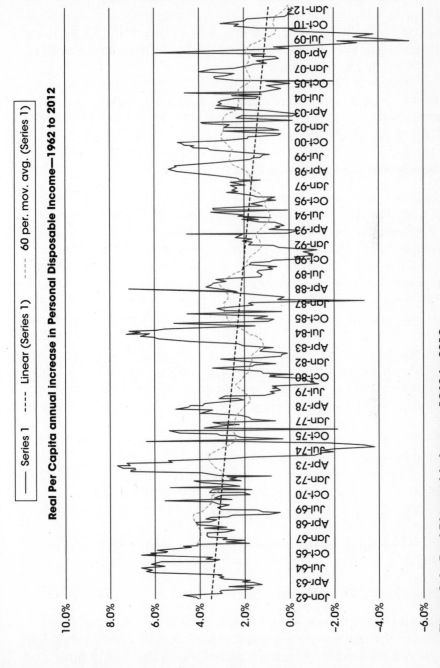

Figure 8.4 Real Disposable Income 1962 to 2012

119

Now, it isn't enough for one working parent and one staying home with the kids to maintain a solid middle class standard of living as was the norm in the 1950's. Today, while the kids are in daycare or with grandma and grandpa, both parents are working, struggling to keep up with the rising cost of living, which represents a real decline in the standard of living.

The Wealth Code solution is to focus on inflation-adjusted income. We can expect prices to continue to rise and we need our paychecks to rise as fast or faster if we are going to maintain our current standard of living, or better yet have the potential to increase it.

Income Needs as Defined by Cash Flow

As stated previously, a major focus for each plan I put together for clients is based on cash flow. As many checks in the mail every month from as many sources as possible is the goal. Many of the wealthiest people have built their fortunes from constant passive cash flow.

What does cash flow allow you to do? You can confidently invest in other ideas, knowing the income streams you are receiving potentially cover your bills, and the excess can be used to add to your wealth bucket. The more your bucket grows, the greater your cash flow becomes, and the cycle repeats itself building wealth over time.

A significant part of determining future income needs is compensating for the effects of inflation. A big problem with a payment stream from an annuity is that the check never increases. What might seem like an adequate monthly income today, say $3,000, might only buy a ticket to the movies, much less pay for your monthly living expenses in 20 years.

A serious problem for CD investors when they live off the interest and leave the principal alone is that the principal never grows. As time passes, they will start to fall far short of meeting their monthly expenses.

Income needs are naturally tied to growth of the portfolio, which I will cover in Step Four in our *Wealth Code* process.

Step Four: Growth Needs

On which conveyance should you travel?

On the highway, cars zoom along at 65 mph. Next to the highway is a bike path, where bicyclists pedal along at 8–12 mph, and

Figure 8.5   Different Pathways

next to the bike path you have a walking trail, where the pace might be a solid 2–4 mph (Figure 8.5).

Most advisors try to put everyone on the highway, trying to double their money the fastest way possible. They use the stock market exclusively because it does have the possibility of doubling your money very quickly. The problem is, how often do you see accidents on the freeway? Everyone is driving so fast that inevitably someone makes a mistake and hits the guardrail or another car and causes a big accident. The freeway is shut down for hours.

Funny, those silly bicyclists who just keep pedaling along the bike path at a solid 8–12 mph seem to get to work a lot faster most of the time. At least the bicyclists can plan their day with the reasonable assumption that they will get to their destination on time. The freeway is a gamble. Some days the freeway is the fastest, but sometimes it takes you three hours longer than expected, and you miss your big meeting and lose your shot at that important job.

Retirement planning is about reaching goals. In my opinion, using the freeway is the worst way to plan, yet for the majority of financial advisors, it is the only path they know for guiding clients.

I like consistency with our investments. By using many asset classes, which are not designed to double your money but are meant to work slowly and consistently and to potentially keep up with the ravages of inflation, we generally choose to travel on the bike path and tend to reach our goals more predictably.

Retirement planning is a lot easier if you use reasonable assumptions and you aim for consistent growth and income. This is seemingly impossible with the stock market. You could have invested for 40 years in the stock market and planned to retire in 2010, but now what? Many baby boomers are going back to work for another 30! How many baby boomers have been forced to downsize their lifestyle or scale back their retirement plans due to the recession?

Portfolio growth does not need to be great, but it needs to be reasonably consistent. Singles and doubles to use the baseball metaphor. In my opinion, the best part of real asset investments is their direct correlation with inflation. Our government has been on an inflation kick since the creation of the Federal Reserve in 1913, and it doesn't plan to change course anytime soon. Real assets generally provide a natural inflation hedge. Why? It costs more to create or develop tangible assets when the price of the raw materials increases with inflation. How many people go for a walk in their neighborhoods and ponder what it would cost to build their same home all over again? Could they even afford to buy it?

Building a portfolio can be thought of as placing your money on the various pathways. Some on the highway (stock market), some on the bike path (real assets), and some on the walking path (cash or cash equivalents).

What you are trying to achieve determines how much of each pathway you should use. Due to its consistency most of my clients choose the bike path for the greater share of their wealth. They want to have reasonable assumptions in place for determining their retirement needs and want to be able to sleep at night without wondering about how the stock market is doing today, tomorrow, or frankly ever!

They know that they can set an objective of 5-10 percent overall returns, and aim for consistent results, never 50 percent, never doubling their money in a year, but they can get a consistent total return. That's piece of mind.

Achieving Total Return

If you are pulling out income of 6 percent per year from your portfolio and reasonably expect a total return of 10 percent, then your portfolio will slowly creep up by 4 percent each year. With more principal to work with each year, there can also be the potential for an increase in cash flow.

KEY WEALTH CODE CONCEPT

Total Return = Income + Growth

Total return is income plus growth. Wall Street wants everyone to focus on growth as the major component of total return, but as mentioned earlier, I feel that growth tends to be a wildcard and not as predictable as you would like it to be.

If your goal was 10 percent per year, and only 2 percent was achieved by dividends, you would have to have growth of 8 percent each year to reach the goal.

If on the other hand, your dividend was 7 percent, now you would only need growth of 3 percent to hit your total return goal. Three percent growth seems like a more reasonable assumption than 8 percent, wouldn't you agree?

Hypothetical example with a 10 percent target total return:

	Total Return	=	Income	+	Growth
Wall Street:	10%	=	2%	+	8%
Tangible Assets:	10%	=	7%	+	3%

If the growth doesn't happen for either investment, Wall Street's version of total return has only achieved 20 percent of the overall goal or 2 percent. For the tangible assets example, if the growth doesn't happen, you've already achieved 70 percent of your goal or 7 percent.

With real assets, you are usually dealing with various forms of cash flow such as rents received. Anyone who has ever rented an apartment has felt the effects of rising rents and their tie to inflation. Each year that little envelope would show up in the mailbox or worse, was slid under the door, and inside was a simple message, your rent is being increased by three to four percent.

For you, the renter, it became a yearly ritualistic disappointment. For the owner of the building, it was good news because raising the rents meant more cash flow—adding to the growth component of the apartment building's total return and keeping pace with inflation. By raising the rents year after year, the building's owner is increasing the economic value of the building, or in other words, the growth component of the real asset.

With any real asset investment, you will not know what the total return will be until the final sale of the underlying investment—whether the real estate in a REIT, the loans in a Business Development Corporation, or other foundation for a particular investment. Let me say that one more time. Until the last asset is sold and the REIT, BDC, et cetera portfolio liquidated, you will not be able to calculate your total return. You will have potentially received distributions over time (not guaranteed) that can be calculated easily, however.

This also applies to a rental house you might own. Until you actually sell your rental, you don't really have anything to compute in terms of total return. On any given day it could be plus $5,000 or negative $5,000 depending on the current economic environment. The day you sell is the day you have the final piece of the equation (the growth component) of total return equaling income plus growth.

Any given year, you can figure out whether the income measures up to expectations and ascertain the investment's strength, but until the pied piper plays, total return cannot be tallied.

When I sit down with my clients and summarize all the legs on their portfolio table (see Table 8.2), it will show the initial investment and cash flow to date, but will not show a current value for any of the real assets. Unlike the stock market, where values fluctuate and reach a final value at market close, tangible assets are different. Again, because until the final sale of the investment, we don't know the true value and cannot compute total return. Of course we show the value of the liquid investments—those being the managed accounts in the stock market which have daily valuations.

I believe this ability to see current value of the stock market and wide swings is what causes so many of us to panic at the wrong time

Table 8.2   Hypothetical Summary Example

Investment Name	Initial Contribution	Distributions	Current Value
REIT A	$50,000	$6,342	N/A
BDC A	$50,000	$5,844	N/A
Stock Market A	$80,000	$3,234	$86,033

and ultimately to make bad financial decisions. For instance selling at the bottom or buying at the top.

The lack of daily valuations with real assets is the primary reason I believe that these illiquid investments may be suitable for my clients. Real estate, notes, oil/gas, and so forth are examples. They generally don't create as many panic attacks and can allow the investment to work until maturity. The illiquid nature of these investments potentially keeps them from being sold at a bad time in an emotional panic.

Other than understanding what total return is, you should be rolling your eyes, thinking to yourself, every adviser says they will make X percent a year. I agree. That is why your education and due diligence are vital. Please take the time to learn about these other asset classes, form an educated opinion, and build a portfolio based on what you've learned.

My goal is to provide the big picture for *The Wealth Code* concept from A to Z, from philosophy to implementation. The introduction through chapter nine and the case studies in Appendix A serve this purpose. Let me make it abundantly clear that these concepts may not be suitable for every investor. This book is designed to provide an overall introduction to the concepts so that you, as an investor, can hopefully make better, more informed decisions. The examples used are general in nature, and the investor is strongly urged to read all the materials provided before investing.

At this point, please don't put the book down and call it a day. Appendix B is vital to your understanding of the various legs on the financial table—the different investment asset classes and their pros and cons. As you gain a better understanding of the various asset classes, you are providing the glue to finish your financial table. Without the glue to hold the legs on your table the resulting portfolio may not be solid.

Step Five: Beneficiary Needs

When it comes to spending, everyone has good kids and not so good kids. Not that they are criminals, but they differ in terms of spending habits. Some beneficiaries are great with money. They save, live within their means, and invest wisely. Others live for today. Every dollar that goes into their pocket goes out the next day for the latest flat screen television or gadget. They live paycheck to paycheck and will probably work until the day they die.

Ferrari Distribution

A fun term I use at my firm for a lump sum inheritance that lands on a beneficiary's lap all at once is a "Ferrari distribution." They get the dough and the next day blow it on a new Ferrari or whatever impulse buy they have always wanted. According to the *Wall Street Journal, Boston Globe,* and several other reputable news sources, over 30 percent of lotto winners spend all their money quickly and are more depressed after winning than before. Most of these winners are depressed because they had a taste of another life and now long for what they no longer can have. Back to buying lotto tickets, I guess.

A great benefit of real assets is their lack of liquidity or difficulty in cashing out quickly. Time and time again, a client dies, and the beneficiaries call wanting all their money in cash as quickly as possible. No consideration for how the money is invested, no consideration for how much it might cost to get out, just give me whatever is left. From observing beneficiaries and their inheritances over the years, I've noted that the longer it takes to pull money out of real assets, the more time the beneficiaries have to enjoy the potential for monthly distributions, which helps them realize the benefit of taking only the income and not touching the principal. Many parents would love to instill this discipline in their adult children or beneficiaries.

If you have been sold an annuity because it can be used as a stretch IRA and will benefit your kids, I have news for you: Any type of investment can be a stretch IRA, not just annuities, but stocks, bonds, REITs, partnerships, and so forth. The reality is that the day you die, your kids have the choice of whether they take only partial payments over their lifetime (Stretch IRA) or take out all of the money much faster. Most choose the latter. They just

KEY WEALTH CODE CONCEPT

Using investments in the HR-CP category, the real assets, provides an added bonus in terms of managing inheritances and beneficiaries. Inherited illiquid investments can potentially serve as a means of protecting your lifelong savings from being spent quickly by beneficiaries, almost forcing them to appreciate the potential for cash flow and not squander the remaining principal.

want whatever is left after taxes, and they don't care if they lose half the money to Uncle Sam. They didn't work to save it and unfortunately they do not respect the loss to taxes by taking the money as a single lump sum.

Putting Together a Financial Plan

At this point, I am ready to implement a plan. I know as much about the client as I believe I can know. I understand their income needs, current investments, level of comfort and experience with different asset classes, their objectives, their lifestyle expenses, their investment time horizon, future liquidity needs, portfolio growth needs, as well as what the beneficiaries hope to inherit. Lastly, I have proposed time lines that I believe are reasonable for having access to the money for other investments, purchases, or income.

To better illustrate putting together a plan, let me use an example. Please note that Appendix A includes a few more case samples to better clarify the process of building a *Wealth Code* financial portfolio.

Case Study: Mrs. Jones

Mrs. Jones is 61 years old and is concerned about her retirement. She retires in five years from a job that pays $75,000 per year, and she feels too much of her money is not working due to a large bank CD position from the proceeds of a previous rental property she sold as well as stagnant mutual funds in her IRA. At her full retirement age, 66, her Social Security check will be $1,800 per month. Her current federal and state income tax bracket is around 28 percent.

A list of her assets includes:

Personal residence	**Fair Market Value (FMV) $600,000 with a $100,000 30-year fixed mortgage at 4.5%**
IRA	$ 375,000 mostly in mutual funds
CDs	$ 600,000
Treasury bonds	$ 100,000
Net worth including Residence	**$1,575,000**
Net worth excluding Residence	**$1,075,000 (Fully Accredited)**

Her equity in her personal residence equals the fair market value minus the mortgage balance. In her case, $600,000 − $100,000 = $500,000.

When thinking of the different legs on your financial table in the High Return-Capital Preservation (HR-CP) category, a good rule of thumb is never to use more than 10 percent of investable wealth in any particular financial tool. Some states have mandated that non-accredited investors must limit their investments to 10 percent in any one type of these assets. Investable wealth would be the investments, not counting the personal residence.

For Mrs. Jones (an accredited investor), her investable wealth is $1,075,000 (IRA, CDs, and treasuries), and thus the maximum for any one non-liquid investment using the rule of thumb should be around $107,500. Rounding up or down a couple thousand is within reason.

Investable wealth:

IRA	$ 375,000
CD	$ 600,000
Treasuries	$ 100,000
Total	**$1,075,000**

Maximum per financial tool = Investable wealth × 10 percent = $1,075,000 × 10 percent = $107,500

Due to the lack of immediate liquidity with most of the investments in the HR-CP category, it is always a good idea to spread the wealth around as much as possible. Using smaller legs on the table, or smaller allocated amounts is what I believe to be a good approach. If any of these investments goes sour, it limits the impact or exposure for the overall portfolio. For instance, for Mrs. Jones, maybe each non-liquid financial tool becomes roughly 5 percent of investable wealth.

More conservative maximum per financial tool = Investable wealth × 5 percent = $1,075,000 × 5 percent = $53,750 or approximately $54,000

In her particular situation I felt it was prudent to go even smaller (2 to 4 percent) for most of the illiquid investments. This provides diversification within the tangible asset classes.

The emotional investments, High Return-Liquid (HR-L), and the banking products, Capital Preservation-Liquid (CP-L) can be larger percentages because of their liquidity. You can always sell at any point and raise cash if needed, and thus, the size of these legs can be larger. Remember, this is only an example of what was done for one particular client. It is not "one size fits all".

Table 8.3 is a recommendation summary for Mrs. Jones.

Please note, the investments which will be described in her plan are fully explained in Appendix B. The goal here is to understand the logic of each one and how they relate to her financial goals.

KEY WEALTH CODE CONCEPT

The key to picking investments is to use common sense and your personal beliefs.

Notice the use of the non-traded REITs. We have chosen to go into three types of real estate, which we feel would do well in times of chaos and going forward. Currently, with millions losing their homes to foreclosure, what do these people do next? They sell or put their belongings in storage and move into an apartment. Storage centers have been one of the most consistent performing types of real estate going back the last 35 years and according to the Self Storage Association, one in 10 United States households currently rent a storage unit. We are a nation of pack rats I guess.

According to CTIA-The Wireless Association, United States consumer data traffic increased 104 percent between July 2011 and July 2012. They estimate it will quadruple in only three years. Everyone has to have the latest iPad or cellphone and needs to be connected 24/7. This bodes well for internet data usage and hence for cloud data storage. We want to own the real estate that stores the data centers for companies such as Apple, Google, Amazon, and so forth.

As for the healthcare REIT, this plays off the fact that there are 79 million baby boomers beginning to retire, and a by-product

Table 8.3   Mrs. Jones' Example Recommendations

Original Position	Amount		Recommended Position	Amount	Asset Class	Liquidity Timeline
IRA	$375,000	⇒	Oil Royalty	$ 50,000	Oil/Gas Royalty	? Years
			Equipment Leasing	$ 35,000	Equipment Leasing	10 Years
			Energy BDC	$ 35,000	Collateralized Note	5 Years
			Small Cap BDC	$ 35,000	Collateralized Note	5 Years
			Health Care REIT	$ 35,000	Institutional Grade Real Estate	4 Years
			Storage Center REIT	$ 35,000	Institutional Grade Real Estate	4 Years
			Data Center REIT	$ 35,000	Institutional Grade Real Estate	4 Years
			Adaptive Asset Management	$115,000	Stock Market	Liquid

Original Position	Amount		Recommended Position	Amount	Asset Class	Liquidity Timeline
CDs	$600,000	⇒	Energy Developmental Drilling	$ 30,000	Oil/Gas Drilling	? Years
Treasuries	$100,000		30-Year Fixed Mortgage Notes	$ 50,000	Collateralized Note	1 Year
			6-month Life Settlement Note	$ 50,000	Collateralized Note	6 Month
			2-Single Family Residences	$140,000	Consumer Grade Real Estate	120 Days
			Adaptive Asset Management	$380,000	Stock Market	Liquid
			3-month CDs staggered in 1 month increments	$ 50,000	Bank	Liquid

of getting older of course can be the need to see a doctor with increasing frequency.

Between the two business development corporations, BDCs, which is a form of collateralized note, I chose one which is based on helping small to mid-cap companies. This BDC has greater potential for upside growth as they usually are given warrants or options of stock along with the loans they make. The second BDC is based on loans to energy companies. Love them or hate them, oil is here to stay, and Mrs. Jones felt making loans to them was a good idea. I chose two other oil investments for her due to her belief that oil would, in the long run, go up in price tied to real inflation (see Table 8.4).

The first is an oil royalty program. There is no liquidity ever with this investment but could potentially provide some level of return for decades (see Tables 8.5 and 8.6). She is fairly young and wanted a part of her IRA distributions to be tied lockstep with inflation. Oil is always a good choice for that.

The second oil investment was placed in her trust account, which is after-tax money. The developmental drilling program should theoretically provide the same type of check the royalty program does, but will have one additional benefit. This program comes with an intangible drilling cost (IDC), a type of income tax deduction. As of 2012, for her investment of $30,000 she could receive an immediate tax deduction of around $27,000 or 90 percent of her investment in the first year of the investment, and potentially receive depletion deductions in subsequent years. Programs that come with an upfront tax deduction should not be used in retirement accounts because you will lose any such tax benefit. In Mrs. Jones' example, however, she was in the 28 percent federal and state income tax bracket and with a $27,000 deduction, she should save approximately $7,560.

$27,000 tax deduction × 28 percent income tax bracket
= $7,560 taxes saved.

Considering Mrs. Jones has experience owning rental property: the rewards of positive cash flow, and the headaches of management, I referred her to a realtor/management firm which specializes in refurbishing single family residences. This realtor/management firm provides turnkey rental purchase solutions, including management, for clients who do not wish to have the day-to-day responsibilities.

Table 8.4   Summary of Recommendations for Mrs. Jones

Oil/Gas Investments	$ 80,000	~ 7% of investable wealth
Equipment Leasing	$ 35,000	~ 3%
Non-Traded REITs + 2 Single Family Residences	$245,000	~ 23%
Collateralized Notes	$170,000	~ 16%
Adaptive Asset Management	$495,000	~ 46%
CDs	$ 50,000	~ 5%

Table 8.5   Summary of Liquid to Illiquid investments

Liquid Investments	$545,000	~ 50% of investable wealth
Illiquid Investments	$530,000	~ 50%

Table 8.6   Approximate Liquidity Timeline for her investments

Liquidity Time Line	$ Becoming Liquid	Total Liquid Investments
Liquid Immediately	$545,000	$545,000
Liquid after 6 months	$ 50,000	$595,000
Liquid after ~ 1 year	$ 50,000	$645,000
Liquid after ~ 4 years	$105,000	$750,000
Liquid after ~ 5 years	$ 70,000	$820,000
Liquid after ~ 10 years	$ 35,000	$855,000
Oil/Gas Annuity Payment Single Family Residences	$220,000 Never Liquid	$855,000

Her attitude with these properties is she will be a collector. Enjoying the potential rental income and thinking of them as a forever investments.

The other investments completed her plan. A mixture of longer-term ideas was used for her IRA as this money is meant for longer-term income needs and not meant to be pulled out quickly, which would cause a huge tax problem. Retirement accounts tend to work well with illiquid investments. The durations of the investments are much shorter in her after-tax investments as this money would be first used in an emergency or for a large purchase such as another rental property. Equipment leasing, adaptive stock market management, and CDs were used to provide what I believe to be a well-balanced financial table with a total of six asset legs.

Mrs. Jones considers her oil payments to be comparable to a lifelong pension payment, like a second social security check. She also considers her new rental property something she'll own until she dies. The rental properties could be liquidated fairly quickly with the price depending on the real estate cycle we are in. In a good time she could sell very fast. In a bad time she would have to wait longer or drop the price to be appealing to a potential buyer. The nice part of single owner real estate is there is always a price you can sell for. It just depends on how much you are willing to accept.

After several meetings with Mrs. Jones, understanding that past performance is no guarantee of future results and with a clear understanding of the prospectuses and risks with each asset class, I put together an income projection for her (see Table 8.7). Using target dividend/distribution assumptions that Mrs. Jones was comfortable with for the various investments, I was able to generate an approximation of her income potential today and in five years when she plans on retiring.

Adding everything up, the income potential for her portfolio is approximately $64,875 per year or 6.03 percent. See Table 8.7.

Table 8.7   Portfolio Income Potential—Hypothetical

Investment	Target Income Assumption	Investment Amount	Income Per Year
Oil/Gas investments	9%	$ 80,000	$ 7,200
Equipment Leasing	8%	$ 35,000	$ 2,800
Non-traded REITs	6.5%	$ 105,000	$ 6,825
Single Family Residence	9%	$ 140,000	$ 12,600
Collateralized Notes	6%	$ 170,000	$ 10,200
Adaptive Asset Management	5%	$ 495,000	$ 24,750
CDs	1%	$ 50,000	$ 500
	Average 6.03%	**$1,075,000**	**$64,875**

Obviously, the low return on the CDs hurts the overall income potential, but their addition for liquidity needs is important.

Since she is still working and does not need the income, reinvesting the dividends and distributions over the next five years compounds or grows her account balances to $1,440,629.

End of Year 1	Year 2	Year 3	Year 4	Year 5
$1,139,823	$1,208,554	$1,281,430	$1,358,700	$1,440,629

If we are able to maintain the dividends at 6.03 percent, her accounts will generate approximately $86,870 per year. Adding her Social Security payments brings her estimated yearly income to $108,470.

$1,440,629 × 6.03 percent	= $86,870 per year
Social Security	= $21,600 per year($1,800 × 12)
Income potential	= $108,470 per year

I like to design plans using only the dividends and not count on any growth. If growth occurs, that would be all gravy on top of the reinvested dividends.

Mrs. Jones liked the fact that almost 83 percent of the investments would essentially be liquid by the time she retires, and when she does retire, she can elect to receive distributions (if they are being made) versus reinvesting potential dividends. In this way, she has the potential ability to dial-in her income from the various investments to meet her needs. For example, if she wants an extra $2,000 per month, all she has to do is call us, and we will set up monthly payments to her from the necessary investments to match the $2,000 desired. Maybe she does not need extra income but is planning a big European trip in six months and will need $10,000 for the trip. By planning ahead and electing distributions versus reinvestment, she could potentially receive the $10,000 from the dividends into her checking account, and by the time her trip comes around, it is already paid for. At that point, she would turn off the investments, that is, suspend the monthly checks, and begin to reinvest them again.

Having many different cash flow generating investments provides a greater sense of control over one's finances and income needs. Of course, the drawback to having many financial investments or legs on your table is that you have many more statements each month. Most of my clients don't seem to mind a bit more paperwork if the goal hopefully is to protect and diversify their wealth more successfully.

You might question the ability to earn a consistent 6.03 percent. Remember I am are not counting on any one investment to deliver this return. I need the average to equal 6.03 percent. Remembering the **Wealth Code Golden Rule**, I expect things to not work out as planned. I expect a distribution to be cut or lowered or one of the investments to not work out as planned. That is why I chose 14 different investments for Mrs. Jones, knowing that if something doesn't go as planned, something else, in all probability, will work better. This has the effect of evening out the returns and helping to keep her potential cash flow in a consistent range.

A question Mrs. Jones asked me was whether or not to pay off her mortgage balance. After factoring in the mortgage tax benefit of her 4.5 percent fixed mortgage and assuming her tax bracket would stay around 28 percent, I was able to show her that the net cost of her mortgage was 3.24 percent.

4.5 percent Interest − 1.26 percent(28 percent Tax deduction of 4.5 percent) = 3.24 percent net cost of mortage

The simplest answer was showing her that potentially most of her investments would reasonably earn more than 3.24 percent and that each dollar earned above 3.24 percent was free money. Factoring inflation into the equation and paying back loans with devalued dollars would boost her net return even more. She saw the logic pretty quickly and looked forward to enjoying the excess free earnings.

Mortgage arbitrage is the concept of borrowing money at low rates, investing it in higher earning investments, and pocketing the difference in earnings.

When thinking about paying off your mortgage or investing the principal amount using mortgage arbitrage, ask yourself the following: "Is it okay to pay $1,000 in mortgage payments when investing that money could, for example, generate $1,200 a month?"

Earning an extra $200 each month seems like a no brainer, doesn't it? For some people, it is a no brainer. For others, the idea of having a house completely paid off has been their goal. Whether to pay off a mortgage or carry a loan is fine depending on a person's circumstances.

This principle behind mortgage arbitrage is exactly how the banks penalize us for keeping deposits in our bank accounts. They pay us practically nothing in interest, yet they get to invest the money in other more profitable endeavors and keep the difference. Funny, when you loan the bank money by putting money into your accounts, they pay you practically nothing in interest, but if you walk into that same bank and ask for a loan, they will charge you lots of interest.

My philosophy is to be the bank with your mortgage. Pay the bare minimum and invest the difference. The extra earnings are gravy in your pocket. Of course, the key to this concept is having a mortgage with fixed payments. Unfortunately, to take advantage of the artificially low rates in effect today, many people have used adjustable rate loans for this concept. The rates are artificially low because the Federal Reserve is buying mortgage-backed securities and keeping the market rates down. When the Federal Reserve stops buying, rates could skyrocket, and people who are using adjustable mortgages to arbitrage will be hurt by payments that are higher than what they are able to earn in other investments. My recommendation is to use only fixed rate (payment) loans for mortgage arbitrage.

One other advantage of a fixed mortgage is that eventually when you do pay back the loan you will be paying for it with inflated dollars. I often joke to clients, "On one of my properties there is $1M in fixed loans. Maybe 10 years down the road, I'll put a roll of toilet paper in an envelope, mail it to the lender and pay off my house." We'll call this type of envelope, "Squishy Mail." The lender of course will call it "bankruptcy mail."

This would be due to immense inflation in the United States. The value of the dollar would have to go down so much that a roll of toilet paper becomes valued at $1M to pay off my loans. Though said in jest, unfortunately, hyperinflation has occurred many times in history. Recall the previous story about a roll of toilet paper in Zimbabwe.

Another story I heard about the effects of hyperinflation is hair-raising: A very wealthy lady who lived in Germany had more than $1M Deutsch Marks in the bank. She went to Switzerland for a trip, caught tuberculosis, and did not return to Germany until 1923. When she got home, she opened two letters from her banker.

The first dated 1920 read, "Mrs. Smith, please come by the bank very soon. I feel we should convert your money into another currency to protect its value."

The second, dated 1922 read, "Mrs. Smith, we are closing your bank account as your balance is too low for us to service it." She noticed on the outside of the envelope, the canceled stamp was valued at $1M Deutsch Marks. Thankfully, she had real estate, which protected a large portion of her wealth.

The ones who get hurt the worst by inflation are those who lend money at low fixed rates. When they get their money back, its purchasing power isn't worth nearly what it was when they lent it. Having a long-term fixed mortgage is a way of protecting wealth against a devaluing dollar. The more the Federal Reserve prints, the cheaper it will be to pay back a fixed sum of money. Again, we'll start a revolution and call it "Squishy mail," and all of us will mail toilet paper to our lenders and pay off our houses.

A second recommendation is important when considering mortgage arbitrage. Only invest dollars in the same asset class as those dollars against which are being borrowed. For instance, real estate (tangible asset) should only be arbitraged against other tangible assets. Often, people borrow money against their homes to invest in the stock market only to lose half of the money. Not a good idea.

Aside from the concept of mortgage arbitrage, there's another concept of wealth that the very rich have mastered. That's the principle of using other people's money to build their personal wealth, which dates back to the origin of money and investing.

Here's a thought. Would you rather have a 401(k) or a 401Condo?

People are told that they should invest diligently into retirement accounts and receive the tax deferral today on current income tax. Wall Street loves most retirement accounts because it gives them control over your wealth and the ability to charge all their fees for managing it. As mentioned previously, who do you think spearheaded all the various retirement programs out there? 401(k)s, 457s, profit sharing plans, 403(b)s: All were promoted and implemented by Wall Street and the insurance industry.

The sad reality is that most people put hard-earned money into 401(k)s, and the only choices they have are mutual funds, with average internal costs approaching 2 percent according to a Deloitte 401(k) fee study conducted in 2009. If someone has had money in a 401(k) for more than 15 years, almost a quarter of their account has been eroded by fees.

Table 8.8   401(k) Summary

Investment into 401(k) for the year	$ 10,000
Earnings at 10%	$ 1,000
Taxes deferred at 20%	$ 2,000
Employer Contributions	$ 1,000
Total at the end of the year	**$14,000**

Most of the financial talking heads and books say to put your money into your 401(k) because you effectively earn 40 percent. This is the math they use to rationalize it: Assume you divert $10,000 each year from your income into your 401(k), you earn 10 percent each year, you are in the 20 percent tax bracket, your investments have no fees and lastly, your employer contributes $1,000 (see Table 8.8).

It would appear you made 40 percent on your original $10,000. Now the disadvantages:

- You cannot touch the money without Federal penalties until you reach the age of 59½.
- Good luck making 10 percent each year in the stock market and not paying fees.
- Taxes are only deferred. Funds you eventually withdraw will come back out of the account as ordinary income, and thus you will be taxed at your highest marginal bracket. The IRS is rooting for you to invest very wisely because they will get all the taxes owed and a lot more. Notice THE IRS put together is "THEIRS."

Let's compare this to an investment in a 401Condo. If we think about cash flow, we know you are already contributing to your 401(k), so instead of that income going into the company plan, what if you took out the income and used it to pay for a mortgage and property taxes on an investment condo? This could be any type of investment real estate.

If we assume a 30-year fixed rate mortgage at 6 percent interest, with $10,000 to spend, that easily would cover the mortgage payment and property taxes on a $100,000 property somewhere. According to the Case-Shiller home appreciation index averaging

Table 8.9   Condo Cash Flow Summary

Investment (cost) for the year (Mortgage payments and property taxes)	$10,000
Rent received: $1,000 × 12 months	-$12,000
Appreciation: **3% of $100,000**	$ 3,000
Management costs	-$ 1,200
Miscellaneous costs	-$ 1,000
Total at the end of the year	**$ 2,800**

around 3.4 percent between 1987 to 2012, assume the property will appreciate at 3 percent each year; you can rent it out for $1,000 per month, and property management costs are 10 percent.

Purchase Condo for $100,000 with down payment of $20,000. I'll address the down payment in a minute. For now, let's work through the exercise.

Adding everything up, you realize $2,800 within one year (See table 8.9). On the surface that seems far worse than the 401(k)'s $14,000 sum.

The difference in real wealth becomes apparent over time as which scenario is more realistically achieved.

Since both investment strategies defer the same taxes on the pre-tax $10,000, those gains are negated.

In the 401(k), over 10 years if you have diligently paid $10,000 each year into your 401(k), your employer has contributed their portion ($1,000) and hopefully overall earned 10 percent per year, you will have approximately $175,000 saved in the pre-tax 401(k).

$11,000 per year contribution at 10 percent compound return = $175,311

In the 401Condo over 10 years, with the $80,000 mortgage having been paid down to $67,000 and the property fair market value (FMV) having appreciated to $134,391 at 3 percent per year and if you invested the net rents ($9,658) after the depreciation deduction and taxes paid say at 3 percent net after tax, you will have approximately $182,820 between 401Condo equity and cash saved.

After 10 years the 401Condo total return is equal to $182,820 as compared to the total value of the 401(k) being $175,311

Table 8.10   401Condo Total Return Summary

$100,000 FMV condo × 3% appreciation for 10 Years		$134,391
Condo Equity = $134,391 − $67,000 (mortgage balance after 10 years of payments)	$ 67,391	
Condo Depreciation per year = $100,000 (purchase price) ÷ 27.5 year rate		$ 3,636
Taxable Rental Income = $12,000 (rents received) − $3,636 (depreciation offset)		$ 9,658
Income Taxes Paid = $9,658 (taxable income) × 20% (income tax bracket)		$ 1,931
Net after-tax income = $12,000 (rents received) − $1,931 (taxes paid)		$ 10,069
$10,069 × 3% (after-tax investment return) for 10 years	$ 115,429	
Total Return = Income ($115,429) + Growth ($67,391)	**$182,820**	

Here's the good news:

- You don't have to wait until you are 59½ years of age to sell the property.
- Taxes on condo appreciation, after selling the property, are based on the favorable long term capital gains rate. Or better yet, do a 1031 exchange into another property and defer the taxes. If you do this until the day you die—I call it, "swap until you drop"—then the capital gains are eliminated due to a step-up basis of the property at death.
- You can raise the rents while enjoying depreciation offsets on the income.
- If you lose your renters, the bills are already paid because of your consistent $10,000 retirement contributions covering the basic bills, mortgage, and property taxes.
- It's not hard to realize a 3 percent annual growth rate on real estate over a period of 10 years; most properties will appreciate at a greater rate than that.
- The $115,429 is AFTER-TAX funds, unlike the 401(k) funds which are all pre-tax and eventually the tax piper will have to be paid (see Table 8.10).

The point of this example is which situation is realistic for most investors: 401(k)s earning 10 percent each year in the stock market with no fees being paid, or earning 3 percent each year in real estate appreciation while never increasing the rents? Most investors will probably be more successful with the 401Condo versus the 401(k).

One of the keys to the potential success of the 401condo is leverage, or using other people's money. You can get loans on real estate. Try going to the bank and getting a loan to invest in mutual funds. Note the bold print in Table 8.9. Appreciation (**3 percent of $100,000**) is the true meaning of leverage. You are no longer earning appreciation based on the $10,000 contributions but on the leveraged/total value of the investment property.

This can be a double-edged sword, of course, and leverage can easily work against you if you buy a property that is a liability and not an asset. Again, a property is an asset as long as it pays for itself and puts money in your pocket each month. I always recommend to clients looking to buy individually owned rental properties that the properties should have positive cash flow from day one. People have made fortunes from fast appreciation in real estate, but they are also generally the ones you hear about who go bankrupt in bad times.

Clients often ask me how they can come up with the money or cash flow to buy real estate. I look at their 401(k) contributions and point out they already have a negative cash flow being paid each and every month, which we can divert to another investment. Since mortgage interest and property taxes are deductible, they will receive the same tax benefits at the end of the year as if they were still contributing to a 401(k). In the example above, both the $10,000 contributed into the 401(k) and the $10,000 invested in mortgage payments and property taxes are deductible for income tax purposes.

It's appropriate to address the issue of the down payment and to answer other questions you might have. Many people I meet have money tucked away in emergency accounts, CDs, or other after-tax investments. They would like to buy real estate but are worried about whether they can get renters. What if the property stays vacant? If you are making the major payments with the contributions you would have put into your 401(k), in terms of your cash flow you are in a neutral position and frankly it doesn't matter if you have renters. You own a piece of real estate, which in the long run will potentially inflate in value. Sure, there might be real estate pull backs, but most will agree, if you have time on your side, real estate is a solid investment and has done far more for building wealth in this country than any 401(k) ever has.

If your job is not very stable or if you don't consistently add money to a 401(k) or other retirement plan, the 401Condo is probably not for you. But for those who contribute religiously to retirement plans, this idea might benefit your wealth bucket.

In Summary

The goal of this chapter was to take you through an example of putting together the multitude of financial ideas into a working model. The success of a plan depends on taking into account everything, from understanding the background of the client and their goals to their liquidity needs; income and growth targets; as well as having the knowledge, depth, and insight into this turbulent economy we are trying to navigate.

Appendix A includes a variety of other investment plans for different individuals and will provide more exposure to building a successful financial table. You will see that everyone is different and no two plans will be the same, yet at the same time, many of the plans follow consistent themes of investment exposure, time lines of liquidity, and balance. Working with an experienced financial advisor is imperative to the process. If your current advisor does not offer these other types of investments, which are needed to build an ASSET class diversified table, you can always call us at 800-737-8552 or go to the website www.thewealthcode.com, and we will be happy to refer you to someone versed in this philosophy.

CHAPTER

Life Insurance, Annuities, and How They Relate to Your Wealth Code

Life insurance and the various products that come from life insurance companies have always been a great source of debate among financial advisors, as well as the general public. Some call it a necessary evil, others say it is the Holy Grail, while still others say it is a complete waste of time and money.

As with everything, no two people will have the same needs, but many of us could potentially benefit from some form of life insurance or life insurance products, such as annuities, at some point depending on our situation. When used appropriately, insurance is most certainly a part of a successful financial table. A problem we see consistently is the sale of life insurance products by insurance agents who are not licensed in securities, or by insurance representatives who are licensed in securities yet only focus on life insurance products. One-trick ponies one might say. Their answer to all financial questions comes back to either life insurance or annuities, either fixed or variable.

I view insurance products as another tool in the financial toolbox to be used when appropriate and suitable for the client's needs. Here again, one size does not fit all.

This discussion will serve as a brief opinion on this very complicated basket of financial tools, tools that all too often are sold by representatives and agents who tell only a part of the story. This is a common problem with the sale of annuities.

There are countless books that cover all aspects of life insurance products, and it is not the focus of this book to dive deeply into this topic but to provide a primer or reference on which to build your understanding.

General Need for Life Insurance—Family Liabilities

Why is life insurance part of most everyone's financial journey at some point? Because we all take similar paths in life in one form or another. We grow up, go to school, find jobs, and eventually, many of us start families. As we follow our financial road, many check points deem life insurance to be a vital part of protecting our wealth and our family's financial well-being.

Family liability is generally the first major reason to get life insurance. If you have young children, a spouse, or other dependent(s) who would suffer financially if you died, you have what is called an insurable interest. That is, a need for life insurance protection.

Ask yourself a question. If you had the misfortune of being run over by a steamroller tomorrow, what would the financial liabilities and needs of the following be:

- Spouse
- Children
- Other beneficiaries who might depend on your support
- Your estate and possible tax consequences to your heirs

Family liabilities include everything from income needs to education, health care, and so on. If you earn significantly more money than your spouse and you are run over by that steamroller, think of where that would leave your spouse. Besides needing a spatula to get you off the road, your income and future earnings potential would be gone overnight. Will there be money to pay for the bills such as the mortgage and utilities? How will his/her lifestyle be affected? Some would say it's unfortunate but they can go to work. That's one view, but most would probably prefer to leave a spouse with the lifestyle you both had before the accident. The spouse will face many other challenges, and financial hardship doesn't have to be one of them.

What would happen to your children and their future needs? Do you envision them going to college? If yes, then how would they pay for it? If you think they can work, just like you did, then great, more power to you. But if you had financial help going through school from your parents, wouldn't you like to extend that same support to your children?

Life insurance allows you to hedge a bet. The bet is that you will live a long time and it will be totally unnecessary and, thus, some will view it as a waste of money. We believe the smarter way to view it is that it is cheap protection in case the unthinkable happens. By the way, I use silly examples of death as being run over by a steam-roller because one day I was discussing with a client the future issue of death and said, "Let's say you get hit by a truck."

The client's face dropped and he said, "My dad was hit and killed by a truck."

Needless to say, after I pulled my foot out of my mouth, I have never used a real-life situation like getting hit by a truck ever again. In case someone's loved one *was* actually run over by a steamroller, the shear amazement of that form of meeting your maker, I hope, would outweigh the foot in mouth disease.

All forms of insurance are hedges against a bet that something bad will happen, and the current price you pay will be small compared to the future value. For instance, you have a heart attack and need heart surgery. You've purchased health insurance at work or privately. Isn't the $5,000 deductible better than the $1M in hospital bills?

Estate planning uses life insurance for the very reason that it is cheap money and it bypasses the probate process. Your beneficiary or estate gets a check from the insurance company. Many people who have built sizable estates are facing a dilemma with the estate tax, also commonly known as the death tax. We will all kick the bucket at some point, and if we have estate tax consequences, life insurance can be a real blessing.

For instance, if you have a $10M estate and, as of 2012 with current laws on the books, the exemption is only $5M, what would your estate tax liability be? In this scenario, $5M is in excess and will be taxed at roughly 40 percent nine months after death. How's that for a parting shot from this planet? Thanks for building a great estate and paying all your tax along the way. For one last congratulatory pat on the back, please send us $2M. Where will the money come from?

Will your beneficiaries have the cash, will they need to sell your vintage car collection, paintings, real estate or other investments at fire sale prices, or will they have to borrow the money and pay interest over many years?

The answer to these questions is based on the actual cost of money. Bottom line, insurance is generally the cheapest form of money.

Federal Estate Taxes

There are four ways you can pay Federal Estate Taxes, which can run as high as 55 percent on the portion of the estate that is over the exempt amount. Currently, the exempt amount for 2012 is $5M per person, but remember that in 2013 it will revert back to $1M unless Congress acts again to change the amount.

If you are thinking, no way, of course they will keep it at the higher amount, I challenge you to think again. In 1901, the estate death tax exemption was $1M per person. As recently as 2001 it was $625,000. The reality is the estate death tax is based on whatever direction the political winds may blow, and they are heavily influenced by the economic state of the government. If the government is running surpluses, then they might be generous and lift the exemption amount. If they are broke, well, it doesn't take a rocket scientist to figure out where the exemption is heading.

Today, is the government awash in surplus budgets or starving for tax revenue? That should help you form an opinion on which direction the estate tax exemption will go. The key to the death tax is planning and understanding what are the best methods for paying Uncle Sam the final bar tab on your life.

The four ways to pay for estate taxes are as follows:

1. Using liquid assets (money market, savings, checking)
2. Using illiquid assets (real estate, art, antiques or jewelry, home furnishings, cars, etc.)
3. Borrowing the funds
4. Adding Life Insurance

Here are the costs of each choice:

1. Use of Liquid Assets

The cost of using liquid assets is generally one dollar for each dollar paid in taxes. Since these assets are being held in easily accessible forms (checking, money market or savings), the problem is they are only making around 1 percent interest. For the following example, let's just presume that you could be investing those liquid dollars at a hypothetical 7% compounded annually. Let's see what the effect is.

The additional cost is lost opportunity. If you are making only 1 percent, the difference over 10 years could be hundreds of thousands of dollars, that is,

- $1 million at 1 percent for 10 years = $104,622 potential interest earned.
- $1 million at 7 percent for 10 years = $967,151 potential interest earned.

The opportunity cost is the difference, which is $862,529 in this case.

$$\$967,151 - \$104,622 = \$862,529$$

Therefore, the cost was actually $1.86 dollars for each dollar paid in taxes.

$$\$1,000,000 \text{ tax paid} = \$1,000,000 \text{ liquid savings plus} \\ \$862,529 \text{ opportunity cost}$$

For simplicity, let's not count opportunity cost and just assume that each dollar paid in tax ONLY costs one dollar held in liquid savings.

- Cost = $1 for each $1 paid in taxes

2. Forced Sale of Assets

There are two faces to forced estate sales: the buyers who are happy they are getting such great deals and the sellers who are losing heirlooms at pennies on the dollar to raise cash for taxes due in nine months. If you happen to die when the economy is booming, then perhaps prices are at a high point, but what if you happen to die, say, in the middle of another recession. Prices could be at an all-time low-just when your family needs to raise cash. So selling real estate or long-term bonds or stocks at depressed values can be another big problem.

Most forced sales raise only 50 to 70 cents on the dollar. For instance, selling a piece of real estate in a quick sale may only bring in 70 percent of the fair market value of the property (leaving 30 percent on the table as a loss). Let's use the upper estimate of 70 cents on the dollar.

- Cost = $1.30 for each $1 paid in taxes

3. Borrow Funds

Paying long-term interest escalates the true cost of the estate settlement. Suppose you borrow $1M at 7 percent amortizing interest for 10 years. The actual cost is repayment of $1M, plus an additional $400,000 in interest, for a total of $1.4M paid.

- Cost = $1.40 for each $1 paid in taxes

4. Life Insurance

Life insurance is one of the best ways to leverage your dollars. Usually, for each 20 to 30 cents you pay out, you will receive $1 in return. If life insurance is not part of the estate, it is free from federal and state estate taxes. As an added bonus, the premiums you pay for life insurance reduce the estate by like amounts and therefore further reduce the portion of the estate that is taxable.

It is important to note that life insurance, to be excluded from your estate, must be part of a more comprehensive trust arrangement. If you purchase a life insurance policy, you must place the policy in a special IRS exempt trust, so that the death benefits will not be included in your estate and will therefore not be subject to the estate tax. When you set up these life policies, you must insist on setting up all of the necessary parts and not cutting any corners. Use of an estate planning attorney, licensed in your state of residence, is critical.

Many insurance agents love to sell estate tax policies because they are generally very large. The problem occurs when an agent focuses on the sale and is not well versed in estate planning and does not include an estate planning attorney in the process. For fear of complicating the sale, or to speed up the time to receive their payday, he or she may skip necessary steps, such as an Irrevocable Life Insurance Trust. This probably sounds like the opinion of someone who is very jaded. I am. I have seen many examples of people who were sold a life policy and had the right idea, but due to an incomplete process on the part of the sales person, the client's situation was not protected and he or she was left vulnerable and little improved.

The bottom line for using life insurance is that estate liabilities are paid FOR the estate but not FROM the estate! The estate receives the funds it requires to meet its liabilities, and the estate beneficiaries receive their full inheritance, undiminished in any way.

- Cost = $0.20 to $0.30 for each $1 paid in taxes

The order of importance when designing your estate plan should always be:

1. Estate Planning Attorney
2. CPA
3. Life insurance

The goal is to reduce your estate tax liability as much as possible via trust and accounting work. After reducing the estate tax liability using the first two estate-planning priorities, use life insurance to cover the taxes that are left. This is not a popular belief among insurance agents because using this priority system will most likely drastically reduce their commission and could save you a lot of money each year in lower insurance premiums.

Annuities

Life insurance is the financial tool that protects you from living too short. Annuities are the life insurance tool for protecting you from living too long. Anyone who has retired from a company and is being paid a monthly check has an annuity. The annuity was purchased by your previous employer from the pension funds available for your retirement, and now you are benefiting with a monthly payout.

Most people know of annuities as lifetime investments, a payout that stops the day you die, leaving nothing to your beneficiaries. Though this is one path you can take with annuities, many people use them instead as tax-deferred savings, vehicles that work similar to a CD. You save your money, it potentially grows over time, and, eventually, the CD or annuity matures and you can withdraw your money and move it somewhere else.

The annuitization features can be implemented, or they may never be used. Annuitization means converting the annuity policy from a deferred-savings vehicle to an income-paying vehicle. You can pick from different periods for the payout to continue, from five, ten, to fifteen or more year increments for various life payout options.

Again, this book is not intended to teach everything about annuities and life insurance, as there are hundreds of others you can easily pick up at your local bookstore or library or go online to further your education.

This chapter is intended to give you my opinion from personal experience and hopefully introduce you to some of the little-known features of annuities, which few if any insurance representatives will share with a client before they buy.

Index Universal Life and Index Fixed Annuities

These versions of universal life (UL) and fixed annuities (FA) have the potential to earn interest based on common indexes such as the S&P 500, the NASDAQ 100, or others. They are sold as the ideal product. They will make money for you if the stock market goes up, and they will protect your principal if the stock market goes down. Sounds like the ultimate investment vehicle.

The single biggest problem we see with these financial tools is the ability of the insurance company issuing the products to change the way they calculate the interest. To explain in more detail, each Index UL and Index FA has different means of calculating what interest you earn each year based on the various stock market indexes.

We like to describe the different means of calculating interest as engines in a car. Imagine you have a garage with four cars, maybe all Toyota Camrys. From the outside, they appear exactly the same, but on the inside, each car has a different type of engine. One has an electric motor, one a 4-cylinder, one has a V6, and the most powerful one has a V8-turbo. Each engine will perform differently under different road conditions.

One of the engines in Index UL and FA is called the participation rate. Again, this is a method of calculating the interest that a particular UL or FA will earn based on the performance of an index such as the S&P 500.

Assume an annuity has a participation rate of 80 percent of the S&P 500. On the anniversary of your Index UL or FA, they will record the value of the S&P 500. On the next anniversary, they will again record the value of the S&P 500, and calculate the return. Let's say for example that the markets rose 10 percent, and then apply the participation rate, 80 percent, to the market gains and you have a total return for the annuity of 8 percent.

$$\text{Market gains} \times \text{Participation Rate} = \text{Index credit for that year}$$
$$10 \times 80\,\text{percent} = 8$$

This 8 percent interest rate is then applied to your annuity contract value for that year. If you have an annuity starting at $100,000 and you gain 8 percent, your new contract value is $108,000 for the next year. This value can never drop due to poor market conditions in the future; it is locked in! Sounds good so far, right?

This is usually where the story ends when most insurance agents sell these products. The problem, buried in the Index UL or FA contract, is that the insurance company has the ability to change the participation rate on each contract anniversary at its discretion. This is sort of like changing the governor on an engine.

A governor is a device that limits the performance or top speed of a car's engine. A particular BMW might be able to drive 175 mph, but the manufacturer puts a governor on the engine to limit it to a maximum speed of 125 mph.

On each anniversary insurance companies have the ability to change the settings on the governors they placed on their Index UL policies and Index FA policies. The reason they do this is to limit the upside potential of the contract, and frankly, keep the difference.

Agents will say the companies will not do this because it would not be good for the clients and thus not good for them, but in my experience this means nothing.

More often than not, the first year in these contracts, the engines are set for full power. It makes them easy to sell. But once you have purchased a particular Index UL or FA, and are committed to the policy for five, ten, or fifteen years or longer, with high surrender charges for canceling the contract early, I have seen virtually every insurance carrier crank down the governors so much that the up-side potential of the policies is almost insignificant in most normal stock market years.

For one particular Index FA, I saw the insurance company set the governors on the contract so low that if the S&P 500 rose 30 percent in a year, this contract might earn 4.5 percent. Remember, the insurance company keeps the difference. Sounds like these Wall Street companies are stacking the deck against the client, doesn't it?

Other crediting methods or engines in Index UL or FAs are called spread fees and cap rates. The engines are usually mixtures of these three methods of calculating the rate of return of an index like the S&P 500.

Before buying one of these Index UL or FAs, find out the minimum rates to which these methods can be reduced. Ask for a history from the company on existing policies. There are a few companies that have maintained an honorable co-existence with their policy owners. That is, the insurance company has kept its side of the bargain and has not lowered rates very much, if at all.

Why is it important to have some upside potential with an Index UL or FA? Sure, your principal is protected in bad years, but in good years, if you are not making anything, you are basically going sideways or barely up, and inflation will eat you alive. This is why I do not include these products on the teeter-totter because they don't really match the three main asset categories. They are not able to achieve our goal for high return but rather a low to mid-return.

According to the rule that you only have to give up one of three attributes—High Return or Capital Preservation or Liquidity—Index UL and FAs really only accomplish Capital Preservation. They are not liquid and will not achieve the high return goal. You give up two of the three descriptions.

MVA versus Non-MVA Annuities and Why You Need to Know This

The second important piece of advice to ask concerning Index UL and FAs, is whether a contract is an MVA contract or not.

MVA stands for Market Value Adjustment and is a feature that affects the surrender value of a policy. Since all annuities and life policies are bond based, they are affected by fluctuating market interest rates.

The surrender value is the amount you could walk away with if you decided to cancel the policy early.

For instance, let's imagine you put $100,000 into an FA that has a surrender fee of 10 percent the first three years. If you walk away after the first year, assuming no growth, the most they would give you is $90,000. You are breaking the contract early, and after paying the 10 percent or $10,000 penalty, you end up with $90,000.

In an MVA policy, the surrender value is based on current market interest rates, which are compared to the rate when you got in. As this book goes to print in 2012, rates are at all-time lows. If interest rates take off and rise 3 to 5 percent, you will see the surrender value in an MVA policy fall like a rock.

For instance, in the above example, if market interest rates rise 5 percent, the MVA surrender value might drop from $90,000 to $50,000. Though the contract states a 10 percent surrender charge, it is easy to see how an unaware investor might erroneously presume their worst case scenario for early withdrawal being a $10,000 surrender fee. This investor will be in for a nasty surprise when the $50,000 check shows up from the insurance carrier, not the $90,000 they expected.

In non-MVA contracts, the surrender value is not based on the rising and falling interest rate tide. If the contract states a 10 percent surrender charge, then the surrender value will be 10 percent less than the full contract value. In low interest rate environments, these would be the only FA and UL policies I would generally recommend.

The flipside to this discussion is in high interest rate environments, you would want to buy an MVA fixed annuity or universal life policy because if interest rates came down, you would see the exact opposite effect as described above. The surrender value would actually shrink faster than stated in the contract.

In Summary

Life insurance and annuities serve a purpose and can be vital parts of a well-rounded financial table. From family liabilities and estate taxes to the need for another pension or CD-like investment, the most important tip when buying insurance products or any investment for that matter is to ask questions. Every financial situation is different and calls for different solutions. No investment is always bad or always good; it depends on each client and their personal situations as well as the current economic landscape.

From the gentleman who loves watching unaware ATM users looking at his $1M checking account balance, to the engineer with the 401(k), which after close inspection had lost money over the last 14 years, each situation is different. The job of your financial advisor is to help guide you through the twists and turns of the financial maze and to pick ideas that make common sense. For instance, I would not buy a fixed annuity or bond in the extremely low interest rate environment we are currently experiencing. That being said, if interest rates go above 8 to 10 percent, I would unwind as many of my clients investments as possible and load the boat with bonds and fixed annuities. In high interest rate environments these are probably the best ideas to be in.

Always apply common sense, an open mind, and the current economic landscape to determine your pathway and which financial tools you use to build your *Wealth Code* portfolio.

Conclusion: Time to Take Action!

Many people are driving around with broken portfolios, just as some people drive a car with the clutch slipping. We hire mechanics to fix our cars, and if they don't, we either have them redo their work or find a new mechanic. In my opinion, you should not accept a financial advisor who has a bury-your-head-in-the-sand approach to investments and your estate. Considering the years ahead and the turmoil we have yet to experience, doing nothing is doing something. You are admitting defeat, or worse, accepting the fact that you have lost a lot of money and there is nothing you can do about it except wait for things to improve.

Do you remember that US Airways plane that managed to land on the Hudson River relatively unscathed? Did the passengers give up and wait it out? Of course not. One would reasonably agree that crash landing a passenger plane is about as bad and unfortunately lethal as it gets. But, when they hit the water and came to rest, instead of thinking that it was hopeless, admitting defeat, and remaining in their seats hoping for rescue, the passengers immediately crawled out the exits and onto the wings and stepped into the waiting boats in an orderly fashion. In spite of what most would expect would be the outcome of being on a plane forced to make a crash landing, they chose to alter their futures and survive. If someone had chosen to wait inside the plane, we all know what happened next. The plane eventually sank.

If you have a broken wealth bucket, just as the passengers had a broken plane, you can choose to alter your financial future. With the understanding of building financial tables and using as many asset classes or legs as are suitable for your situation, no matter what comes our way in the future, you will stand a better chance of protecting your wealth, plugging the holes in your bucket, and potentially growing your financial security.

No one knows the future. Our economy might greatly improve from this point forward, go sideways, or fall even further into despair.

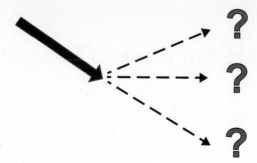

Three Possible Economic Futures

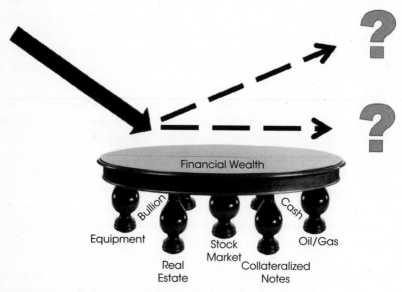

Try to Protect Against a Bad Economic Future

The main reasons to reassess your financial table is to lower your exposure to categories that don't match your financial goals and to strengthen your table by diversifying into other asset classes. Of the three possible scenarios for the future—up, sideways, or down—an asset class diversified table can reasonably help buffer the worst of the three economic outcomes.

According to *Merriam-Webster,* "common sense" is defined in the following way:

Sound and prudent judgment based on a simple perception of the situation or facts.

I believe the most important guiding principle when building your financial table is to use common sense, along with your newfound "Uncommon Knowledge." The investments I have discussed in this book each have strengths and weaknesses, and many of them will work for some people but not for others. The key is to determine which one works for you. The goal of this book is to provide a more complete framework for you to take control of your financial destiny.

The key to everything is education. You are never too old to learn. And, as many other wealthy individuals and families have learned, successful wealth building can be accomplished by gaining enough of an understanding of finance to navigate and overcome the challenges along the way. If life were a placid lake where you could get from Point A to Point B without a single ripple affecting your crossing, there would be no need for guides, mentors, or this book. We all know this is not the case. Life is more like a turbulent Class 5 rapid through the Grand Canyon, with rocks and trees in our pathway. Hopefully, this book will provide a new guide for the back of your raft, a guide to help you potentially steer around unforeseen obstacles, and provide a new foundation or perspective on which to build your own strong financial table.

Appendix A: Case Studies

The following are additional examples of building what I believe represents a strong financial table using my methodology of asset class diversification. Please note that these examples are based on the individual circumstances of each investor. They are not meant to be blanket recommendations and are for educational purposes only. Rates of return will vary and are not guaranteed, and the models used are hypothetical in nature. The math I use is simple, in an effort to help you understand the basics so that the door is open to learn more details as your interest in this methodology grows. Please consult with your financial advisor, or feel free to call us at 800-737-8552, or go to my web site, www.TheWealthCode.com, for more information.

Appendix B holds the detailed descriptions of each investment asset class. As you read through the case studies, I suggest you flip to the various investments in Appendix B as they are brought up and complete your education. I've always felt the best way to understand an investment is to see it in a real life example and then to read about the nitty gritty pros and cons. More glue for your *Wealth Code* table building adventure.

Mr. Johnson

Mr. Johnson is 78 years old and concerned about his income. He is living off his social security checks and doesn't like to touch his stock portfolio because he never knows when it is a good time to sell. He would like more income without touching his principal, yet feels the dividends from most stocks are too low and will not keep up with rising costs.

At my request, Mr. Johnson invited his two daughters to be part of the portfolio discussions. He calls the shots but I always like to include the adult children/future beneficiaries in on any changes we might recommend for an older client. Though I feel I'll get to bug him for another 20 years, you never know, and considering I would potentially be recommending some illiquid investments, it is always a good idea to let the future beneficiaries understand the choices being made and to have their say.

After analyzing his stocks and mutual funds, he realizes he hasn't made a dime in the last 10 years. His portfolio has followed the markets up and down, like the majority of investors with similar portfolios. If he were to sell everything, there would only be a small amount of capital gains tax due on a few of his older stock positions and nothing on his mutual funds. Because the cost basis for mutual funds increases each year with each taxable dividend, his basis now exceeds the current market value of the funds and no taxes would be due.

When it came to the capital gains issue on the older stocks, he agreed with me that it was better to pay a little tax today and get the money working harder for him going forward, rather than sitting in an investment earning nothing year after year and continuing to defer the tax. By paying the tax, he was free to invest the proceeds into investments with a more reasonable probability of providing income and growth.

One point to remember: I believe that tax considerations should always be secondary to the right investment choice. Time and time again, I've seen clients hold on to poorly performing investments because they didn't want to realize any taxable gains. Year after year they sat, making no further gains, but would not sell due to an embedded tax bill on the capital gains. There is an old saying, "You can't go broke taking a profit." Many times the best advice is to pay the tax bill and get the stagnant money potentially working harder for you in another investment.

A last consideration is he feels he might have some health issues and wants to keep a fair amount of his after-tax money liquid for emergencies.

A list of his assets includes:

Personal Residence	Fair Market Value (FMV) $400,000 and paid off
IRA	$ 50,000 mostly in mutual funds
After tax Stock and Mutual Funds	$ 300,000
CDs	$ 50,000
Net worth including Residence	**$800,000**

Investable wealth:

IRA	$ 50,000
After tax Stock and Mutual Funds	$ 300,000
CD	$ 50,000
Total	**$400,000**

Maximum per Real Asset financial investment:

$$\text{Investable Wealth} \times 10 \text{ percent} = \$400,000 \times 10 \text{ percent}$$
$$= \$40,000$$

As always, being more conservative in the amount per illiquid investment is being prudent. Using 5 percent as our target for these investments leaves us with around $20,000 per leg.

Designing Mr. Johnson's plan was based on several criteria.

First, he is only state accredited, which means he is not allowed to invest in financial tools such as oil/gas programs, per SEC guidelines. Second, because of his age and always keeping in mind the uncertainty of sudden medical issues which was a concern to him, I kept a significant amount of his portfolio liquid.

If liquidity was one of the three attributes (High Return, Capital Preservation, Liquid) I had to use for a big piece of his money, I am left with choosing from the bank products (goal is Capital Preservation and Liquid) and the stock market (goal is High Return and Liquid).

Using the most conservative adaptive manager I have worked with who only trades fixed income, became a good place to start for a big chunk of his portfolio. In choosing this manager, the single biggest factor was looking at their performance in the bad years such as 2000 to 2002 and 2008 as well as the intermediate rough patches of time such as May through June 2010, August through September 2011 and May 2012.

I care much more about how a group has performed in the bad times than in the good. Everyone can thump their chests and say how great they are when times are good, I care far more about the performance when times are tough. How far did they drop? If and when did they move out to cash? This ability to move to 100 percent cash is the major advantage of adaptive managers.

KEY WEALTH CODE CONCEPT

To see how well a mutual fund, stock, or money manager will perform in the future, start with their performance during the rough times in the stock market.

Years like 2000 to 2002 (S&P 500 negative 52 percent) or 2008 (S&P 500 negative 38 percent).

Bad periods such as May through June 2010 (S&P 500 negative 15 percent), August through September 2011 (S&P 500 negative 20 percent) or May 2012 (S&P 500 negative 11 percent).

If the stock market drops 20 percent as it did in the 2011 rough patch and your particular investment choice also dropped 15 to 20 percent, should you expect a different result the next time the market swoons?

As Einstein was quoted saying; "*The definition of insanity is doing the same thing over and over again and expecting a different result.*"

The particular manager I selected for Mr. Johnson has a 10-year average return of more than 10 percent net of fees as of January 2012 with a beta of 0.18. If a money manager has been able to generate those types of returns in the same time period where the S&P 500 index has barely made over 2 percent, even though we have stated time and time again that past performance is no guarantee of future results, at least we have something to feel more confident about.

Beta is a volatility factor which essentially measures the amount of risk a manager is taking. With a beta of 1.00 being the S&P 500 benchmark, the lower the number the less volatile a particular group's performance has been compared to the general stock market.

2008 was this manager's worst year where they lost about 1 percent. A far better result than the negative 38 percent of the S&P 500, but a loss nonetheless. I know that investment results are going to vary, but again I look at how they've weathered (or not weathered) prior economic storms. After the appropriate manager was selected for this leg of Mr. Johnson's new portfolio, we focused on the other legs for his Wealth Code table.

The other investments available to him include a fixed annuity, banking products, non-traded REITs, equipment leasing companies, various collateralized notes, and consumer grade real estate. Of course, I could add variable annuities and static stocks and bonds, but I tend to avoid these categories for most of our clients due to the current economic climate and outlook going forward. In addition, I make no claims to be a "stock picker" nor will I ever claim to be one.

Liquidity is important, and considering that he is 78 years old, I stuck to investments with durations of no more than five years. The equipment leasing category is excluded due to longer maturation dates of eight years or more and Mr. Johnson did not want to have a rental property where possible headaches are potentially part of the equation. The potential for this type of returns wouldn't justify the nuisances for him personally. We choose to leave his CDs alone, sacrificing return for liquidity. The maturity dates for his CDs were generally laddered appropriately so that a number of them would mature over the years to provide liquidity if needed. All were of reasonably short duration as well.

Although fixed annuities do not normally play a part in plans I craft for clients, I added a small piece in a three-year non-MVA annuity, which could be annuitized in the future, adding another income stream for life. Due to his age, the payout for Mr. Johnson would be around 9 percent each year, lasting his remaining lifetime. If he waits to start the income stream, called annuitization, his payout percentage would increase due to a shorter life expectancy. For the meantime, the annuity will stay in deferral and pay out interest at a guaranteed 2.5 percent per year. Again, I am sacrificing return today to have the annuitization option in the future and liquidity at a small price in case he needs the money.

Within his $50,000 IRA, I used $20,000 of the money in an illiquid Business Development Corporation (BDC) and the other $30,000 in the liquid adaptive management account. Since he is required to pull out increasingly larger required minimum distributions (RMDs) each year from his IRA, we will use the managed account to satisfy the amount above the expected cash flow from both of the investments. He cannot take out more than the BDC earns so any additional amount required to satisfy the RMD will have to come from the liquid adaptive management account.

The goal of the IRS with RMDs from retirement accounts is to eventually drain out your account and force you to pay the deferred taxes. Eventually everyone will have to cut into principal each year as we get older unless you can earn more than the RMD. In Mr. Johnson's case, at age 78 he only has to pull 4.9 percent, which the potential distributions from the two investments in his IRA will satisfy if they perform as expected.

My proposed plan for Mr. Johnson was as follows:

Original Position	Amount	Recommended Position	Amount	Asset Class	Liquidity Timeline
IRA	$ 50,000	BDC	$ 20,000	Collateralized Note	5 Years
		Adaptive Asset Management	$ 30,000	Stock Market	Liquid
Stocks, Mutual Funds	$300,000	Storage Center REIT	$ 20,000	Institutional Grade Real Estate	4 Years
		Single Tenant Big Box REIT	$ 20,000	Institutional Grade Real Estate	4 Years
		30% LTV Mortgage Pool	$ 20,000	Collateralized Note	5 Years
		Life Note	$ 25,000	Collateralized Note	2 Years
		Non-MVA Fixed Annuity	$ 50,000	Insurance	3 Years
		Adaptive Asset Management	$165,000	Stock Market	Liquid

Summary of Recommendations for Mr. Johnson

Fixed Annuity	$ 50,000	~ 13% of investable wealth
Non-Traded REITs	$ 40,000	~ 10%
Collateralized Notes	$ 65,000	~ 16%
Adaptive Asset Management	$195,000	~ 48%
CDs	$ 50,000	~ 13%

Summary of Liquid to Illiquid investments

Liquid Investments	$245,000	~ 61% of investable wealth
Illiquid Investments	$155,000	~ 39%

Liquidity Time Line	$ Becoming Liquid	Total Liquid Investments
Liquid Immediately	$245,000	$245,000
Liquid after 2 years	$ 25,000	$270,000
Liquid after 3 years	$ 50,000	$320,000
Liquid after 4 years	$ 40,000	$360,000
Liquid after 5 years	$ 40,000	$400,000

Mr. Johnson paid $45,000 for his house, 30 years ago, and likes the idea of real estate as a part of his plan, as it has earned him more money than any other investment he has ever owned. He believes rents will generally increase over time and will help offset his income needs with rising inflation. The two REITs chosen for him match his beliefs of what will hold its value over the coming years. The big-box REIT purchases single tenant real estate for stores he frequents a lot such as Wal-Mart, Walgreens, and Home Depot. He feels that no matter how bad the economy gets and even though their stock values might go down with a falling market, they should be able to stay in business and thus keep paying their rent on time.

The mortgage pool represents a collection of 30-year fixed mortgages on residential real estate. The maximum loan to value (LTV) of these properties was 30 percent as an average per their prospectus as provided to the client before investing. That is, the real estate market across the country would have to fall a collective 70 percent from 2012 prices to jeopardize the principal in this investment. This is one of the more conservative investments he chooses. It will never pay an exorbitant amount, reasonably around 5 to 6 percent, but I feel the risk is commensurate with the return.

Though the annuity will probably not perform as well as the non-traded REITS or the collateralized notes, 2.5 percent is better than current CD interest rates in the low 1 percent range. More importantly, he can annuitize the contract to begin a much higher payout for the rest of his life, currently around 9 percent. This again is due to his life expectancy, when calculating the payment percentage. The older you are the higher the percentage and vice versa.

I chose a short-term annuity, which I can change in just three years if the economic environment warrants it. The surrender charges on this particular annuity were 4 percent, 3 percent, and 2 percent and 0 percent after year three and since this policy did not have a Market Value Adjustment (MVA) we did not have to be concerned with the negative effects on the surrender charge if interest rates rose. If necessary, he could surrender the policy at any time and, worst-case scenario, give back 4 percent. Again, this is a worst-case scenario. How many people would like to know their worst-case scenario with a stock or bond was only to lose 4 percent?

If interest rates rise dramatically within the next three years, he would be able to close the annuity penalty free after year three and move the money to a harder working financial vehicle.

Finally, I left the $50,000 CD alone because this is an account that provides him piece of mind. That is always worth more than gaining an extra couple of percentage points by moving the money. Always design a plan around your beliefs, not somebody else's.

Using target dividend/distribution assumptions for the various investments, I was able to generate an approximation of his Cash Flow potential today.

Investment	Target Income Assumption	Investment Amount	Income Per Year
Fixed Annuity	2.5%	$ 50,000	$ 1,250
Non-traded REITs	6.5%	$ 40,000	$ 2,600
Collateralized Notes	6%	$ 65,000	$ 3,900
Adaptive Asset Management	6%	$ 195,000	$ 11,700
CDs	1%	$ 50,000	$ 500
	Average 5%	**$400,000**	**$19,950**

Growth assumptions must be used to generate an expected total return for Mr. Johnson's new *Wealth Code* portfolio. Nothing is ever guaranteed of course but having 10-, 20-, even 30-year histories of actual performance at least gives us warm fuzzy feelings about a particular group's ability to generate returns.

In Mr. Johnsons plan, three of the four new investments have growth attributes: The non-traded REITs, BDC, and adaptive manager. The non-traded REITs and BDCs have generally tacked on another 2 percent for growth and the adaptive managers we currently work with have 10-year returns of more than 10 percent net of fees going back to 2001. Being conservative and cutting the adaptive manager's historical performance down to 8 percent suggests we should see another 2 percent for growth on top of the 6 percent distributions we will take from that category.

Asset Class	Growth Assumption	Investment Amount	Growth per Year
Non-traded REIT	2%	$ 40,000	$ 800
BDC	2%	$ 20,000	$ 400
Adaptive Asset Management	2%	$ 195,000	$ 3,900
	Average 2%	**$255,000**	**$5,100**

The potential total return for Mr. Johnson's plan equals income plus growth. In his case, $19,950 plus $5,100 for a total of $25,050.

$25,050 divided by his investment amount of $400,000 equals a total return goal of 6.26 percent.

My job for Mr. Johnson was not to light the world on fire but to provide an investment platform that I believe could potentially provide a consistent return that would be comparable to the real rate of inflation. He was more concerned with the return *of* his principal rather than the return *on* his principal. With the designed portfolio, I feel he'll have a fighting chance to realize both.

Ms. Smith

Ms. Smith is 55 years old and single. She does not work and lives off an inheritance she received from her deceased parents. She loves to travel and maintains a condo in a downtown high rise. The condo works nicely with her lifestyle, as it allows her the flexibility to leave town on a moment's notice.

A list of her assets includes:

Personal Residence	Fair Market Value (FMV) $1,000,000 and paid off
Muni Bonds	$2,300,000
Rental Property	FMV $800,000 with $100,000 in loans Cost basis of $300,000 Net Cash Flow of $18,000 per year
Net worth including Residence	**$4,000,000**

Investable wealth:

Muni Bonds	$ 2,300,000
Rental Property	$ 700,000 ($800,000 — $100,000 Mortgage)
Total	**$3,000,000**

Maximum per Real Asset financial investment:

$$\text{Investable Wealth} \times 10 \text{ percent} = \$3,000,000$$
$$\times 10 \text{ percent} = \$300,000$$

KEY WEALTH CODE CONCEPT

Clients have muni bonds in their portfolio for the obvious benefit of being federal tax free and potentially state tax free. Even though their returns may be only three of four percent with realistically no upside potential due to probable rising interest rates, the justification for accepting the low yields is the net tax benefit.

As previously mentioned, in order to get higher yields on a muni bond, you have to extend out the term of the bond. A 20-year muni bond will most likely pay more interest than a 10 year bond. Whatever the term of the bond, if interest rates happen to rise quickly, an investor will most likely be stuck in the bond until its maturity date, ten, twenty, or more years into the future, all the time losing purchasing power due to the effects of inflation.

What if there was an alternative investment which, after tax, yielded more than a particular muni bond and was far shorter in expected duration?

A difference between the stock market-traded REITs and the non-traded REITs is the pass through of tax advantages to the end investor. The non-traded REITs use 1099 reporting of their income each year. On the 1099, an investor will see their total distributions or reinvestments broken into two pieces. Taxable distributions and non-taxable distributions.

For instance, let's say an investor receives 7 percent or $7,000 of income from a $100,000 non-traded REIT in a given year. Their 1099 might report the taxable distributions as being $3,000 and the non-taxable distributions as being $4,000.

$7,000 total distributions = $3,000 taxable distributions
+ $4,000 non-taxable distributions

The non-taxable distributions result from items such as depreciation, mortgage interest, and other real estate tax advantages being passed through to the investor's tax return.

Ultimately, you are lowering the cost basis of your investment until the eventual sale of the properties where you will recapture the off-set income.

The investor will have to pay tax on the $3,000 and not on the $4,000 until much later and at potentially more favorable tax rates.

Assuming the investor is in the 35 percent effective tax bracket today, they would pay $1,050 in income tax. Subtracting this from their total distribution of $7,000 results in net income of $5,950 in their pocket.

$7,000 (distributions received) − $1,050 ($3,000 taxable income
× 35 percent) = $5,950 net or 5.95 percent

Compare the example non-traded REITs 5.95 percent after tax return to the longer-term muni bond maybe only yielding 4 or 5 percent.

There are two major differences between a non-traded REIT and a longer-term muni bond:

1. Length of investment is generally much shorter, generally in the four to eight year range;
2. Principal growth potential.

Most will agree real estate, if held long enough, will appreciate in value. The goal of the non-traded REITs is to sell the underlying properties for a potential profit and return more than the contributed capital to the investors on top of the received distributions. The goal is to have appreciation of the principal, something muni bonds today, in today's potentially rising interest environment, will most likely not experience.

The bottom line question for an investment is, whether it is tax free or taxable, what's in your pocket after Uncle Sam has taken his piece of the pie? If a muni bond is paying 5 percent and another taxable investment, after taxes have been paid, is earning more, isn't it better to have the higher paying investment if the risks and rewards are suitable?

Though I am not a fan of muni bonds in a probable rising interest rate environment, Ms. Smith' bonds were appropriate for her. Her current advisor had chosen an ultra-short duration portfolio of individual bonds, with the longest maturation date a mere two years out. She had more income than she knew what to do with and was comfortable with the portfolio.

Going back to Ms. Smith, I recommended doing nothing with the short-term muni bonds and instead focused our attention on her property.

Discussing her rental property, she said it was the one nuisance in her life. The terrible Ts (tenants, toilets, and trash) were driving her crazy. She felt tied to the property due to the capital gains she would owe when selling it. If she sold, she would realize $500,000 in capital gains, and with the recapture of depreciation, her tax bill would be more than $125,000. The taxes paid would represent a huge leak in her financial bucket of lost opportunity.

We taught her about 1031 exchanges, (discussed in detail in Appendix B and Appendix D) and showed her options using co-ownership real estate via Delaware Statutory Trusts (DST). These securities allow her to sell the property and do a 1031 exchange, deferring all the taxes, into multiple co-ownership real estate properties for investment diversification.

Our recommendations for Ms. Smith were as follows:

Original Position	Amount		Recommended Position	Amount	Asset Class	Liquidity Timeline
Rental Property	$700,000	→	5 "Dollar" Retail Stores DST	$200,000	Institutional Grade Real Estate	5–8 Years
		1031 tax deferred exchange	Single AAA Credit Tenant Office DST	$200,000	Institutional Grade Real Estate	5–8 Years
			400 Unit Apartment Complex DST	$200,000	Institutional Grade Real Estate	5–8 Years
			Oil Royalty	$100,000	Oil/Gas	? Years

Using target distribution assumptions for the various investments, we are able to generate an approximation of her cash flow potential.

Investment	Target Income Assumption	Investment Amount	Income Per Year
5 "Dollar" Stores	7.1%	$ 200,000	$ 14,200
Single AA Credit Tenant Office	6.5%	$ 200,000	$ 13,000
Apartment Complex	6.4%	$ 200,000	$ 12,800
Oil Royalty	8%	$ 100,000	$ 8,000
	Average 6.86%	**$700,000**	**$48,000**

The average target yield for the properties selected was around 6.9 percent. By exchanging the equity in one property into four distinctly different properties, she was able to diversify her holdings and raise her net cash flow from $18,000 to around $48,000.

The part that surprised her was how large commercial properties can accelerate depreciation via a cost segregation study.

This study effectively identifies and reclassifies real estate assets into four categories: personal property, land improvements, building components, and land. The first three have accelerated depreciation deductions and easier write-offs when an asset becomes obsolete, broken, or destroyed. The net effect of using a cost segregation study for DSTs in general is that, for Ms. Smith' income of $48,000, she may only have net taxable income of $15,000 to $20,000. Basically, the same situation she was in before the 1031 exchange.

The other headache she was relieved of was that of tax reporting, which is essentially prepared by the sponsor of the DST and mailed to the owners. The owners just hand the forms to their accountants and they are done.

There are trade-offs for DSTs, the biggest one being a very limited ability to sell one's ownership share during the duration of the investment, typically between four to eight years or longer. This wasn't a concern for Ms. Smith, considering she had owned her previous property for more than 20 years and understands real estate is a long-term investment.

DSTs require a lot of education concerning the pros and cons and should only be considered after careful due diligence and working with a financial advisor experienced in DST investments.

Other negative attributes are the same negative attributes that affect all real estate investments. Income can be suspended if the property loses tenants, additional cash requirements may be needed if significant issues arise with the property, and real estate values go both ways, up and down.

Though Ms. Smith didn't really care about the increase in income, she was thrilled to no longer have to deal with the terrible Ts. The DSTs she purchased all came with professional management. Now, she is truly free to leave town without any of the headaches of managing a property and being on call to deal with them.

Mr. and Mrs. Jaspar

Mr. Jaspar is 38 years old, a graphic artist with income around $45,000 per year. He is married and has a 4-year-old son. His wife, Mrs. Jaspar, is 35 years old and works as a nurse part-time earning $36,000 per year. The family rents a two-bedroom apartment for $1,500 per month.

Many times when younger clients come into my firm, my first goal with them is to look at the basics, things like estate planning and insurance planning. Being in California a basic revocable trust is a good starting point. In other states a simple living will is most likely sufficient. I strongly urge you to consult with your own estate planning attorney in your own home state.

It is important to remember that more than just the living trust or will you get the other vital documents which come with it such as a medical power of attorney and durable power of attorney. Both cover the situation if one of the spouses is incapacitated and the other needs the authority to make medical and financial decisions on their behalf.

You might question why, since the Jaspars are so young, we start with things like estate planning. Bottom line, not having your estate in order is a train wreck waiting to happen for any age group. It is never too early to start. As we are not attorneys, we referred the Jaspars to a number of competent, yet very reasonably priced small law firms and let them choose who they worked with.

Because the Jaspars have significant family liabilities, we also recommended term life policies for both spouses, due to their having similar incomes. Because of their ages, both applied for 25-year term policies for $1M each, with a cost at the time the policies were put into place of around $600 for him and $400 for her. Anytime a family has young children at homes, life insurance, in my opinion, becomes a necessity.

Does an additional cost of $1,000 per year or $83 per month cut into the amount they could be saving? Of course it does, but it is an inexpensive hedge against either or both of them being killed and leaving the other or their son facing financial hardship. It is important to consider the loss of future income and costs associated with college or other typical expenses of raising a child.

I recommended the 25-year term policies to cover them to around age 60 and past the college years for their son. At that point, family liabilities generally tend to ease as does the need for life insurance. If there are still other liabilities remaining, such as mortgage, job, estate, and so forth, this may deem a continued need for insurance or changing the coverage to a permanent policy.

A list of their assets includes:

Mr. Jaspar's 401(k)	$ 12,000 (contributing $300 per month)
Mrs. Jaspar's 401(k)	$ 4,000 (contributing $200 per month)
After tax Mutual Funds	$ 39,000
Net worth	**$55,000**

With a combined income of $81,000 per year and net worth of $55,000, the Jaspars are considered non-accredited investors. They wish to start building wealth and feel they are going nowhere at this moment with their current investments.

Because of the security laws for accreditation, they do not have access to most investments that are part of the *Wealth Code* table. Again many of the illiquid investments have rules of net worth and income requirements. Typically the state of domicile minimum is $70,000 income *and* $70,000 net worth *or* $250,000 net worth to have access to the non-traded REITs, BDCs, note programs, and so forth. The higher accreditation standards of $1M net worth apply to most of the partnership deals.

That being said, one of my favorite categories for an investor is consumer-grade real estate, real estate valued at less than $5M. In this case we are looking for single family rentals in the range of $60,000 to $80,000.

Since the real estate bubble peaked in 2006, many areas of the country have now fallen more than 30 percent in value. In several areas of the country, houses which used to be $100,000 plus are now in the $60,000 to $80,000 range. As the values continue to fall, the gross rents as a percentage of the value of the homes continue to rise.

For instance, a house which rents for $8,000 per year and used to be worth $100,000 had at that time a gross rent of 8 percent. That house, having fallen in value to $70,000, now has a gross rent of 11.4 percent assuming the rent stays the same.

$8,000 Rent/$100,000 Previous Home Value = 8 percent Gross Rent
$8,000 Rent/$70,000 Reduced Home Value = 11.4 percent Gross Rent

Historically, when gross rents approach 15 percent, you are getting very close to the bottom of a local real estate markets cycle. Local can literally mean a particular zip code.

This is not speaking for the country as a whole being at the bottom of its real estate cycle, just the particular area where the gross rents are now approaching 15 percent.

Why 15 percent? Maybe it is a psychological number where investors will start to buy. Can the rest of the country continue to fall? Absolutely! Places which still have large numbers of foreclosed properties waiting to hit the market as well as gross rents that are in the single digit percentages have a ways to fall in my opinion. California, Las Vegas, Arizona, and Florida come to mind that match this criteria.

The opportunity lies in the fact that today loans are extremely difficult to get. You need solid income, high credit scores, and low debt to qualify for even the smallest loans.

The biggest barrier to entry is the required down payment. Many of the potential buyers, families with local jobs and kids in the nearby schools, have some money saved, but not $20,000 to $30,000, so are forced to keep renting. They do not wish to be in apartments and would rather raise their kids in a single-family residence. The unfortunate aspect is the rents in these homes are rather high, again, roughly 15 percent of the value. Not having the down payment forces them to pay rent, and this is the opportunity for investors with sufficient cash whether in a self-directed IRA or after-tax dollars, to purchase these investment homes.

The Jaspars' were straddling both sides of this fence. They did not have sufficient down payment to purchase a home in Los Angeles, due to the relatively high home values, but had enough saved and the credit to buy a rental in one of the more reasonably priced rental markets.

Mr. Jaspar was also rather nervous of taking on a multi-thousand dollar mortgage and property taxes that would be associated with buying a primary residence in Los Angeles. Though they would like to buy a house, they know it is out of their reach at this moment and are content in their current living arrangement.

After teaching them the difference between a liability and an asset, which is something that has a net negative cash flow versus something that puts money in your pocket each month respectively, the Jaspars were very interested in purchasing their first rental property and beginning to build real wealth and positive cash flow.

We referred the Jaspars to a few different real estate management groups in the mid-west. Why the mid-west? Because the overall cost of homes there was substantially less than the local Los Angeles market. In other words, similar sized homes (3-bedroom, 2-bath, for example) were hundreds of thousands of dollars cheaper in other metropolitan markets. At one of the real estate management groups, they were able to find a newly rehabbed three bedroom single family home with a long-term tenant in place renting for $825 per month.

At a purchase price of around $80,000 and a required down payment typically of 25 percent for investment properties, they would only need $20,000 for their down payment. The only debt they had was a revolving credit card which they paid off each month. With their good credit and low debt payments, the Jaspars could qualify for the loan of $60,000. The monthly payment for a 30-year fixed mortgage, with current interest rates for investment properties around 4.65 percent, would be around $308.

Why this number is important is because it is roughly the same amount Mr. Jaspar is contributing to his 401(k). That makes him feel financially comfortable because he knows, even if there is a vacancy at the rental property, he could divert their 401(k) contributions ($300+$200) to pay the home's mortgage and property taxes, and his overall cash flow as well as tax situation would stay exactly the same. That is, their living needs would be covered by the same effective take home income since they were not using the amount contributed in their 401(k)s anyways. Their tax situation stays the same because even though they are taking more home in their paycheck, paying the mortgage and property taxes neutralizes the increased income.

The summary of the property is as follows:

Rental home purchase price	$80,000
Investment (Down payment + Mortgage costs)	$22,000
30 year fixed mortgage balance	$60,000

The summary of the estimated potential cash flow is as follows:

	Annual Payments
Rental Income: $825 per month	$9,900
Mortgage Payment: $308 per month	−$3,696
Property Management at 9%: $75 per month	−$ 891
Property taxes at 1.25%: $83 per month	−$1,000
Property Insurance: $35 per month	−$ 400
Miscellaneous costs: $50 per month	−$ 600
Net Cash Flow: $276 per month	**$3,313 per year**

Looking at the net cash flow and dividing by the investment made gives the Jaspars' a healthy net return of 15 percent.

$3,313 net cash flow ÷ $22,000 initial investment ($20,000 Down Payment + $2,000 closing costs) = 15 percent

Here's the icing on the cake. If the property over the next 10 years averages three percent compounded appreciation, their total return will equal more than 27 percent per year.

3 percent compounded appreciation × $80,000 (Initial FMV) = $2,751 average per year growth

$3,313 net cash flow + $2,751 average per year growth = $6,064 per year total return

$6,064 ÷ $22,000 (Initial Investment) = 27.56 percent annual return

I ask you, as the reader, to tell me that their own 401(k) has matched that performance over the last five years or longer.

Another question they had was funding future college costs. I have always been an advocate of the philosophy that a client should build their personal cash flow as much as possible by passive means. By using that cash flow to continue to build additional income streams, the day college rolls around, you may be able to divert some of that income to help pay the costs. Once college is over, you still have the potential for income streams for yourself in your retirement. This is the same strategy as paying for a car, buying assets to pay for liabilities, except college is not a depreciating liability but rather a long-term asset for your children. Thus you get the best of all worlds. You bought assets to pay for another asset.

My personal problem with typical college accounts such as 529s is that the principal is spent and gone forever. The asset value gets drawn down to zero as college is paid for. Yes, you hopefully have a college grad, but you do not have the principal to provide future cash flow. If an asset such as a rental property helps pay the tuition, the property is hopefully still there after the child graduates. Using the checks in the mail approach provides for both the higher education expenses and personal retirement needs.

In summary, the most important education I provided to the Jaspars was to teach them to shift their focus from making only 401(k) contributions as their primary means of building wealth to buying a real asset which would produce its own paycheck for them today and not only after age 59½. This extra paycheck comes to the door whether they get out of bed or not. Generating additional passive cash flow is a tried and true wealth building principle.

Many people might argue that we should have guided them into purchasing a home for themselves first. While this is desirable for many, I teach my clients to buy assets first, liabilities second. If successful, the Jaspars may eventually have enough cash flow coming from various rental properties (assets) to equal a mortgage payment on their own house (a liability). Then they would be effectively mortgage-free!

Mr. Warbucks

Mr. Warbucks is 67 years old, married, with lots of grandkids. He recently sold a patent to a big turbine manufacturer for $50M. He had excellent tax and estate planning already in place and was looking for a financial advisor to help guide him in investing the money. Needless to say, this client was shopping all the big names, and they all were putting on their best dog and pony shows for him.

This client came to me after seeing the proposals from the major wire houses and most of the boutique firms in the area. His comment to me was that the plans from everyone so far were pretty much the same: stocks and muni bonds. They all discussed the need for lower taxes and over emphasized muni bonds.

His concerns about the proposals presented:

- Interest rates were at the bottom and would put downside pressure on stocks and bonds when they eventually rise.
- Income needs for himself and his family would always be going up with inflation, and he wanted a better hedge for the future.
- He wanted a lot of flexibility for the majority of his money within five years, due to the unpredictability of the economy.

Here is the plan proposed to Mr. Warbucks:

Original Position	Amount	Recommended Position	Amount	Asset Class	Liquidity Timeline
CASH	$45,000,000	Oil/Gas Royalty	$ 4,000,000	Oil/Gas Royalty	Generational
		Energy Drilling	$ 4,000,000	Oil/Gas Develop-mental Drilling	Generational
		Equipment Leasing	$ 3,000,000	Equipment Leasing	8–10 Years
		DST Single Owner- 5 Properties	$10,000,000	Institutional Grade Real Estate	5–7 Years
		Collateralized Notes	$10,000,000	Collateralized Notes	6 Month to 5 Years
		Non-Traded REIT	$ 6,000,000	Institutional Grade Real Estate	4 Years
		Silver/Gold	$ 3,000,000	Bullion	Liquid
		Muni Bonds	$ 5,000,000	Stock Market	Liquid
CASH	$5,000,000	FUN MONEY	$ 5,000,000	Reward	Goal: Spend within one year

Alternate Idea: Replace some real estate with money management to provide more liquidity.

CASH $5,000,000 ⟹	Adaptive Asset Management	$5,000,000	Stock Market	Liquid

Hypothetical Income Analysis:

Investment	Target Distribution	Investment Amount	Income Per Month	Income Per Year	Depreci- ation %
Oil/Gas Royalty	8%	$ 4,000,000	$ 26,666	$ 320,000	15%
Oil/Gas Drilling	10%	$ 4,000,000	$ 33,333	$ 400,000	15%
Equipment Leasing	8%	$ 3,000,000	$ 20,000	$ 240,000	70%
Real Estate—DSTs	6.5%	$ 10,000,000	$ 54,166	$ 650,000	50%
Non-traded REITs	6.5%	$ 6,000,000	$ 32,500	$ 390,000	60%
Collateralized Notes	6%	$ 10,000,000	$ 50,000	$ 600,000	0%
Bullion	0%	$ 3,000,000	N/A	N/A	N/A
Muni Bonds	4%	$ 5,000,000	$ 16,667	$ 200,000	0%
	Average 6.22%	$45,000,000	$233,333	$2,800,000	

Approximate Taxable Income After Depreciation Deductions	$1,765,000
After applying Energy Drilling tax deduction of $800,000 per year for five years	−$ 800,000
Approximate Taxable Income	**$ 965,000**
Effective Tax Bracket: 31.32%	**$ 302,725**

Gross Annual Income	$ 2,800,000
Minus taxes owed	−$ 302,725
Approximate Net After-Tax Income	**$2,497,275**

When looking through my plan, the first thing he noticed was the smiley face and fun money category. My comment to him was, "Congratulations, you just won a very well-deserved spending spree. Spend all the money in this category within a year. Blow it on every frivolous idea you can imagine, spend it on your kids, grandkids, the neighbors' grandkids, your favorite charity. Enjoy it. You worked very hard for this accomplishment." With a smile on his face, considering the spending possibilities, we got down to business.

After describing to him my philosophy on wealth and the use of numerous legs on one's financial table to potentially provide stability and income, I broke down the individual pieces and how they related to the overall plan.

Starting with the real estate portion, we decided on a combination of single-owner DSTs, and non-traded REITS. The single owner DSTs were meant for him to have total control over the buildings and the final say. There would be no other owners to cloud discussions about management, possible sell dates, and so on. The money that went into these properties would potentially grow effectively capital gains tax-free over many years due to the planned use of 1031 exchanges whenever a building would be sold. Remember, using DSTs for 1031 exchanges has risk, and the PPM must be read thoroughly before investing.

As previously mentioned and further explained in Appendix D, when Mr. Warbucks passes away, those buildings will receive a step-up in cost basis per current tax law, and the next generation will inherit them without any capital gain tax burden. Both the DSTs and the non-traded REITs provide a high degree of current income tax sheltering via depreciation and other pass through tax advantages.

We used the non-traded REITs for a smaller but significant chunk of his money for the shear diversification among hundreds of institutional grade real estate properties across the country, and in various categories from multifamily, storage, big box retail, student housing, to office and data centers.

The plan consisted of two types of energy DPPs I commonly use for clients. The oil/gas royalties would generally provide for inflation-adjusted income streams we could plan around and the energy drilling was used for two purposes. The first being the possibility of higher income distributions, the second being the favorable income deductions available from intangible and tangible drilling costs associated with these programs. Per current tax law, one option someone has when investing in an energy drilling program is to amortize the purchase amount over five years and receive 100 percent income deductions without concern for Alternative Minimum Tax (AMT) holdbacks. By placing $4M into various energy drilling programs and amortizing the intangible and tangible drilling costs over five years, Mr. Warbucks will receive $800,000 of income deductions each year until they are exhausted.

$4,000,000 Oil/Gas Drilling investment amortized
÷ 5 years = $800,000 per year

Given that the price per barrel of oil has a strong correlation with inflation both royalty and drilling oil/gas programs should potentially provide a high degree of inflationary income protection. If inflation moves up quickly, oil prices tend to follow fairly closely, which would correlate into higher distributions from his oil/gas programs.

The collateralized note investments (a combination of BDCs, mortgage and life notes) are designed to be shorter term in duration and have a higher sensitivity to rising interest rates. Considering many of these programs are short-term loans to corporations, as the money comes back in and if interest rates have risen, these investments will lend out the capital at higher rates and potentially pass the higher earnings on via distributions. The shortest investment was a six-month life note and the longest a BDC with an expected duration of five years. The biggest problem with the collateralized note programs is they do not have any tax advantages. Any earnings they have are passed through to the investors as pure interest reportable either on a 1099 or K-1 tax filing. What we gain in terms of shorter term investments we have to sacrifice a bit in tax planning. Of course, if someone used these in a retirement account, that would neutralize the tax issue, but in the case of Mr. Warbucks, he only had after-tax cash to work with.

Mr. Warbucks lives very modestly for someone who is worth so much. He agreed that he does not have liquidity needs he could possibly foresee beyond a million or so. I placed $5M into muni bonds and $3M in gold/silver bullion for the just-in-case needs he might encounter immediately. Better safe than sorry. Who knows, he might on a whim want to purchase a house for each of his grandkids.

The target projections were discussed in detail and he felt they were reasonable but understood that nothing was guaranteed.

When adding all the projected dividends/distributions along with the tax benefits, Mr. Warbucks was looking at cash flow approaching more than $233,000 dollars per month, $2.8M annually.

Most of the investments have depreciation or mineral depletion deductions, so of the $2.8M, only around $1.765M is taxable based on current tax laws.

From $1.765M we subtract the annual $800,000 oil/gas drilling IDC leaving just $965,000 exposed to a combined effective Federal and State income tax bracket of 31.32 percent. This results in income tax of $302,725 due.

Netting everything out leaves Mr. Warbucks with annual after tax income of around $2,497,275.

$2,800,000 gross income − $302,725 Federal/State income tax
= $2,497,275 after tax income

Even though muni bonds only represented 11 percent of my *Wealth Code* portfolio for him, dividing $2.497M by the starting principal ($45M) results in an after-tax distribution of approximately 5.55 percent.

This is an income higher than most muni bond portfolios will pay, with one added advantage. There is the potential for growth of his principal in the rising interest rate and inflationary environment he expects, something the bonds will not likely achieve given the current economic policy of the Fed as of late 2012.

Also, consider he is using such a small portion of his after tax income. At the end of the fifth year when our oil/gas drilling deductions ($800,000) go away, it is very likely Mr. Warbucks will invest in other oil/gas developmental drilling programs to keep the oil and tax benefits flowing.

Lastly, the plan for Mr. Warbucks included a significant amount of advanced estate planning and asset protection, charitable gifting, and life insurance. Though he had done a significant amount of the above planning, I still managed to find several holes in his plans. For the scope of this book we are just focusing on the diversification of the assets and generation of cash flow.

Summary of Recommendations for Mr. Warbucks

Oil/Gas Investments	$ 8,000,000	~ 18% of investable wealth
Equipment Leasing	$ 3,000,000	~ 7%
Non-Traded REITs & DSTs	$16,000,000	~ 35%
Collateralized Notes	$10,000,000	~ 22%
Gold and Silver Bullion	$ 3,000,000	~ 7%
Muni Bonds	$ 5,000,000	~ 11%

Summary of Liquid to Illiquid Investments

Liquid Investments	$ 8,000,000	~ 18% of investable wealth
Illiquid Investments	$37,000,000	~ 82%

Liquidity Time Line	$ Becoming Liquid	Total Liquid Investments
Liquid Immediately	$ 8,000,000	$ 8,000,000
Liquid Between 6 months and 5 years	$10,000,000	$18,000,000
Liquid after 5–7 years	$16,000,000	$34,000,000
Liquid after 8-10 Years	$ 3,000,000	$37,000,000
Oil/Gas Investments	$ 8,000,000	$37,000,000
	Never Liquid	

Please note that when we were dealing with larger amounts like this and with someone who lives on only a very small portion of the cash flow generated, it can be suitable to invest a substantial amount of the principal in illiquid investments, as in Mr. Warbucks' case, only needing about $400,000 per year. The client was looking for stability and income, the primary goal of the High Return–Capital Preservation category. The tradeoff again was limited liquidity and long-term commitments to the investment programs.

As we finished up our meeting, the most gratifying thing Mr. Warbucks said about the plan was the use of the fun money category. "*Astonishing*," he said, "*you were the first advisor who looked beyond the money and thought of me and my family and how we could improve our lives.*"

I believe many of the grandkids now have new homes.

Appendix B: Different Investment Asset Classes

Static Stocks, Bonds, Mutual Funds

This refers to any stock, bond, mutual fund, or derivative that is held for more than one year. I call this the "hope and pray" leg of the financial table. The vast majority of investors only know this asset class. This asset class tends to do well in bull markets. Since 2000, however, the problem is that we have been in a bear market, and this secular trend will most likely continue for many years.

This is the asset class that most applies to the classic brokerisms, "Buy and hold," "Dollar Cost Average," and so forth. Since most people know this category well, we won't spend much time on it. I will reiterate a few points from previous chapters for clarification.

As with all investments, you should be aware of the real investment fees. Over time, fees tend to be a factor that makes or breaks a financial tool's long-term performance. If you hold equity positions within a wrap account (assets which are charged a fee based on account value), be aware of the hidden stuff, which further compounds the issue. If you are pulling income from stock and bond positions, as previously discussed in the leaks chapter, be aware of the long-term effects of sideways markets and how pulling income and fees intensify the losing years and detract from the winning ones.

With bonds, consider that we are at historic interest rate lows in 2012, and the only reason rates are where they are is due to the Federal Reserve's quantitative easing programs. That is, they are legally printing money to buy Treasury bonds and thus forcing interest rates to artificial lows.

Contrary to popular belief, other countries are not buying all of our debt. According to the 2011 Federal Reserve Flow of Funds report, the Federal Reserve purchased 61 percent of the total net treasury issuance in 2011. This creates the false appearance of demand for U.S. debt which has the effect of reducing yields. With the 10-year Treasury's yield pricing around 1.5 percent, the 30-year around 2.7 percent, at what point does this manipulation of the free market stop and yields reset themselves to a proper level? In my opinion, the day this happens will be a blood bath for the price of long-term bonds, munis, and other debt instruments.

One particular client with a large municipal bond portfolio asked why we would suggest that she sell now that all her bonds were doing so well and were priced at a high. I responded with the old market saying, "Buy low and *sell* high." People are used to selling when their stocks and bonds are low and have sustained losses. The losses compel them to take action. They will hesitate to sell at the top for fear of leaving money on the table, but isn't that the point?

If the Federal Reserve believes printing money is good for the economy, why do they arrest people for counterfeiting? You think they would give them an award! Just a thought . . .

As with any financial concept, it is important to apply common sense in a rational, systematic approach. If one believes interest rates could effectively go below zero, which they hit in December 2008, then they should stay in their bonds hoping for more gains on the principal.

However, a reason to stay in bonds in these environments is if you already hold short durations that will mature reasonably soon. You should be protected fairly well, unless of course the municipality, corporation, or other debt issuing entity goes bankrupt. Stockton and Mammoth Lakes in CA and Harrisburg in PA are examples of cities that have gone bankrupt. As discussed previously, the tax-free benefits of muni bonds can essentially be replicated with other investments that have tax advantages, such as depreciation or other income deductions, yet respond favorably in rising interest rate environments.

Variable Annuities and Life

Essentially, the same as static accounts except issued by insurance companies and accompanied by more bells and whistles, such as death benefits and income guarantees. The more bells and whistles, generally, the more fees associated with a contract. Variable annuities can be considered liquid for a price, generally a high surrender fee which does decrease over time, usually a period of six to seven years. You can get your money fairly quickly but the insurance company is going to take their pound of flesh.

With variable contracts, you will have your typical mutual funds called sub-accounts. Many variable contracts use standard funds, which are easily found in Morningstar or other financial research tools. But with many variable contracts, they will use hybrid funds, which are similar in name but impossible to find through a standard search on the internet. You will have to go to the prospectus for the particular variable contract to find what the holdings of the funds are, some performance history, and so forth.

I personally own a variable universal life contract, mainly for the insurance provisions and loan attributes, and not for the sub-accounts or mutual funds from which I can pick. In order to see how a particular fund has performed over a period in time, I literally have to plot out the sub-account unit values every few days. Forget just pulling up Yahoo! Finance and looking at the six-month chart. It is impossible without hand mapping the data points. Most people are not interested in doing this much work to follow their investments and the insurance companies know this and depend on consumer complacency to keep the contracts in force.

Most of these contracts are sold with numerous bells and whistles, all for a fee of course. I urge you to get out the magnifying glass and review the fine print in your insurance contract and any prospectus describing the sub-accounts and their investment choices.

As described in Chapter 5, Leaks in the Bucket, knowing all about the various bells and whistles of these variable contracts is important. Make sure, if purchasing one, to listen not only to your advisor, who has a vested interest in your buying it but also to call the insurance company issuing the product. Ask for customer service and inquire as to the various benefits in the contract. The service representative will not be earning a commission on your purchase and usually will tell the whole story, the good and bad. I've found that this is usually a good practice no matter what investment product you are purchasing. Call the customer service department and ask lots of questions.

Other than the guaranteed growth rider we discussed in the fees section of Chapter 5, another commonly added benefit is the guaranteed income rider. This rider may be added to your contract so that, at a point in time, you can annuitize the contract. That means you can start a payment system, which will be based on a value generally equal to your original contract value or more with some small guaranteed growth component.

Having seen the market get clipped almost in half in 2008 and the following market rally the next few years, many of the variable annuity contracts are nowhere close to their previous highs from 2007. Mainly due to investor emotional buy and sell decisions as the DALBAR study described in Chapter 5 demonstrated, but also, in my opinion, the relatively high internal fee structures of variable annuities eating the principal each year.

In some of these variable contracts though, the guaranteed income rider can work to the investor's advantage. I've seen that it's possible to initiate the payment system on someone's contract that is upside down more than 30 to 50 percent. By beginning a payment system that is around 6 percent or so, they effectively start the process of getting back their entire original principal with some to boot. Not the best option, but at least the client knows they will eventually get their money back. If they stay in the variable annuity without initiating the guaranteed income rider they will realistically have no means of seeing their original value ever again, unless of course they die.

One client who walked in my door in 2010 is a good example. In March of 2008, she put $228,000 into a particular variable annuity contract. By April 2009, she had $130,000 left and had positioned her funds within the contract in the money market sub-account out of fear of additional loss. For her to get back to even, she would have to earn 5.78 percent for the next 10 years. Add on top of that a fee of roughly 4 percent she is paying each year to be in the contract while it is in deferral, and now she has to average almost 9.8 percent every year to get back to even. How is any growth on her original principal going to occur?

The particular variable contract she was in had the guaranteed income rider attached, but there was no provision for required holding time, a big mistake this insurer overlooked when underwriting the contract. This income rider stated she could pull out 107 percent, her original principal plus growth of 7 percent for the previous year over a 14-year period. Sounds complicated right? A big complaint of these benefit riders is you have to re-read them many times and practically be a member of MENSA before you can comprehend all the rules and requirements. Long story short, by her initiating the payment system immediately, she stands to get all her money back within 14 years. Now the pressure is on the insurer to perform at least by 6 percent over that time period, and not her.

The main thing to remember about variable contracts is that they are still tied to the markets and are basically static accounts. Yes, there are features of some contracts that make them very appealing to some people, and for others they make no sense at all. Everyone is different and has different needs. As previously mentioned, I have a variable universal life contract for retirement income purposes. One feature of life insurance that is very appealing is the ability to pull income out of a contract via a loan and not have any tax to report.

For instance, you contribute $100,000 into a life insurance contract, have growth over the years, and now your cash value is approximately $200,000, you have $100,000 of taxable growth if you ever surrender the contract. A feature of most life insurance contracts is the ability to borrow from the contract, usually at an effective cost of 0 percent. Let's say your contract reasonably earns 5 percent each year. That means each year, on $200,000, you are earning $10,000.

$200,000 × 5 percent (assumed growth) = $10,000 per year

Most life contracts will allow you to borrow the $10,000 each year from the contract as income, or whatever, and since you took out basically what the contract is earning, the result at the end of the year is neutral. You still have $200,000.

The best part though is that the $10,000 you took out is completely tax-free, since you pulled it out via a loan. That is $833 per month of income you could receive tax-free for your lifetime. Even though there is taxable growth inside the contract, you will never pay it. Eventually, when you kick the bucket, the loan that has built up over time will be paid back via the tax-free death benefits. The other thing to know is that there are no IRS age requirements to begin taking the loans. According to my plan, I will begin taking tax-free loans for income starting at age 50.

This is but one of many ways of structuring income to be protected from income tax. There are dozens of books that spend a great deal of time discussing these insurance strategies. Do a Google search on "income benefits" or "loan benefits of life insurance" to find out more.

Lastly, please remember that the variable contract I own is but one of many different legs on my financial table that will help feed my future income needs. I am not depending solely on this one contract to be my future protection, as it is still tied to the markets and my ability to time them.

Adaptive Managed Stocks and Bonds

There are investment managers who take an active role in changing the portfolio throughout the year to adapt to changes in the economy and the world. The managers I tend to recommend essentially rebuild their portfolios from scratch every quarter or more often and do not have restrictions in terms of which type of equity classes they can use to build the overall portfolio. For instance, they can use bonds, stocks, or commodities. They have the ability to mix and match any of the three equity classes as they see fit. The main criteria for the advisors I hire is that they cannot use leverage, only cash. This eliminates hedge funds.

Please note, not all hedge funds are bad. Many have excellent track records, and some have access to financial vehicles that most people wouldn't believe could exist, for instance, Leveraged Trading Programs. There is a realm of finance beyond what most of us can comprehend. A Leveraged Trading Program is the use of tremendous leverage on a relatively small amount of money. Say $10 million is deposited into a checking account; this then opens up trading programs with 10 times that leverage. These groups now have $100M to play with. They buy bonds from one group at say 94 cents per $1 and sell that same day to another group for 97 cents on the $1. They pocket 3 cents or $3M on the trade, a 30 percent return on their original $10M investment. Not bad. Now, do this trade 20 times in a year, and *voila,* big bucks. Let's come back to reality for us mere mortals, who will never have access to these types of programs.

Successful investing in the stock market requires a significant commitment of time, energy, and attention. While most investors manage their investments part-time, portfolio management or third party management, as it is called, is a means of hiring a team who spend their entire careers researching the markets and managing portfolios.

Most people don't fix their own cars or learn to perform heart surgery. They hire people who spend their lives perfecting these skills. The same can be said for money management.

As an investor, you *must* stay the course to be successful. While returns on stocks and bonds have been very rewarding over the better part of the last century, the majority of investors have not been successful at growing their wealth in the stock and bond markets because of their lack of patience and emotional decisions on when to buy and sell. According to DALBAR, 20-year average returns of 3.47 percent for the average equity investor support this.

Time and time again, I hear, "I bought at the top and sold at the bottom." Emotion and not following a disciplined, systematic approach are the primary reasons most investors fail to match the general stock market indexes.

There have been three major bull markets in the past 80 years, and each one has ended in a bubble. In each case, stocks moved up too far too fast, aided by borrowed money and greed. When the technology bubble burst in the mid 1960s, a long sideways market followed. By late summer of 1982, *TIME* magazine featured an article concluding that the stock market was like a "*Roller Coaster to Nowhere.*" It stated that the Dow Jones Industrial Average was 1000 in early 1966, but only 760 in August of 1982.

With the real possibility that we have entered another extended bear market, lasting 15 to 25 years, which began in 2000, the need for adaptive managers who have demonstrated the ability to provide reasonable returns in sideways markets is crucial.

How do they do this, you ask?

Within portfolio management, fund selection is one of the most important features designed to enhance overall portfolio performance. Once the manager has identified and targeted specific areas of investment opportunity, a proprietary fund selection process takes over. Your specific universe of mutual funds or sub-accounts is analyzed by applying a series of in-depth processes that rate and rank funds and their managers within a particular peer group. As the ranking screens are applied, mediocre funds are eliminated in an attempt to identify only top-performing funds for placement in your portfolio.

Secondly, the manager will perform the daily research and analysis across the broad equity, fixed income, and global markets, with the intention of maintaining the most accurate financial forecast possible. From this analysis or forecast, the manager will make the investment selection (stocks versus bonds, large cap versus small cap, foreign versus domestic, etc.) and fund selection for your portfolio, as well as monitor and update these selections on an ongoing basis.

Unless one has several hours a day to study the economic universe and constantly select investments, qualified portfolio managers allow for one to place their hard earned money into proven hands and know their money is being carefully reallocated according to prevailing market conditions.

How many times did your investment advisor change your portfolio in the year 2008? How many times did he or she even call you in 2008?

As stated many times before in this text, no single manager is going to be right all the time. I use a number of managers in order to diversify even within this product category.

Consumer Grade Real Estate

In general, this includes real estate valued at $5M or less. This includes residential homes, and apartment buildings, as well as small commercial properties. The prices of these properties tend to fluctuate far more than large commercial properties due to the type of buyer. The typical buyer tends to be less sophisticated than a group purchasing say a $100M property. More emotion is involved, which may cause larger increases in good years but potentially more significant drops in bad years.

Look at the real estate market increases during 2003 to 2006. This was primarily a factor of easy credit, commission hungry representatives, and unsophisticated or wide-eyed buyers. A couple shows up to an open house, looks at the beautiful blue pearl granite countertops with the fancy ogee edge, and sees four other couples also drooling over the ogee edgework. Feeling the urgency to place a bid for the $500,000 home before someone else snatches it up, and knowing they are pre-qualified up to $750,000, they overbid the house by $100,000, taking the price up to $600,000, with the recommendation of their well seasoned, three-month veteran real estate agent.

Thankfully, their stated income, stated asset, negative amortization loan will come through and allow them to afford this great house.

Is the house worth $600,000? Probably not, but that is what they paid due to their emotional desire to buy the house, which enabled the sale. Had the couple used a more rational financial viewpoint, they would have seen the house down the block with the 1970s Formica countertops and old kitchen selling for $400,000 and realized that with a month of rework and around $20,000, they too could have the fancy blue pearl ogee edgework granite countertops, besides having an extra $80,000 to $180,000 saved on the purchase price of the home. This example is similar to the faulty purchase of a car via cash versus buying a rental property to pay for the car, as described earlier. The financially savvy choice is not always the easy, path-of-least-resistance choice.

As stated earlier in the book, one of my favorite categories for any net worth investor is single-family rentals in the value of $60,000 to $80,000 if such a purchase is suitable for their situation.

Since the real estate bubble peaked in 2006, many areas of the country have now fallen well more than 30 percent in value. In several areas of the country, houses which used to be $100,000 plus are now in the $60,000 to $80,000 range. As the values continue to fall, the gross rents as a percentage of the value of the home continue to rise. For instance, a house that rents for $8,000 per year and used to be worth $100,000 had a gross rent of 8 percent. That house, having fallen in value to $70,000, now has a gross rent of 11.4 percent assuming the rent stays the same.

$$\$8,000 \text{ Rent} \div \$100,000 \text{ Previous Home Value}$$
$$= 8 \text{ percent Gross Rent}$$

$$\$8,000 \text{ Rent} \div \$70,000 \text{ Reduced Home Value}$$
$$= 11.4 \text{ percent Gross Rent}$$

Historically, when gross rents approach 15 percent, you are getting very close to the bottom of a particular market's cycle. This is not speaking for the country as a whole being at the bottom of its real estate cycle, just the particular area (zip code) where the gross rents are now approaching 15 percent. Why 15 percent? Maybe it is a psychological number where investors will start to buy. Can the rest of the country continue to fall? Absolutely! Places which still have large numbers of foreclosed properties waiting to hit the market as well as gross rents that are in the single digit percentages have a ways to fall in my opinion. California, Las Vegas, Arizona, and Florida come to mind that match this criteria today in 2012.

The opportunity lies in the fact that today loans are extremely difficult to get. You need solid income, high credit scores, and low debt to qualify for even the smallest loans. The biggest barrier to entry is the required down payment. Many of the potential buyers, families with local jobs and kids in the nearby schools, have some money saved, but not $20,000 to $30,000, so are forced to keep renting. They do not wish to be in apartments and would rather raise their kids in a single family residence. The unfortunate aspect is the rents in these homes are rather high, again, roughly 15 percent of the value. Not having the down payment forces them to pay rent, and this is the opportunity for investors with sufficient cash, whether in a self-directed IRA or after-tax dollars, to purchase these investment homes.

Pitfalls of Distantly Owned Real Estate

There are three big headaches that accompany distant owned rental real estate. The first being repairs, the second being a bad manager who usually exacerbates the first problem, and the last being rental vacancies.

Let's deal with the first major problem, repairs. My goal with clients is to try and find almost turn-key properties. Properties which have had most if not all the significant issues rehabbed or replaced recently—the roof, hot water heaters, plumbing, electrical, air conditioner, furnace, flooring, and so forth. Do not have carpets in a rental. Make sure everything is a hard surface so when the eventual tenant leaves, you do not have to clean carpets each time. Just grab a mop and you're done.

The second problem is a bigger issue: Finding the right property manager. You will want to do background checks, financial checks, and referral checks on the group you eventually hire to maintain and rent your property.

I saw a manager in Tennessee start charging $10 per month for grass mowing. Though there was a foot of snow on the ground, they were supposedly mowing the lawns. What really was happening was this particular manager was short his personal mortgage payment and felt it was acceptable to charge a couple hundred rental properties an extra $10 each to cover his personal financial deficiency. Needless to say, this property manager was fired.

When considering the vacancy issue in the area where you are looking to buy, ask for the records from the property management company showing the rental history for many different properties they manage. Ask to see the inquiry log for a particular house when it became vacant and how many people called on the property. You are looking for multiple prospective tenants wishing to rent the house. The more people putting in applications, the more likely you will be to find a viable tenant. If the logs show few calls for their vacant properties, then you should look for another area to buy in which has more demand for rentals.

There are hundreds of books discussing the topic of buying rental property and it is highly suggested to read a few before jumping into the rental business. With the expected headaches and nuisances can come very significant rewards and long-term stable cash flow.

I have found reasonable levels of success is using real estate investment groups that specialize in packaging these turn-key single family properties with management for the hands-off, distant owner. Again, prudence is imperative in doing your homework and making sure the real estate investment group is top notch.

There will always be good and bad times to buy rental properties. Warren Buffett was quoted in February 2012 as stating one of his favorite investments was single-family residences. His problem was he had no way of managing 200,000 homes, the amount he stated he would need to buy to make a dent for his fund Berkshire Hathaway. The good thing for most of us, we won't have the problem of needing to buy 200,000 homes to make an economic benefit to our personal wealth. One, two, five, or more will suffice.

Buying Your Personal Residence

One small suggestion when buying a home: Consider building it instead of finding the turnkey property. A small secret of wealthy individuals who understand banks and equity is to have the bank fund their down payment. Instead of buying a home for $1M, ready to move in, the road less traveled is to buy the lot and build from scratch.

The turnkey buyer puts up at least $200,000 as a down payment and finances $800,000. The builder potentially buys an old, beaten down shack on a good lot for $500,000 and needs to put down only $100,000. Then with $20,000 in architecture plans, the builder presents the plans and lot to the bank that wrote the first loan and gets an appraisal for the completed house for $1M. Just like the turnkey house down the block.

The house costs $300,000 to build, bringing the total loans to $700,000, one hundred thousand dollars less than the turnkey buyer will have to repay with interest. The bottom line, for $120,000 out of pocket, eighty thousand dollars less than the turnkey buyer, the builder has the same home, worth $1M, and $180,000 of sweat equity courtesy of the bank. Maybe that is why so many real estate builders have the nicest houses on your block.

	Turnkey Buyer	Builder Buyer
Purchase Price:	$1,000,000	$ 500,000 (lot)
Deposit:	$ 200,000 (cash)	$ 100, 000 (cash)
Loan:	$ 800,000	$ 400,000
Plans:	0	$ 20,000 (cash)
Building cost:	0	$ 300,000 (additional loan)
Property value:	$1,000,000	$1,000,000
Loan or New Loan:	$ 800,000	$ 700,000
Equity:	**$ 200,000**	**$ 300,000**

Rare American Coins and Bullion

Two very significant dates have affected this category; March 1934 and August 1971. The first was when Franklin D. Roosevelt made it illegal to own gold, and which established the cutoff date for rare gold coins. The second of course is the day the world entered by fiat into a currency-credit system. The latter is what has led to the financial debacle we are experiencing today, in 2012.

Whether you believe the dollar is going to come crashing down or that the status quo of the global debt explosion can continue on indefinitely, having real wealth, gold, or other precious bullion could be a smart way to protect purchasing power.

If the client feels so inclined, their well-diversified portfolio might contain at least 10 percent to 15 percent of gold or other precious metals. Why gold/silver? Because it has been a foundation of money since the beginning of civilization. Don't just rely on my opinion, check out any religious text or history book and count the number of times gold and/or silver is mentioned. Who believes this? China for one. By mid 2012, China will have more than doubled its gold reserves and is continuing to mine more and more by the day, as well as purchase mines around the world. They realize the massive foreign reserves they hold will need to be offset by something tangible; otherwise, they will be left holding the bag when inflation further destroys their holdings.

There are four easy ways to buy bullion.

The easiest route to own precious metals is to use an exchange traded fund (ETF) such as SIVR, SGOL, or others. When you purchase one share of SGOL for example, you are effectively buying 1/10 oz. of gold. Likewise, when you purchase one share of SIVR you are basically buying one oz. of silver. With these ETFs you never have the right to call them up and ask for the underlying precious metal. You do have the ease of these ETFs trading on a public exchange and the correlating ability to buy and sell quickly.

The most popular metal ETFs are GLD and SLV but I'm personally a fan of the Swiss versions mentioned above. It's nice to know the Swiss government audits the holdings of these two ETFs. Check out their respective prospectus for more details.

Keep one thing in mind. When you own these ETFs, you do not get the same capital gains rate for taxes as with traditional stocks. All bullion capital gain rates are 28 percent under current tax law.

The second way to own gold or silver bullion is to use a bank such as www.Everbank.com or www.PerthMint.com to actually buy the gold at a price close to the spot price of gold, plus a small commission, and they can store the gold in either a pooled account or in a holding account.

A pooled account is a less expensive way to own gold or silver. Your purchased metal is pooled with other investors, saving you from paying storage or maintenance fees. In a holding account, you directly own gold or silver bars and coins with this storage option, which incurs a custodial fee.

For those who wish to know with certainty that they *could* get their gold or silver, you can use an allocated custodian such as Bullionvault.com or Goldmoney.com. They store the precious metals for you in allocated accounts, which are individually audited and guaranteed to be in possession. Their vaults are in places such as London, Hong Kong, and Switzerland. With these types of bullion ownership you could request they send you your precious metals. Of course if all hell is breaking loose, good luck getting the delivery.

The last way to buy gold, silver, or other metals is through physical possession. Whether you are buying American Gold Eagles and Buffalos, Canadian Maple Leafs, or Krugerrands, this gives you something to put in your safe at home. If the value of the dollar goes to zilch, you'll be able to go down to Wal-Mart and buy some milk and cookies. Today, you don't need to bite into coins to make sure they're real; just make sure you purchase from reputable dealers. One thing to keep in mind: commissions can be huge on coins. Make sure you ask exactly what they are charging. Around 2 to 4 percent above the spot price is the norm, but I've seen groups charging in excess of 10 percent.

In terms of which ownership route is best, that depends on the clients' personal feelings. A happy medium between a few of the ownerships is good but for most people, owning the ETFs is sufficient.

To understand a bit about 1934, U.S. citizens were exchanging their gold certificates for actual gold due to concerns about the economy. President Franklin D. Roosevelt, in his first week in office, signed executive orders 6073 and 6102, and the Senate passed the Emergency Banking Act, effectively making it illegal for U.S. citizens to own gold and changing the price overnight to $35 from approximately $20. Please note that these laws are still on the books, and it's interesting to observe that, on the back of American Gold Eagles, it still says a value of $50.

Rare Coins

Rare coins that have collectors' value were exempt from the great confiscation and tend to have a higher multiple in protecting against inflation. The key with coins and collecting is the rarity of the coin. Every day, on late night TV or in the papers, you can see ads for buying coins that are $99 or whatever price. Don't waste your time. These coins are not rare. They are sold in bulk and will probably never have any value other than the metal content. In general, rare coins above $5,000 will have much higher multiples at auctions than smaller coins. The key here is to play off the emotion of the auction when you plan on selling them. People tend to pay a lot more for coins that are unique and have a story, or documented provenance.

Keep in mind, again, that your coin dealer is a critical player in this situation. A dealer must have the knowledge and experience to know when is a good time to sell. It is easy to buy coins; the trick is knowing the timing of when to sell.

Advantages of Rare Coins as an Investment

The following summarizes some of the main advantages of rare coin investments:

1. Rare coins have historically protected or preserved wealth as strong inflation fighters, particularly in countries where the paper currency has been severely weakened. Any time our paper money is threatened, rare coins can protect wealth much like an investment in gold bullion.
2. Rare coins are currently selling at a steep discount to their 1980s highs, and given the cyclical nature of the rare coin market, may be poised for rapid price appreciation in the near future.
3. The beauty of rare coins can be enjoyed much like any other work of art. They are also a very private form of investment, not subject to the government scrutiny common to other types of investments held in banks and by brokerage houses.
4. Rare coins are easy to store and are virtually indestructible. They are also insurable. Rare coins represent truly portable wealth, which can be moved from place to place very quickly and easily.
5. With thousands of coin dealers available, selling most quality, rare coins is quite easy, making them a fairly liquid investment.

Guidelines for Rare Coin Investors

The following are basic guidelines for prospective investors in rare coins:

- Have clear objectives in mind when buying rare coins as an investment. Decide what types of rare coins you should acquire, the total amount you wish to invest in rare coins, and the circumstances under which you will consider selling your coins.
- Keep in mind that the market for rare coins can be particularly volatile. Further, the difference or *spread* between dealer buy and sell prices is normally much higher than the commissions charged by brokers for equity investments. Consequently, for an investor to sell rare coins at a gain, rare coin prices must appreciate at a higher rate than may be the case for other investments.
- Only buy rare coins graded and authenticated by the leading independent grading services, whose standards are accepted industry-wide.
- Buy coins as a long-term investment only. Do not expect short-term profits from rare coin investments. Expect to hold the coins for two to five years or longer.
- Only buy rare coins that are popular with collectors and are actively traded.
- Never buy very expensive rare coins by mail-order. When representing coins, the coin dealer's credentials are vital. How long have they been in numismatics? To which associations do they belong, and can you confirm? Do they have experience selling coins at auction, and most importantly, do they have references?

Many collectors have come across a particular coin from time to time and wondered whether they had something of great value in their possession. This feature describes the main factors influencing a coin's value and provides some guidance in obtaining an estimate of such value. Remember, however, that the mere fact that a coin does not have significant monetary value does not mean that it is not interesting or that it should not form part of your collection.

Factors Influencing Value

The value of a particular coin is influenced or determined primarily by the following four factors:

1. Scarcity or rarity is a major determinant of value. As a general rule, the rarer a coin, the more it is worth. Note that rarity has little to do with the age of a coin. Many one-thousand-year-old Chinese coins often sell for no more than a few dollars because there are a lot of them around, whereas a 1913 Liberty Head Nickel may sell for more than $1M because there are only five known specimens in existence.
2. The condition or grade of the coin will influence its value. The better the condition a coin is in, the higher will be its assigned grade, and the more it will be worth. An uncirculated coin that is in flawless mint state condition might be worth hundreds of times more than the same coin in good condition but which has been circulated.
3. Many coins have a bullion value determined by the value of the precious metal it contains. A gold, silver, or platinum coin does not generally sell for much less than its melt value.
4. The demand for the particular coin, or how many collectors want it, will also greatly influence coin values. Some coins that are relatively plentiful may command higher prices than scarcer coins because the former are more popular with collectors. For example, there are more than four hundred thousand 1916D dimes in existence, as compared to only about 30 thousand 1798 dimes. However, even though the 1798 dime is much rarer than its 1916D counterpart, the 1916D coin sells for significantly more. This is because many more people collect early twentieth century mercury dimes than dimes from the 1700s.

Determining a Coin's Approximate Value

Accurately and properly identify the coin. Is there a summary page describing the history? How much did the value go up and down during the past cycles, for instance during either the 1979 or 1987 run-ups? Any properly graded coin will come with this information.

Online, you can go to Professional Coin Grading Service at www.PCGS.com. You can find many coins and see scale values at different grades.

A firm I've used and have found to be exceptional is Farmington Rare Valley Coin & Investment Co., in New Hartford, Connecticut. They follow our philosophy of "Education first," a mantra to which any coin dealer you work with should adhere.

Other means to confirm general prices is to look up the coin in a coin catalog to find listed retail selling prices or estimated retail values for your coin. For U.S. coins, use *A Guide Book of United States Coins* by R.S. Yeoman, commonly called The Red Book by collectors and dealers. It provides retail prices for U.S. coins. For world coins, the most widely used guide is a series of volumes called *The Standard Catalog of World Coins* by Krause and Mishler.

For more current prices, based on what dealers are actually selling a particular coin for, you should check coin newspapers and magazines or online auction sites such as *Coin World, Coin Prices,* or *Teletrade.* These sites provide price guides for many U.S. coins and some world coins.

Lastly, you should buy coins that have been sealed and barcoded. An example show in Figure B.1 is from the Numismatic Guaranty Corporation (NGC).

Oil/Gas Investments

State of domicile suitability and accredited investor rules apply—not suitable for all investors.

Figure B.1   1912 $20 Saint-Gaudens PF-67

Oil and Natural Gas investments are any type of investment that focuses on the production of petroleum products. These investments can be offshore based, but for most, they are from domestic sources. I feel that sticking within our borders or Canada will help reduce political risk. Political risk includes the threat to an investment's ownership from someone nationalizing the resource, such as Hugo Chavez did within Venezuela.

Oil and natural gas investments come in three varieties, including everything from exploratory to developmental to royalty programs.

Exploratory—New wells in uncharted areas. In general, these were the majority of the programs in the 1980s, which everyone remembers as losing most investors' money. These programs generally have very low success rates, yet when they hit, they have the potential for a large return.

Developmental—New or reconditioned wells in existing fields around existing producing wells. Think oil/gas fields with lots of wells already producing, and these programs are putting more straws in the dirt.

Royalty—Buying land with mineral rights and letting the developmental or exploratory drillers do all the hard work. For their hard work, they generally get 75 percent of the production. Royalty owners sit back and do nothing but collect up to 25 percent of the production coming from their lands. This is generally the most conservative form of energy investment when discussing direct participation programs.

Following is a list of many common questions we have seen over the years with oil/gas direct ownership investments:

Is Investing in Oil and Gas Profitable?

Yes, it can be very profitable, and it can also be a complete loss of your principal. However, I tend to think about which are the largest companies in the world. Chances are a good number of these are oil companies. This could mean that they are making big profits.

There are several areas where you can make oil and gas investments, and all of them have profit potential. You will need to determine which areas to get into by analyzing their risks versus their rewards.

The potential rate of return is also a consideration. A rate of return between 25 percent and 40 percent is considered great. Of course, many exploratory oil/gas programs return 0 percent, not counting a tax benefit. Who cares about a tax benefit when you just lost all your money? All programs have pros and cons and need to be analyzed.

What is your investing goal with oil and gas? This will play a part in determining how profitable it can be because it will affect your choices. You may also want to determine what your desired rate of return is.

One option for investing that may help with your profits is to focus on investing with what are called Independent Operating Companies. One of the benefits of this is that they can help reduce risk by investing in oil companies that are located in several different geographic areas. The companies tend to share the cost of development, which also can reduce risk.

Investing in the oil and gas industry can be very profitable but it's not for everyone. Some invest for the potential tax benefits, and some invest because they enjoy speculating. In order to make it as successful as possible, you need to understand your investing options, as well as learn how to analyze the potential risks and benefits.

Top Four Reasons to Invest in Oil and Gas Ventures

There are several reasons why you may want to invest in oil and gas.

1. Investors are usually eligible for tax benefits.
2. Energy is in high demand throughout the world.
3. Financial return potential increases as technology expands.
4. Potentially a good way to balance your portfolio.

Investing in hard assets, such as oil and gas, in my opinion, is important to avoid some of the volatility of the traditional markets and investments today. Another important quality is the relationship of the dollar to commodities like oil and gas. Since the U.S. Dollar is the world exchange currency, the further the dollar falls, the more dollars it takes to purchase a barrel of oil. Therefore, commodities tend to be a great inflation hedge. Unless of course, the Chinese Yuan becomes the world exchange currency, then we better all learn to speak Mandarin.

Tax benefits are usually one of the most talked about qualities of these types of investments. Below is a basic example of some of the benefits you may realize from investing in an oil and gas program based on current tax laws. Remember to work with your financial advisor and tax professional regarding your potential benefits and risks prior to investing.

According to *Worth Magazines April 2010*, drilling is one of the best tax-advantaged investments. Oil and gas investments are generally 100 percent tax deductible. You can usually write off 65 percent to 90 percent in the first year of certain investments.

Risks

- Interests in these types of programs are speculative and involve a high degree of risk; investors should be able to bear the complete loss of their investment.
- There may be restrictions in transferring the Interests, and some Interests are not liquid investments.
- The performance of the investment could be volatile as a result of commodity pricing, the depletion nature of oil and gas investments, and operation of the oil and gas wells.
- There are a number of significant tax risks and tax issues involved with the purchase of energy programs; investors should consult their own tax advisors and legal counsel.
- The direct or indirect purchase of oil wells and/or royalties involves significant risks, including market risk and commodity pricing and risks specific to a given oil field.
- Cash distributed to you may constitute a return of your own capital and may be paid from proceeds of the offering.
- Energy programs involve the risk that the mineral production will not provide enough revenue to return the amount of your investment.
- The revenues are directly related to the ability to market gas and oil and to its price, which is volatile and cannot be predicted. If oil and/or gas prices decrease, then your investment return will decrease.
- There is a potential for lack of liquidity or a market for the units.

How is a standard oil & gas transaction structured?

1. The Mineral Owner "leases" his/her property to an oil/gas company for development and receives a royalty interest in any future production, for example 25 percent.
2. The oil/gas drilling company now owns 100 percent of the working interests in the lease.
3. The Net Revenue Interest (NRI) in the lease is 75 percent, (100 percent minus 25 percent paid to royalty owner = 75 percent left for NRI).
4. The 75 percent NRI is responsible for paying 100 percent of expenses. Therefore, the higher the NRI, the better the economics of the deal.

Summary: For Every 100 BBLS of Oil

25 BBLS go to Mineral Owners and other Royalty Owners

75 BBLS go to Working Interest Owners

What is the difference between working & royalty interests?

Working Interests

Cash flow equals revenue minus lease operating expenses (LOEs), capital expenditures, admin and marketing costs, and severance taxes.

- Responsible for all expenses
- Takes active role in development
- Less expensive to acquire than royalty interests due to market availability
- Working interests programs have the potential to generate payout in three to five years or longer. Remember this could be a return of capital.

Royalty Interests

Cash flow equals revenue minus severance taxes

- No expenses/No liabilities
- No role in development
- Generally more expensive to acquire than working interests due to limited market availability

I've heard U.S. domestic production is heavily funded by direct Investments.

1. Major oil companies have gone offshore in search of reserves.
2. Many onshore players are independents with little or no bank backing.
3. Independents raise money through direct investments vehicles to:
   a. Lease additional acreage to secure additional reserves
   b. Access additional reserves through drilling and/or reworks
4. Value Proposition
   a. Investors may receive value with cash flow, ROI, and tax advantages or lose it all.
   b. Independents enjoy funding that promotes additional activity

How long before I receive income from my investment?   This depends on a number of factors, but the type of investment: Royalty Interest or Drilling Program has a bearing on the investment timeframe. The Royalty programs typically will have a three to six-month window. Payments will generally start small and progressively build to the final amount, which depends and fluctuates based on current oil/gas prices. The reason for the buildup is that once the lands (Mineral Rights) are bought, the oil/gas that comes from the ground from that point in time is payable to the new owners. The oil/gas that is currently in the system (pipes, trucks, so forth) is the property of the previous owner.

With a drilling program, the timelines can vary depending on the ability of the sponsor to drill the wells, establish potential production, get the oil/gas sold and transported, collect the revenues, and disperse the payments to both the royalty (land) owners and drilling investors. Typically, once a well is drilled, there is a 90-day (or more) lag to receipt of the revenues for that well. Then the payment can be made to the investors. Some drilling programs are designed to generate payments very quickly, in two to four months; others are much longer terms of one to three years. Make sure you understand the anticipated timeline for potential payments before investing in any oil/gas partnership.

How long are these investments?   Although some energy-direct investments have seven- to 10-year terms, it's not unusual for these investments to be open-ended. A well produces oil or gas on a diminishing basis over time, but its duration or rate of depletion can only be estimated. When the well stops producing, the income stream of the investment ends too. So there is no single event that results in a final cash distribution or capital gain.

In my opinion, going into an oil/gas program with 20 or more wells or more helps mitigate the possibility of one or two or more dry or poorly-producing wells significantly affecting a program's distribution potential.

What does "a barrel of oil" mean anyway?   According to the Energy Information Administration of the U.S. Government, "One barrel (42 gallons) of crude oil, when refined, produces approximately 19.6 gallons of finished motor gasoline, as well as other petroleum products" (See Figure B.2).

What are the products and uses of petroleum?   There are many ways that petroleum (oil) is used. Oil is refined into useable petroleum products, most of which are used to produce energy. Other products made from petroleum include: ink, crayons, bubble gum, dishwashing liquids, deodorant, eyeglasses, records, tires, ammonia, and heart

One Barrel (42 Gal.) of Oil Yields:

43% Gasoline
21.5% Distillate
11.5% Residual
6.9% Jet Fuel
4.7% Feed Stocks
3.8% Still Gas
3.1% Asphalt
2.6% Coke
2.3% LPG
1.3% Kerosene
1.3% Lubricants
0.67% Misc.

Figure B.2   Products from a Barrel of Oil

valves. From a barrel of oil, 47 percent is refined into gasoline for use in automobiles; 23 percent is refined into heating oil and diesel fuel; 18 percent is refined into other products, which includes petrochemical feedstock such as polypropylene; 4 percent is refined into propane; 10 percent is refined into jet fuel; and 3 percent is refined into asphalt. Percentages equal more than 100 percent because there is approximately a 5 percent processing gain in refining.

Won't electric cars reduce the need for gas?   A client of mine drove up in his new 100 percent electric car. He steps out and asks my opinion of his *electric* car.

My response, "What electric car? I see a natural gas and coal burning car, with tires made from six barrels of oil each along with plastics, fibers, paint and dyes all made from petroleum products. I see parts made of metal, mined using diesel-powered equipment. For sure, though, the welders were indeed electric."

Where does the electricity come from to recharge the batteries in his "fully" electric car? Do a little research and see how lithium is produced—a major component of today's battery technology. Almost all the electricity used to recharge his car comes from burning fossil fuels!

The point being, everything we use today, from cosmetics to dyes to plastics to rubber, comes from petroleum products. I believe it is impossible for us to get away from the use of oil and gas in our modern lives.

Tax Benefits of Oil/Gas Programs—2012 tax year

The Basic Tax Considerations Involved in an Oil & Gas Investment

- *Intangible drilling* Costs (IDC) are any costs associated with the drilling prospect that cannot be re-sold. These costs may be deducted against active, passive, or portfolio income in the year incurred. Consult with your tax advisor.
- *Tangible drilling* costs include all items associated with the drilling of the prospect that can be re-sold, such as tanks, wellhead equipment, and so on. These costs may be depreciated over seven years, currently 20 percent the first year and the balance over the next six years.

- *Depletion allowance* allows you to receive the first 15 percent to 24 percent of your revenue income tax-free. This means you are paying income taxes on only 76 percent to 85 percent of your potential well income.

Example of Tax Benefits (Hypothetical Illustration of $100,000 investment)

$100,000	Investment
– $ 17,500	Leasehold Cost & Tangible Drilling Cost (17.5 percent)
$ 82,500	**Intangible Drilling Costs**
$ 82,500	First-year deduction for Intangible Drilling Cost
+$ 3,500	First-year depreciation for Tangible & Leasehold Costs
$ 86,000	**Total first-year tax deductions**
$ 86,000	
× 28%	(enter your tax bracket. We assume 28% for this example)
$ 24,080	**Total first year cash value of deductions (estimate)**
$100,000	Original Investment in Drilling Working Interest
– $ 24,080	First-year cash savings from tax deductions
$ 74,095	**After-Tax Cash Investment (estimate)**

What are the current oil and gas tax incentives from Congress? The United States is still heavily dependent on foreign oil and gas reserves. In order to help minimize this, the U.S. Congress has historically been devoted to encouraging the use of domestic reserves. To help do this, they create tax laws which offer tax incentives and benefits to people who are investing in oil and gas. These benefits are listed in the official tax codes put out by Congress, which are listed here.

What are the current tax deductions for intangible drilling costs? Intangible drilling costs include such expenses as the cost of labor, grease, chemicals, and so on. These costs are usually 65 to 85 percent of total drilling costs. All of these drilling-related expenses are completely deductible in the first year. The first year is considered to be the year that the investment was first started (Section 263 of Tax Code).

What are the current tax deductions for tangible drilling costs? The tangible costs for drilling consist of the remaining percentage of the total drilling costs and are deducted over a five year time span.

Active Versus Passive Income   The Tax Reform Act of 1986 introduced into the Tax Code the concepts of *passive* income and *active* income. The Act prohibits the offsetting of losses from Passive activities against income from Active businesses. The Tax Code specifically states that a working interest in an oil and gas well is not a passive activity; therefore, deductions can be offset against income from active stock trades, business income, salaries, and so on (Section 469(c)(3) of the Tax Code).

Self-Employment Tax Exemption Information   This section has to do with the self-employment tax exemption and the concept of converting a general partner to a limited partner.

The net income or net loss of the investments is considered "earnings from self employment." It is likely that there will be a loss taken the year that the initial well is drilled. This loss can be used to offset any employment income that was generated.

Once a general partner becomes a limited partner, self-employment tax does not apply (IRC Section 1402, Rev. Rul. 84-52, 1984-1 C.B. 157).

Tax Exemption for Small Producers   This section relates to the 1990 Tax Act, which allows certain tax advantages (called the Percentage Depletion Allowance) for individuals and smaller companies. This tax benefit exists to encourage their participation in oil and gas.

Who is not eligible:

- Large oil companies
- Petroleum marketers
- Large refiners (more than 50,000 barrels a day)

Alternative Minimum Tax   Prior to the 1992 Tax Act, working interest participants in oil and gas ventures were subject to the normal Alternative Minimum Tax, to the extent that this tax exceeded their regular tax. This Tax Act specifically exempted intangible drilling costs as a tax preference item.

Alternative Minimum Taxable Income generally consists of adjusted gross income, minus allowable Alternative Minimum Tax itemized deductions, plus the sum of tax preference items and adjustments. Tax preference items are preferences existing in the Code to greatly reduce or eliminate regular income taxation. Included within this group are deductions for excess intangible drilling and development costs and the deduction for depletion allowable for a taxable year over the adjusted basis in the drilling acreage and the wells thereon.

Equipment Leases

In general, State investor suitability rules apply for this type of investment and they are not suitable for all investors.

Leasing offers businesses an alternative to purchasing hard assets vital to the operation of their business, especially items that are extremely expensive or those that become obsolete within a relatively short period of time. An Equipment Leasing Trust gives the investor an opportunity to invest in the operational equipment that a company may need to operate. This type of program creates income from the lease payments, which is potentially paid out to the investor as dividends. Remember that dividends are not fixed and can be increased or decreased as the advisor to the lease trust deems necessary for operations.

Leasing gives a company greater flexibility by freeing up capital because lease payments are less than purchase payments. A company leasing its operational equipment also has the tax advantages that come with lease payments. Unlike bank loans taken out to purchase equipment, lease obligations don't appear as debt on a company's financial statements. This can be helpful, as major debt can make a company less attractive to investors. Additionally, because lease payments are typically less than purchase payments, this frees up capital to be dedicated elsewhere.

Equipment Leasing programs offer an alternative that is not as prone to the volatility of the stock market. This is generally due to the equipment values themselves not fluctuating with the broader equities market. For example, the aircraft that FedEx leases to fly packages around the world didn't necessarily decrease in value during the most recent recession. FedEx still needed to pay their lease obligations or risk losing the aircraft. Equipment leasing programs are typically an illiquid investment that requires a longer time commitment, but that commitment may potentially provide a platform for greater stability.

What Is the Leasing Business?

The terms of a leasing deal are spelled out in a contract signed by the equipment provider, called the **lessor**, and the equipment user, called the **lessee**. The contract generally provides that the leased item will be returned in good condition. Then the lessor either sells it or re-leases it to a different lessee. Some contracts, though, give the lessee an option to purchase the equipment, usually when the lease ends, or to renew the lease at a residual value and at a favorable rate.

Companies lease equipment instead of buying it for several reasons. Capital intensive industries—airlines, utilities, railroads, transit authorities, factories, shipping, and healthcare facilities—may find that purchase prices are prohibitive, even though they need the equipment. Or they may own some of the equipment they need and lease the rest to conserve cash.

Leasing also gives a company greater flexibility in meeting its capital commitments in times when it's difficult to forecast business volume.

What are the benefits of this type of investment?

One of the appeals of a direct leasing program is that you and other participants potentially collect a stream of rental income from the leased equipment. In most cases, you may also realize additional income from re-leasing or selling the equipment at the end of the lease term. These residual values may vary from estimations, so I don't usually include any upside in my financial plans. If it happens, then I just consider it gravy.

In addition, you can take advantage of accelerated depreciation and the tax benefit it provides. Usually, you can write off your share of the cost of the equipment at a relatively fast rate, offsetting income you receive in the early years of the program, thus potentially reducing your tax bill. That situation changes, however, as the leases mature and the equipment is sold. While you may continue to collect income, an increasingly larger percentage of that income is taxed at your regular rate. You must plan for this tapering effect.

A diversified leasing program can be an attractive investment because it is long-term, and because it's not traded, it can help insulate your portfolio from market volatility. Further, because hard assets underlie the return, investment risk is generally reduced. In instances where a lessee can't pay, the equipment can be reclaimed and leased again or sold.

Equipment leasing can also serve as a hedge against both inflation and recession. In inflationary periods, the hard assets may sell at a higher price and exceed expected yields. During recessions, companies typically defer new equipment purchases in favor of holding onto leased equipment, so lease renewals may increase. In addition, when interest rates are low as they are now, equipment leasing programs may be an attractive substitute for fixed-income securities, though they are likely to be significantly more difficult to liquidate than bonds or other interest-bearing investments.

What Happens in the Beginning of a Leasing Trust?

As the leasing company begins operations, it pools investments from hundreds or thousands of participants and uses the money to buy the equipment it will lease. Be aware that any dividends or distributions will come from infused capital until the trust begins buying and leasing out equipment.

When you invest, you generally don't know in advance exactly what equipment the company will be offering. But most equipment leasing DPPs invest in a wide range of equipment types to achieve the greatest possible diversification and help reduce the risk of concentrating in a limited number of sectors or industries.

I've Never Heard of These Investments. Are They New?

Among the earliest equipment leases were those for Phoenician merchant ships, the first example of the now-common practice of leased transportation equipment. Today, the list includes not only ships but airplanes, trucks, container ships, trailers, train and subway cars, and buses. Many of the pieces of equipment in your office building could very well be leased. The computers and large copiers you use daily all could be leased from an equipment leasing trust.

My personal experience with a large copier I purchased used for my business taught me the value of leasing equipment. I paid more than $6,000 for a copier which was previously sold brand new for $12,000. After only 18 months my copier was broken and unrepairable. I thought I was getting a good deal when in fact I was paying $6,000 for a giant doorstop. My bad luck, but again it taught me an important lesson on equipment leasing.

It is better for my firm to lease a $12,000 copier for $500 per month, ($6,000 per year), than to buy it out right. Why would anyone pay 50 percent per year? Simple, after the firm deducts the expense for the payment, in reality I'm only paying $250 per month and I free up the use of the other capital I didn't spend. The best part, the equipment is warranted and serviced by the owner for my benefit.

It is not a bad deal for the owner either. They receive over two years 100 percent of their purchase price of the equipment and their goal is to sell it at the end of the second year for about 30 percent of what they paid. In this case around $4,000, which is their profit on the copier. If they are able to do this, they would have made approximately 15 percent per year return on their initial investment.

Institutional Grade Real Estate

In general, State investor suitability rules apply for this type of investment and they are not suitable for all investors.

This is generally real estate valued at $10 million or more, including either single or portfolio properties, Tenant-in-Common, Delaware Statutory Trusts (DST), or non-traded REITs. The key to the REITs in this category is that they are *not* traded on the stock market. The REITs that trade on the stock market are classified as static mutual funds. Though they are real estate, since they trade on the markets, they tend to follow the markets in general and lose much of their non-correlation status.

A Real Estate Investment Trust (REIT) is a tax designation for a corporation investing in real estate that reduces or eliminates corporate income taxes. In return, REITs are required to distribute 90 percent of their income to the investor, of which a portion may be taxable. These earnings are distributed to the REIT shareholders as dividends. The REIT structure was designed to provide a vehicle for investment in real estate much as mutual funds provide for investment in stocks. REITs can invest in real estate, mortgages (loans), or both (hybrid). A REIT pools money from investors to purchase real estate investments. A REIT has a management team that is responsible for overseeing the day-to-day operations and investment process.

The overall goal of a REIT is to manage and build a portfolio of income producing buildings in order to generate income and potential appreciation when the assets are divested at some point in the future. REITs allow smaller investors to own small pieces of large, institutional grade income properties. They also allow for geographic and building-type diversification.

There are three different types of REITs: publicly traded, public non-exchange traded, and private.

Publicly traded REITs file with the SEC and trade on one of the national stock exchanges. Private REITs are not available on any exchanges and are not registered with the SEC. I primarily work with public non-exchange traded REITs that are registered with the SEC but not traded on a national exchange.

Public non-traded REITs typically require a longer time commitment, but are generally not correlated to the stock market like their publicly traded counterparts. They may provide the investor an opportunity to invest in a type of REIT that is not subject to the volatility of the stock market. As a result, they may potentially be more stable than a publicly traded REIT. Because the public non-traded REIT does not sell on a national exchange, it may be a more illiquid investment. It is important to note that Public non-traded REITs qualify for IRA funds and offer a diversifying alternative to traditional stocks and mutual fund portfolios. Bear in mind, however, that global economic meltdowns and panics that impact the US Economy as a whole, will potentially effect the valuations of the assets held within these REIT's.

Here are the common questions asked about REITs:

What's the Difference Between Traded or Non-Traded?

Most REITs are publicly traded. Their shareholders range from individuals to large institutions, such as pension funds, insurance companies, and mutual funds. And there's an active secondary market, where REIT shares trade at a discount or premium to—that is, for less than or more than—their *net asset value (NAV)*, or worth on paper.

Non-traded REITs are available to investors who meet certain suitability standards. Here too, the list may include both institutions and individuals. But there is no formal secondary market for these REITs, and shares trade infrequently, though most programs have a mechanism for selling shares to other buyers. These REITs tend to be non-correlated with traditional investments, which means that they don't tend to be affected by the forces that affect other securities, such as changing interest rates or corporate earnings reports.

The valuation of the underlying assets don't generally change every second of the trading day.

When REITs are publicly traded, however, they are subject to the pressure of meeting short-term Wall-Street analyst expectations, just as other listed investments are. If these REITs seem to be providing stronger returns than other securities, they may attract added attention and their share price might rise. But if their returns are weaker than those of other securities, they face the risk that investors will sell—even if it means taking a loss—or put pressure on management to make changes.

Because the price fluctuations affecting publicly traded REITs tend to be driven by changing economic conditions and investor emotional sentiments rather than changing real estate values, these REITs tend to rise and fall with other equities in the marketplace, rather than providing a hedge against volatility.

Do REITs Pay Income?

REIT income flows to its investors in the form of monthly or quarterly distributions based on rent or mortgage payments from the REIT's investments. Equity REIT distributions often increase as rent payments increase, which can provide a hedge against inflation, though the distributions can drop in a market downturn or if the properties lose value. Bear in mind that as these programs start up, dividends or distributions may be a return of capital until such a time as all the funds raised have been deployed into assets which may potentially add to the overall net operating income of the REIT and thus may flow to the investor.

If you're interested in potential income investments to supplement your annual earnings, REITs may be able to provide a relatively stable cash flow. Similarly, you can use REIT income to fund college expenses or charitable remainder trusts. And, of course, you can use REIT income to make additional investments.

What Are the Tax Benefits?

REITs don't have to pay corporate income tax. Instead, they are subject to an IRS rule that requires these corporations to pay out 90 percent of their taxable income as distributions. As a result, REITs can provide higher returns than other corporations because once stabilized, they may have more cash available for distribution. That, in part, is what makes them attractive investments.

A special benefit of investing in REITs is that you can claim depreciation of real estate assets against your dividend income. As a result, you may not have to pay tax on the income until no depreciation value is left, at some date in the future, when your income tax rate may be lower. Or you may be able to defer payment until the REIT holdings are sold. Then the income is taxed at the lower long-term capital gains rates.

Another advantage of REITs is that they don't generate unrelated business taxable income (UBTI), an important consideration for investors who own these investments in a tax-deferred or tax-exempt account, such as an IRA or 401K, or in a charitable remainder trust. (UBTI results when an otherwise tax-exempt organization realizes any income from a taxable subsidiary or if substantial leverage (debt) is used to generate potential distributions and profit.)

Because a REIT does not pay corporate taxes, taxable REIT dividends don't usually qualify for the low rate that applies to most equity dividends, currently a maximum of 15 percent. Rather, when tax is due, it's at your current rate for regular income, up to 35 percent at the federal level. Long-term capital gains distributions, on the other hand, are taxed at the lower rate.

How Diversified Are REITs?

The majority of REITs own property and often specialize in a particular type of real estate, such as apartment buildings, hotels, shopping centers, self-storage units, office buildings, hospitals and other healthcare facilities, data centers, timber, student housing, or low-income housing developments. Some equity REITs are geographically focused while others are national or global.

You can diversify your REIT investments by buying REITs concentrating in different geographic regions, different areas of real estate, or different industries or market sectors.

What Kind of Due Diligence Should I Be Doing?

Before you invest in a REIT, you and your advisor should review the quality and depth of the management team and the company's business plan. You'll want to consider the managers' experience in overseeing the types of properties the REIT owns, as well as their experience in the industry, market sector, and geographic region where the REIT does business.

Because so much of a REIT's cash goes to pay dividends, the business generally needs access to outside sources of capital. Therefore, in evaluating a REIT's business plan, you'll want to consider the provisions it has made for growth, specifically how it plans to raise new money.

The options are:

- The sale of additional shares
- Mortgage debt secured by its real estate assets
- Corporate debt dependent on the company's overall creditworthiness

The REIT's overall debt level is another factor to consider. As the debt level increases, so does the business risk, and hence, the risk to your investment.

Debt service reduces the amount of net operating income, or funds from operations. The higher the level of debt, the more drag is placed on any income available for distributions. You should check to see if a REIT's debt is at the portfolio level or at the individual asset level. Portfolio-level debt can be riskier than asset-specific debt because when debt is linked to a particular asset, the lender doesn't have any recourse beyond that asset if the tenant defaults.

How Do the Surrender Charges Work Within a Non-Traded REIT?

Most (but NOT all) non-traded REITs follow the following surrender charge schedule from Date of investment (DOI):

DOI to year 1 (day 365)	No access to principal other than dividends
Year 1 to Year 2	7.5% surrender fee
Year 2 to Year 3	5% surrender fee
Year 3 to Year 4	2.5% surrender fee
Year 4 plus	Liquid

Non-traded REITs, at the discretion of their board of advisors, may suspend redemptions in any year, or even permanently, based on how well their properties are performing or whether or not they are able to deploy capital as quickly as it can be raised. Generally, this does not happen in normal times but only in periods of economic uncertainty, when investors are panicking and trying to sell everything. I have seen the suspension of redemptions in 2009–2011 for several of the non-traded REITs. In most cases, the REIT's Private Placement Memorandum (PPM) discloses quarterly or annual redemption limits. These limitations allow the REIT management to plan on maintaining access to at least 95% of the trust's funds each year. When investors pulled out 5 percent of the total value of the REIT in any given year, they will shut off the redemptions until the upcoming January or longer, a cooling off period, so to speak. The board of advisors for a non-traded REIT will not allow panicking investors to force them to take actions in unfavorable times.

A risk to these investments, as any non-exchange listed investment, is the inability to sell your shares if you need to in the above situation. In the REITs which suspended their distributions, though the rent was still being paid to investors, they did not have a means to sell their shares for a return of principal. These REITs are waiting for better economic times before they list the shares to provide liquidity. Just as one would not want to sell a house at the bottom of a real estate cycle if one was not forced to, the non-traded REITs which have suspended redemptions are following the same logic. Protect the principal, collect rents and pay out or suspend distributions, and wait for a better day to eventually sell.

Looking at the surrender charges another way. Even an investor who had an unforeseen event in their life needing money and did not have sufficient liquid reserves to meet the immediate need, if they redeem their shares in a non-traded REIT—which redemptions are still possible—depending on how long they have been in the REIT, they still may potentially come out ahead of a typical CD or bond.

Let's work on a hypothetical example. An investor puts $10,000 into a non-traded REIT and needs to pull out the money between year two and year three. This particular REIT had been distributing 7 percent in dividends.

The investor has earned a combined 14 percent over the last two years and now must surrender with a 5 percent penalty.

The net return is 9 percent, or roughly 4.5 percent per year.

Year one return	7%
Year two return	7%
Surrender in beginning of year three	–5% penalty
Net Two-Year return	**9%**

Keep in mind, the investor is potentially giving up something much greater by selling the non-traded REIT before the sponsor has determined it to be the right time to sell. The appreciation of the buildings, growing inside the REIT, is forfeited by an investor selling early. This can be substantial if the investor has been in the REIT for more than four years and sees it as an easy exit since the surrender penalty is now 0 percent. The real penalty for leaving early may be internal appreciation which will be realized as soon as the sponsor sells the portfolio.

Co-Ownership Real Estate (CORE)

The Co-Ownership Real Estate (CORE) structure is an increasingly popular choice among real estate investors. Whether you are seeking a replacement property to satisfy a 1031 Tax Deferred Exchange or looking for a suitable "turn-key" passive real estate investment alternative, the CORE structure provides a host of options that should be researched.

CORE investment properties employ a professional asset and onsite property manager, guided by an owner agreement, which sets forth the management of the overall investment as well as the decisions that would require a vote by the property owners.

The CORE structure provides an opportunity for smaller investors to potentially own institutional-grade, class-A real estate, with national credit tenants and professional property management. These types of properties have typically been available only to the larger institutional grade investors like Real Estate Investment Trusts (REITS) and Pension Funds and Life Insurance Companies. CORE Investments generally offer the same rights and benefits of individual ownership but without the headaches of day-to-day property management.

A CORE Investment strategy combined with a 1031 Tax Deferred Exchange can potentially provide an opportunity for an individual owner to exit one property and step up into multiple properties, thereby diversifying their real estate portfolio by location and property type.

Example CORE Property Types

- Triple Net (NNN) Lease Properties
- Multi-Family Apartment Communities
- Self Storage Facilities
- Internet Data Centers
- National Single Credit Tenants and Franchises
- Multi- and Single-tenant Office Buildings and Corporate Centers
- Industrial Complexes, Warehouses, and Manufacturing Facilities
- Retail Shopping Centers and Malls
- Medical Office Buildings
- Hotel and Hospitality Properties
- Restaurant and Food Service Facilities

CORE investment properties are assembled by real estate investment companies referred to as Sponsors. I employ an extensive due diligence process to evaluate each Sponsor according to its track record, management team and expertise, financial strength, property selection, industry access to properties, and essential business relationships (i.e., financing).

Reasons for CORE Ownership

- May be suitable for those who realize the importance of real estate as an investment tool but who are dedicated to a career that may not allow them to dedicate the time required to building a successful real estate portfolio. This type of investment allows a part-time real estate investor to purchase and build a portfolio of properties. Through the repeated use of the 1031 exchange process, the portfolio can potentially grow tax deferred while providing passive income and tax advantages.
- Eliminates the headaches associated with day-to-day property management. May be a viable solution for those rental property owners looking for relief from active property management and the burdens that come with being a landlord.

- For estate planning purposes, the heirs of a CORE investment get a stepped-up basis in the inherited property, thereby wiping out the built-up tax liability resulting from one or many prior 1031 Exchanges.
- In some cases, properties that are available for co-ownership are institutional grade, class-A properties that typically would not be available to the smaller investor. By pooling funds and aligning with a Sponsor, the smaller investor has access to properties, management resources, and financing that would not normally be available to them.
- You may be searching to purchase a new investment property outright or looking to trade-up via a 1031 Exchange. A CORE property will allow you to expand your consideration pool and offer more opportunities to find property that has a favorable return on investment. Additionally, you may currently own a property with a significant amount of equity but with an income stream that is maxed out. CORE properties may offer a better cash-on-cash return than your current options. Depending on the properties you select, you may have the potential for greater cash flow and/or appreciation, combined with renewed tax benefits.

CORE Risks

A CORE investment is a real estate investment and shares similar risks inherent to the overall asset class of real estate investing. These risks include loss of tenants and rents, possible need for additional capital for unforeseen expenditures, and lack of liquidity or formal secondary market to sell you ownership stake.

As always, work with an experienced adviser well versed in CORE properties as well as 1031 exchanges. Ask lots of questions and get other opinions.

1031 Exchanges

In my opinion, the 1031 tax-deferred exchange is one of the most powerful wealth-building tools currently available to U.S. taxpayers. It is the IRS-approved method that allows you to sell an investment property and defer capital gains and depreciation recapture taxes, providing you reinvest 100 percent of your equity into "like kind" property of equal or greater value within a specifically defined timeframe.

Any property held for investment purposes or for productive use in a trade or business generally qualifies as "like kind" property for 1031 exchange purposes. A 1031 exchange is also referred to as a tax-free exchange, tax-deferred exchange, tax exchange, or Starker exchange, named for T.J. Starker, an Oregon timber man and Oregon Agricultural College forestry professor who taught my grandfather and who first used this exchange mechanism and won its approval in the courts, including delayed exchanges, in the late 1970s.

To read more about this powerful deferral of taxes on real estate, please see Appendix D.

Collateralized Notes

In general, State investor suitability rules apply for this type of investment and they are not suitable for all investors.

There are three basic types of collateralized note programs: mortgage notes, business development corporations (BDCs), and life settlement notes.

Mortgage Notes

The types of First Trust Deed Investments I generally work with are geared toward building a portfolio of many loans, as opposed to investing in individual notes. They are structured as a fund with pooled money from investors. The portfolio provides a collateralized note investment vehicle, which is diversified in an effort to balance risk and provide consistent returns. The types of mortgages that are in the fund are acquired through a defined process, using conservative acquisition criteria. They are generally hand-picked, first positions only, that can be purchased at a potential discount to loan value, have low Loan-to-Value (LTV) ratios, include borrowers with excellent track records, and a seasoned successful payment history.

These funds seek to provide investors with a consistent monthly income and attempts to achieve this by investing in a managed portfolio comprised of mortgage notes secured by real estate. These investments are typically not available directly to individual investors. The funds invest in fully collateralized first deeds of trust for residential, commercial, and land mortgages, thereby providing the investors with collateralized hard assets.

It is essential that the fund acquire *good notes* with *good collateral*. A *good note* has a track record of making payments on time. The borrower has been making the payments on a reliable basis; it must be a seasoned note by its successful payment history. This is important because a note is purchased for the payments, not for the collateral. The function of collateral is to secure the principal investment. The function of getting payments each and every month is to receive the interest.

A reliable payment stream helps bring the *return* on the investment; the collateral helps guard the *principal* of the investment.

Good collateral does not refer so much to the specific secured property as it does to the degree of certainty that the property can be readily converted to cash to prepay the debt.

The fund's acquisition and operation criteria are generally as follows:

- Select a note with a good payment history to secure the stream of payments
- Select a note with a healthy collateral margin to secure the principal investment in the note
- Buy the note at a discount to secure an attractive yield on the note
- Monitor the note collections, to assure realizing all the benefits that were negotiated when the note was purchased
- Share the benefits with the investors

These, in a nutshell, are debt instruments collateralized by real estate. They can be first, second, or greater positions.

Business Development Corporation (BDC)

Investor portfolios often include investments in the stocks and bonds of public companies. But did you know that, like institutional and high net worth investors, individuals can invest in privately owned companies as well?

There are 5,000 publicly traded companies in the United States, but more than 300,000 privately owned companies. Using a BDC greatly expands the potential investment landscape. The privately held companies are in recognizable industries, ranging from major retailers and food stores to health service, utilities, and beyond.

Private companies contribute significantly to the American economy. In fact, the 200 largest private companies alone employ more than 4 million people and have combined revenues in excess of $1 Trillion. Cargill, Chrysler, Toys "R" Us, Enterprise Rent-A-Car, Fidelity Investments, Publix Super Markets, and Hilton Hotels are just some of the recognizable private companies that do not trade their debt and equity on the public stock exchanges.

Investors can invest in either traded or non-traded BDCs. Unlike exchange-traded BDCs, non-traded BDCs are illiquid investments and are not directly tied to fluctuations in the stock market.

What is a BDC?   A BDC is a category of investment company created by Congress in 1980 under the Investment Company Act of 1940 to facilitate the flow of capital to private companies. The investor essentially "owns" small pieces of each loan made to the private companies by the BDC. Basically a BDC allows an investor to act like a bank and loan money to a private company. These companies use the proceeds for any number of reasons such as growing the business, buying manufacturing plants, managing cash flow, and so forth.

A BDC provides investors with exposure to the private equity and private debt investment markets, which typically have been dominated by institutional investors, such as pension funds and endowments. These institutional investors have been able to meet the high minimum requirements imposed by private equity firms and private debt investment funds, and have had specialized investment expertise at hand to evaluate these types of investments. I believe that institutional investors participate in these funds for a number of reasons, including their use as a potential source of risk diversification within a portfolio and for their inflation-hedged return potential over the long term (Figure B.3).

Until recently, if you didn't have a billion in your pocket, you were excluded from these sought-after investments. With the economy in turmoil over the last several years, the traditional sources

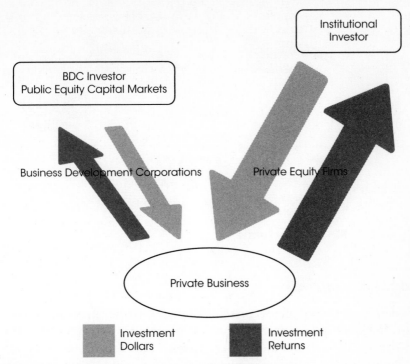

Figure B.3   **BDC versus Private Equity Capital Flow**

of capital for private companies have become much tighter. This paved the way for other groups to gain access into these types of deals, and allow smaller investors the ability to participate.

How do they work?   A non-traded business development company (BDC) allows individuals to invest in privately owned companies, similar to using stocks and bonds to invest in public companies (Figure B.4). Investors are able to pool their capital to invest in the private debt of companies. These companies seek to make earnings or pay interest back to the BDC. The BDCs objective is to pass the earnings or interest to the investors primarily and to a lesser extent capital appreciation.

Private debt positions the investor as a lender to the company. It provides a contractual return and repayment back to the investor with priority over the equity investors in the company.

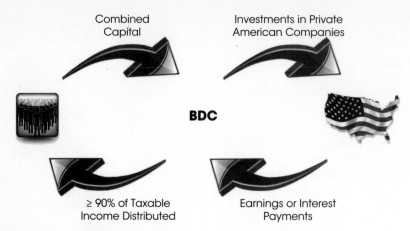

Combined Capital

Investments in Private American Companies

BDC

≥ 90% of Taxable Income Distributed

Earnings or Interest Payments

Figure B.4   BDC Flow of Funds

BDC Investment Focus

The primary area of focus is first lien senior secured loans, second lien secured loans, and to a lesser extent, subordinated loans, of private U.S. companies. These investments are part of a typical company's capital structure whereby senior secured loans represent the senior-most obligations of a company and have the first claim on its assets and cash flows. As such, first lien senior secured loans carry the least risk among all investments in a firm. This is in contrast to preferred stockholders and bond holders, who generally get paid last, or in the case of GM bondholders, paid at all.

First lien senior secured loans are followed in priority by second lien secured loans, subordinated debt, preferred equity, and finally, common equity.

Senior secured loans carry the least risk among all investments within a company's capital structure.

Due to this priority of cash flows and claims on assets, an investment's risk increases as it moves further down the capital structure. Investors are usually compensated for the risk associated with this sliding scale of cash flows, or junior status, in the form of higher returns, either through higher interest payments or potentially higher capital appreciation. As depicted in the chart in Figure B.5, you should look for BDCs which focus on components of the capital structure with higher priority of cash flows, and therefore potentially less risk.

**Typical Capital Structure
of a Company
Investment Type**

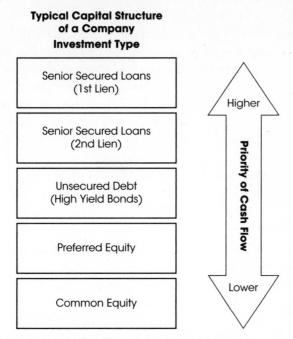

Figure B.5   Typical Capital Structure of a Company

Many of the BDCs during times of economic distress will weight their portfolios heavily toward senior secured debt, where investments are secured by collateral and recovery rates (i.e., the amount of principal a lender recovers after a default) are strongest among all types of corporate securities in the event of default. However, when the economic outlook is strong and corporate profits are expected to grow, many BDCs may broaden their focus to include more junior forms of debt, such as subordinated loans, which offer less downside protection but generally offer more attractive total returns. Subordinated loans offer returns both through high interest rates and potential equity appreciation in the borrower (they often award lenders equity interests at little or no cost).

Understanding First and Second Lien Senior Secured Loans

The goal of most BDCs is to maintain significant exposure to first lien senior secured debt and second lien secured debt, which represent the senior-most obligations in the capital structures that they occupy. These loans generally pay variable rates (a natural hedge against rising interest rates and inflation), are secured by the company's assets, and are generally entitled to receive payment in full before all other security-holders of a company, including public bondholders. Senior secured loans are marked by strict investor protections in the form of loan covenants and enjoy the highest recovery rates (i.e., the percentage of principal recovered in a company defaults) among all classes of debt securities. Institutional investors have traditionally accessed senior secured loans both through approximately $1+ trillion secondary market and through active origination channels.

Understanding Subordinated Loans

In addition to first lien senior secured and second lien secured loans, BDCs may invest a portion of their assets in subordinated loans if the views on the economy or other factors suggest it is in the interest of the BDC stockholders to do so. Subordinated loans usually rank junior in priority of payment to first lien senior secured and second lien secured loans and are often unsecured, but are situated above equity and common stock in the capital structure. In return for their junior status, compared to first lien senior secured and second lien secured loans, subordinated loans generally offer higher returns through both higher interest rates and possibly equity ownership in the form of warrants, enabling the lender to participate in the potential capital appreciation of the borrower. Due to these attributes, subordinated loans tend to outperform senior secured loans and other forms of corporate debt in a growing economy.

The warrants typically require only a nominal cost to exercise and are used as a loan sweetener for the BDC.

An example of the potential protection of secured loans is the bankruptcy of General Motors in June of 2009. Shares of GM common stock, which peaked in 2000 at $90 per share, became worthless. Holders of GM unsecured bonds did not fare much better than the stock holders, ultimately losing almost 90 percent of their investment. The only bright spot in GM's capital structure, the secured loans, which had a first priority security interest in its assembly lines, robotic welders, paint systems, other equipment, fixtures, documents, general intangibles, all books and records, and their proceeds, were ruled in the bankruptcy court proceedings to be paid in full, nearly $6 billion in all. The nice part of being the highest in the pecking order of a company backed by real assets is that most of the time you will be paid back in full. At least you will be paid first before anyone else gets a penny.

Is a Non-Traded BDC Similar to a Non-Traded Real Estate Investment Trust (REIT)?

A BDC is a pooled investment vehicle that invests in equity or debt of private companies, whereas a REIT invests in real estate. Nonetheless, a REIT and a BDC share many characteristics. From a regulatory standpoint, they both must file periodic SEC reports such as Forms 10-K and 10-Q, and comply with the Sarbanes-Oxley Act of 2002. Non-traded varieties are also both subject to state and FINRA regulations.

From a tax perspective, most BDCs and REITs are structured to provide tax-advantaged, pass-through treatment of ordinary income and long-term capital gains directly to stockholders. No corporate tax is paid if at least 90 percent of taxable income is distributed in a timely manner and applicable tax rules are complied with. In addition, a BDC is a highly accountable and transparent form of investment. It is required to place assets with a qualified independent custodian—employees and managers do not handle company funds.

Finally, both BDCs and REITs are governed by an Independent Board of Directors to ensure the proper alignment of interests. Here is a list of these and other characteristics shared by both non-listed structures in Table B.1.

Table B.1   Common Characteristics Shared by BDCs and REITs

	Non-Traded BDC	Non-Traded REIT
Underlying Investments	Private Equity or Debt	Real Estate
SEC Registered	Yes	Yes
Standard SEC Financial Reporting (10-K, 10-Q)	Yes	Yes
Subject to State and FINRA Regulations	Yes	Yes
Distribute 90% of income to investors	Yes	Yes
Inflation and Interest Rate Hedge	Yes	Yes
1099 Tax Reporting	Yes	Yes
Tax Advantages for investors	No	Yes

As you can see, the only significant difference between REITs and BDCs is foundation for the investment, that being private debt/equity or real estate. Since the BDCs are passing interest earned from loans, they generally do not have any tax advantages whereas the REITs are able to pass through property depreciation and other real estate tax advantages.

There is one important difference, however. Unlike REITs, BDCs are restricted in the amount of leverage they can employ to 50 percent of the BDC's asset value. REITs, which are not governed by the Investment Company Act of 1940 as BDCs are, may employ substantially more leverage than BDCs.

Life Settlement Notes

According to the American Council of Life Insurers, individual consumers in the United States owned $10.3 trillion in life insurance policy benefits in 2009. In that same year, consumers lapsed and surrendered 7.52 percent ($752 billion) in life insurance policy benefits back to the insurance companies.

Think about that. How many premium payments did these consumers make keeping their life policies in force, only to wind up with nothing at the end? The number is staggering.

Years back, investment groups realized there was a significant opportunity in these policies that the original buyers no longer wanted. If they bought the life policy from a consumer who was going to get rid of it anyways, the investment group could continue to pay the policy, keeping it in force, and eventually, when the insured (consumer) dies, the investment group collects the death benefits as the named beneficiary on the policy.

They always say the only two things in life guaranteed are death and taxes. I'm not so sure about taxes but the other, I'm pretty darn sure. That is the logic behind these investments. They are called life settlements.

Life Policy Analysis When an investment group is analyzing whether or not they want to buy a particular insurance policy, they are mainly concerned with two pieces of information. How much the policy costs each year and how long do they expect the insured to keep getting out of bed?

Table B.2   Life Insurance Policy Expected Return Analysis

Cost to Purchase	-$ 200,000
Expected Premium Payments	-$ 320,000 (8 year life expectancy X
	$ 40,000 per year premium payment)
Total Assumed Investment	-$ 520,000
Death Proceeds	$1,000,000
Life Settlement Profit (death on 8th year)	$ 480,000
Percent Return per year	**12.34%**

A simple example goes as follows. Suppose you have an 80-year-old man who owns a $1M life insurance policy which he no longer wants to keep, thus alleviating him from the monthly premiums due. The investment group will perform a medical examination and profile on the man to determine what his life expectancy is. Say in this example eight years. Looking at the costs to maintain the policy, in this example, $40,000 per year, the investment group makes an offer to the man of $200,000 to purchase his life insurance.

The investment group will buy the policy becoming the new owner, change the beneficiary to become themselves, and continue to pay the premiums, keeping the policy in force. The man is still the insured, that is, the policy will pay out the death benefit to the investment group on his death.

The amount the investment group is willing to pay is based on their expected return with the assumed life expectancy, in this case eight years (Table B.2).

As you can see, death can be profitable. A bit of a morbid investment, but consider the 80-year-old man's alternative choice. He could lapse his insurance policy and get nothing. In this case he is walking away with $200,000.

Two Common Versions of Life Settlements

Looking at the above example you will start to recognize potential problems with the investment group's analysis for their return potential.

The main one is life expectancy. That is the wild card in the analysis. If the person lives too long, longer than the original expected time frame, the investment group has to continue paying the premiums until the insured eventually kicks the bucket. The longer they have to pay beyond their expected time frame, the lower their return will be. In the above example, if the man lives for 16 years, the investment groups return is now only 1.79 percent per year. Hardly worth the headache factor and effort.

On the flip side, if the man gets hit by a steam roller in year three, the results are far different. Their return is now 58.48 percent per year in the above hypothetical example. Makes you think they would want to go and hire cousin Vinnie to take care of business. Thankfully there are rules and structures these life settlements have to follow. Blind trusts and other entity structures hopefully prevent the nefarious situation of an investment group speeding along their investment returns.

There are various versions of these being pitched to the general public. The most common ones investors will hear about on the radio or TV are either the single policy purchase or fractional policy purchase.

The single policy purchase investment is the previous example. One insured and one policy. These carry the most risk as the statistical life expectancy variance for any one individual is boundless.

However, the actuarial results improve the more life policies you have in your investment pool, the more statistically accurate your payouts and return will potentially be.

Generally it works out that if an investment pool has more than 250 policies; their results will be +/- 2 percent of their projections.

Obviously the fewer policies in the pool the greater the risk and more random the results.

Fractional policy investments are simply spreading your investment over more insurance policies. Suppose you have $100,000 and are presented the ability to purchase a portion of 10 life policies. You would put $10,000 into each one and now participate in 10 different people's lives. The statistical odds are still not any better, but at least you have 10 chances of the steam roller coming around versus just one.

I am not a fan of either of these investments for a few simple reasons.

First, the odds are great either your single policy or fractional policy life settlement will go much longer due to the limited number of policies the investment return is based on. The odds are good the insured(s) will live longer than expected.

Second, other than an occasional account statement reporting your ownership in one or more policies, you get nothing else. Until a policy pays out, you will receive no regular cash flow or distributions. It could be a month, it could be seven years. Not receiving anything for an undetermined amount of time is not the typical investment I try to place into our *Wealth Code* plans. Remember, I love the idea of checks in the mail.

Lastly, most of the life settlement groups will plan for five years of premium payments with either the single policy you purchase or the multiple policies you purchase. This means they have enough money to pay the premiums for five years and if none of your policies pay out, then they will send you a bill for your prorated portion of the premium payment due to keep the policies in force. How's that for insult to injury. You buy and investment, see no returns, and five years later get a bill requesting more money. Instead of positive cash flow, we are dealing with a potential negative cash flow situation indefinitely until a policy pays out.

You can see the single policy purchase issue here being the high odds that the insured lives much longer than expected and you the investor keep getting a bill. This again reduces your expected return on investment year after year.

An Alternative—Life Settlement Notes   You might gather from the above descriptions of the single or multiple policy direct ownership, there are a lot of unknowns so why bother.

Yet, every TV and radio ad touting these investments discusses returns around 16 percent. It is true, that is the investment return most life settlement groups are targeting.

You will hear in the ads that Warren Buffett is a big buyer of life settlements. This is true. The difference with Warren Buffett and Berkshire Hathaway is they most likely have a lot more money than you do, and they don't buy one or two policies, they buy hundreds at a time. By doing so, the statistical odds are in their favor.

An improved version of life settlement investments came out around 2010, and they are called Life Settlement Notes.

You were ascertaining from the name that they are *notes* of life settlements. That is, something collateralized by something real, in this case, the hundreds of life insurance policies.

Basically, what a few life settlement investment groups realized was that they could monetize their previously purchased life policies. Knowing they have hundreds and hundreds of policies and knowing their odds are very high, greater than 98 percent, that the payouts will happen consistently, they created a series of CD-like term notes with definitive time spans and cash flow potential.

For instance, if a group's target return for an entire life settlement pool is 16 percent, they could offer a six month term note with a payout of approximately five percent per annum. Effectively they will pay out 2.5 percent in the six month window. Compared to current treasury prices and bank CDs this is a great return.

The six-month life note investor knows the exact term and how much they will be paid out, taking care of the second concern of cash flow and the unknown duration of your typical single or multiple policy direct ownership.

By the note being collateralized by hundreds of policies, an investor truly is participating like Warren Buffett. A particular settlement pool might be worth billions of dollars of life insurance face value, much more than the average Joe will have to invest. Therefore we are getting the proper diversification necessary to make these attractive investments.

Why would a group be willing to shave off five percent of their expected return? Simple, the money you invest in the six-month term note will allow them to buy additional longer-dated life policies in their investment pool and keep their program going. A problem with a life settlement pool is eventually all the insured will pass away and their 16 percent return comes to a halt. By adding longer-dated life expectancies into their pool, the investment group will keep collecting the difference between what they pay out to the life settlement note investors and the ultimate return of the larger life settlement pool.

In the above example, even though they pay out five percent per annum, assuming they are hitting their return target of 16 percent, the investment group is still making close to 11 percent per year.

16 percent Life settlement pool return – 5 percent investor note payout = 11 percent retained earnings.

As the saying goes, "*It is better to make 50 percent on something rather than 100 percent on nothing.*"

Things to Look for in a Life Settlement Note

The biggest risk to a life settlement note is the constant distributions to the investors whether they have policies paying out or not. The major way these investment groups will cover themselves in this situation is to have an established line of credit with a large bank to handle the withdrawals and interest payments.

As a general rule, I make sure our clients who meet the suitability requirements, only invest in life settlement notes with shorter maturation terms than the renewal date for the established line of credit. When the notes come due, reassess the line of credit. If the investment group has already elongated the term for the line of credit, then you can more confidently renew your life settlement note. Again, keep the life-note term shorter than the renewal period for the line of credit.

No matter how much we believe people will eventually kick the bucket, revolutionary changes in medical treatment, which are occurring every day, is serving to elongate our expected lives. We are living longer due to better healthcare.

This was always one of my greatest concerns with my background in biochemistry. We keep getting better and better at solving diseases and people by nature are living longer. Take AIDS for instance. Back in the 1980s it was a death sentence. Today it is manageable and individuals such as Magic Johnson have been living with the virus for more than 20 years and counting.

A sad reality though, even if the cure for cancer takes place, according to life insurance industry research, that miraculous event will only extend life expectancy rates by just more than two years.

Don't get me wrong, if I had cancer, I would appreciate every second more I get to spend with the grandkids, but the overall impact on population life expectancy is not that great. Not enough to throw the life settlement notes into a tizzy.

To recap the biggest two things to look for with life-settlement note investments:

1. How many policies in the investment pool? Again, I need to see more than 250.
2. How secure is the line of credit and for how long? Ultimately, it won't matter if a single policy pays out as long as the line of credit is in place and has available balance.

Strategy with Life Notes

Many of us are familiar with a bond or CD ladder. That is, buying varying dated maturities with different yields.

For instance you might put $100,000 into a bond ladder with $25,000 in four different maturation dates. Maybe three, four, five, and six years. Let's presume the bonds don't get called by their issuer, and the issuer remains solvent. As the bonds mature, you get back your principal and can invest it in potentially higher paying bonds if interest rates have risen by that point. Of course if rates have fallen further, you are stuck getting a lower yield than previously enjoyed.

Life settlement notes can be used the same way, sticking to the first rule for any investment slice, that being total invested cannot be more than 10 percent of investable net worth. And of course using a smaller allocation of five percent or less is potentially even more prudent.

For instance with an investable net worth of $1M and the size for your individual legs on your financial table being no more than five percent, than the most you can put into the life settlement note program is $50,000. You can apply the idea of creating a ladder with the investment by splitting the $50,000 into five different term notes of $10,000 apiece to achieve a blended return (Table B.3).

Always keeping money liquid in stages is the goal.

In this example, an investor will have $10,000 coming due every six months with larger amounts all coming due at the same time on the yearly anniversaries.

Table B.3   Hypothetical Example Life Settlement Note Yield Ladder

Investment Amount	$50,000	Stated Yield
6 month Life Note	$10,000	5%
1 Year Life Note	$10,000	5.5%
2 Year Life Note	$10,000	7%
3 Year Life Note	$10,000	8%
4 Year Life Note	$10,000	9%
Blended Yield:		**6.9%**

Certificates of Deposit

These are bank instruments that are FDIC insured. Most people know what a CD is. It's a time deposit with a bank. A newer component of this category, which has come out in recent years, is called a structured CD. These are CDs with stock market indexes for determining the potential growth or interest earned in the CD.

For instance, I will use a five-year structured CD that is tied to the S&P 500. If you put $100,000 into this CD, it would be protected by FDIC, in case the issuing bank goes kaput. If the S&P 500 goes up during those five years, you would get the gains of the market as a percent of the growth, as determined by a formula established by the bank for that particular CD. If the S&P 500 tanks during the five years, you would be handed back your original $100,000 and not have any interest credited to the CD's final value. Sounds too good to be true, right? Yes, there are drawbacks to these accounts, which have to do with the underlying securities protecting them, namely bonds. These investment vehicles are very similar to Index Fixed Annuities, and those are thoroughly described in Chapter 9.

The biggest issue with structured CDs is if interest rates move up quickly, the formula that determines how much interest you will earn in the CD as a factor of the growth of the S&P 500 is generally only a portion of the full market upside. You will not earn close to what the market makes in a rising interest rate environment.

Needless to say, these are very complicated investments that are sold as simple concepts. Nothing is simple when it involves complicated formulas tied to bonds or options that are tied to the markets. Also, be aware that structured CD's may also be designed around the performance of a certain basket of stocks. Not the full S&P 500 mind you, but a small number of stocks—like Google, Microsoft, IBM, Yahoo, Apple, and Intel for example. The CD would earn interest based on a formula which only uses the small basket of stocks for upside/downside calculations.

Another version of structured CDs are bank notes. These allow an investor to play an individual stock, commodity, market index (such as S&P 500, INDU, Nasdaq, . . .), or other equity investment with a formula wrapper around the performance. Typically an investor will get a set amount of potential upside return over a time span as short as a couple of years. They will also get a floor, so they will not ultimately lose value if the underlying equity stays above that floor.

These protection levels are created by using equity options, such as puts and calls. The issuer is essentially using puts and calls to manage their returns on your money, and paying you the difference based on a formula they have devised.

For instance, an investor buys a structured note on gold. The issuer develops a formula that, over the course of the two-year term, this investor can participate up to 30 percent absolute return on the upside with a floor above negative 20 percent. That is, as long as gold does not lose more than 20 percent of its value on the day the structured note was purchased, the investor will not lose. Incidentally, some of the more interesting notes will actually give the negative 20 percent as a positive return on top of their principal.

If gold in this example falls below 20 percent of the value on the day the note is purchased, you the investor are no longer protected and when the invested structured note matures, whatever the price of gold is on that day is your positive or negative return.

When purchasing these investments, again, do your homework and ask lots of questions.

Underlying these products are sophisticated call and put options being placed on individual equities, commodities, or market indexes and are designed to simplify the ability of the average Joe to participate without them needing to understand complex stock option theory and application.

These products are potentially appropriate additional legs on the table for investors looking for stock market participation with some downside protection. You are giving up some of the upside in doing so but may be a fair tradeoff. The terms for the bank notes, the upside and downside protections, change frequently depending on the overall stock market volatility and other economic conditions. Take your time, educate yourself and see if they serve a purpose for your *Wealth Code* table.

Cash

"Cash is King," the old saying goes. It gives the holder the power to buy and sell almost everything with total freedom. The main problem with cash is the issue of inflation. When you are liquid and you are protected, the tradeoff of course is you don't earn anything or barely anything on your money. If you stuffed your mattress full of cash 20 years ago and took that money out today, how much purchasing power would you have you lost? If you had stashed away $1,000 in a tin can in 1913, you could only buy around 56 equivalent dollars' worth of goods and services today according to *The Privateer*. That is, you would have lost more than 94 percent of your purchasing power on your $1,000.

The one point we want to make in this section is very basic. Cash does not necessarily have to be denominated in U.S. dollars. If inflation does become a significant problem, commodities will tend to move up in value from a falling U.S. dollar, and the currencies of oil-exporting countries such as New Zealand, Australia, and Canada might offer reasonable protection. The Switzerland Franc has generally been a safe haven but sadly, with the global competition to devalue all currencies, even the Swiss started printing money in early 2011 to keep their currency from appreciating too much. That being said, their currency may still be a good place to park excess cash.

Most of the citizens of Germany in the Weimar Republic lost everything because they didn't realize the significance of exchanging their Deutsch Marks for any other currency during the hyperinflationary years of 1921 to 1923. The same thing goes for Rubles in Russia during 1998, Mexican pesos in 2002, and so on.

Realizing you do not have to keep cash sitting in any one particular countries currency is an important step in potentially protecting your purchasing power.

Appendix C: Discounted Roth Conversions

In my opinion, pre-tax retirement accounts may be responsible for a giant leak in your wealth bucket. This leak takes years for you to become aware of and can become increasingly difficult to plug as your pre-tax accounts potentially grow over the years.

Anytime a decision is made to take action which necessitates an increase in taxable income, one must evaluate all possible measures to minimize or mitigate the resulting tax due.

Most CPAs—and many financial advisors, including certified financial planners (CFPs), investment advisors, and even tax attorneys typically view the Roth-conversion equation in a single dimension. How much did you convert, what will the tax be, and how long will it take for the tax-free growth to overcome the payment of taxes in the year of the conversion?

The problem with this single dimension viewpoint is it assumes you will have to pay tax on 100 percent of the Roth rollover amount and thus pay dollar for dollar the tax due. *Both of these assumptions are wrong.*

With respect to Financial Advisors, Warren Buffett has been quoted as saying "*What makes them good is not their predictions, but their strategies for dealing with an uncertain future.*" This could be no more true than in this single area of Roth conversions.

Roth Conversions—An Overview

Let's review what the experts have been saying about Roth IRAs:

- "By allowing Roth IRAs, they also created the single most powerful estate-building and wealth-transfer vehicle available today. By not imposing RMDs on the owner, they gave the American taxpayer one of the greatest income tax 'loop-holes' in existence today." (Douglas Warren, Roth IRA Notes for Advisors, Winter 2007)

- "The advantage of a Roth IRA over a regularly taxed account is obvious. Either way you pay income tax up front. But with Roth, you're then done paying taxes; with a regular account you're just getting started." (Understanding the Roth IRA, Moneychimp.com)
- "The essence of a Roth IRA is that you pay tax on the seed, but reap the harvest tax-free." (James Lange, *Retire Secure! Pay Taxes Later. The Key to Making Your Money Last as Long as You Do*, 2006, Wiley.)
- "The Roth IRA is the single best gift Congress has ever presented to the American taxpayer." (Ed Slott, *The Retirement Savings Time Bomb . . . And How to Defuse It*, 2007, Penguin Books.)

On point with the above concept of "tax the seed, not the harvest" consider the following analogy:

Most folks know who Johnny Appleseed was. He was a man in the 1800s that planted thousands of apple trees, primarily in the Ohio region. What if the tax man said "Thanks Johnny, for all that you are doing to plant apple trees. Unfortunately, you have to pay tax on your activity. You have a choice. We'll either tax your seeds now or you can wait and we'll tax the harvest." What would you choose? Let's see how this choice applies to retirement strategies.

Here's a hypothetical example. Let's assume we have a 30 year old who has a qualified plan. He wants to put in $6,000 a year for the next 35 years. Let's say his investments yield 8 percent per year and he's in a 30 percent tax bracket. Basically, he's going to save about $2,000 a year in taxes, right? So that means over 35 years he will have benefited from $70,000 dollars of tax benefits. Incidentally, $6,000 over 35 years at 8 percent comes to just about $1M. Now at the backend he says "This is pretty good, I've got my money in there, it grew, and I have $70,000 worth of tax benefits. But I'm afraid of running out of money so all I want to do is take the income off the top of this." He's still getting 8 percent, so that first year he takes out $80,000 per year. What do we know about that money? What we know is that it's 100 percent taxable and if he's still in that 30 percent tax bracket, that's $24,000 of taxes.

What do we notice here? How long did it take the IRS to get back their money? It's less than three years. They gave up $70,000 in tax benefits over 35 years and in less than three years they have it all back. If he lives 20 years longer and keeps drawing that $80,000, he's going to end up paying an additional $480,000 in taxes. If it's 30 years, it's going to be $720,000 in taxes.

So let me ask you this: If the IRS thought enough to invest $70,000 in you, so they could get back between $480,000 and $720,000, would you invest $70,000 in yourself so that you could potentially keep that $480,000 and $720,000 for yourself or your heirs? If the answer is yes then you need to consider a Roth conversion sooner rather than later, and evaluate options that may offset and reduce the taxable income that results. This may be appropriate, whether you plan to use these dollars for retirement living expenses, or pass this wealth on to children and grandchildren.

Also, note that in our example he never spent any of his $1M. He only took the income off the top, so at his death that $1M will also be income taxed to his estate or beneficiaries. That would mean potentially hundreds of thousands more in additional taxes at his death.

You might be thinking "Wait! The income tax doesn't have to be paid at death if he has children because you can do a stretch IRA." If you're not familiar with that, it simply means, from our example, that when he died, that $1M can be transferred to his children and they will take out distributions at that point over their lifetime. Sounds pretty good at first glance, doesn't it?

Again, the IRS has done the math. If that really did occur and his child was 50 when it was inherited, there would be an additional $700,000 in taxes coming out during that child's lifetime. So it's almost $1.5M of taxes simply because it's in IRAs or other qualified plans. So is it any question that the IRS loves qualified plans?

Roth IRA Fundamentals

With a Roth IRA, after-tax dollars are deposited or rolled over from an existing IRA or other retirement fund and all subsequent growth is tax-free based on current tax laws as of when this book was written. When you make the contributions to a Roth IRA those contributions are not tax deductible. The growth can be taken out tax free as long as you have remained in the Roth IRA for a period of at least five years and are above the age of 59½.

Taking out the growth of the Roth IRA before the five-year test will result in it being taxed at ordinary rates and if you pull out the potential growth before the age of 59½, you will be subject to a federal penalty of 10 percent on the withdrawn amount.

There are income tests which need to be met before an individual or couple filing jointly can contribute to a Roth IRA or roll over an existing retirement account or IRA to a Roth IRA.

In 2012 the Modified Adjusted Gross Income (MAGI) was $110,000 for a single individual and $169,000 for a couple filing jointly. These are the lower limits where you can contribute up to the maximum allowed, whereas if your MAGI increases, there are upper boundaries where you cannot make any contributions at all or use the IRA rollover.

These income levels change almost every year and there are exclusions to the withdrawal rules, so it is important to either look up the current levels or discuss with your financial adviser or CPA to see if you qualify.

MAGI Reduction Strategy

Please note that it may be possible to use alternative strategies to reduce your MAGI below these income thresholds and thus allow contributions or rollovers.

These alternative income-tax-reduction strategies include the previously described Oil/Gas intangible drilling deductions (IDC) and a few others I will discuss in this appendix section.

The use of oil/gas investments has to be appropriate for a given investor's financial situation before the consideration of the tax benefits these programs will generate. Who cares if you get an income deduction if the investment is not right for your situation!

But for arguments sake, let's demonstrate the use of oil/gas IDCs to qualify for a Roth IRA contribution or rollover.

Assume a couple filing jointly earns $200,000 in 2012, are fully accredited by means of their net worth, and a particular oil/gas developmental drilling program is appropriate and suitable for their financial table.

If they invest $50,000 into this particular program which happens to have a 90 percent IDC, they will have a $45,000 self-employment income loss to report in 2012.

The effect of this loss will be a drop in their MAGI from $200,000 to $155,000.

$200,000 − $45,000 ($50,000 × 90 percent IDC) = $155,000

Since their MAGI is now below the $169,000 income threshold, they are free to convert an existing IRA to a Roth IRA or make a maximum Roth IRA contribution.

In general, the younger the individual, the more beneficial a Roth conversion may be. That's because there are more years available to recoup the taxes paid on the conversion. If it's fairly early in the prospect's retirement, longevity runs in the family, and the individual won't need to access IRA assets for five years or more, a conversion may well be worth it because there is a higher likelihood of recouping the tax hit.

For those who are already retired and taking Social Security, converting to a Roth could potentially reduce the tax owed on Social Security income. Although the conversion could bump up the amount of Social Security benefits that are taxable in the year of the conversion, the conversion could potentially reduce taxes owed in subsequent years. That's because Roth distributions don't factor into the calculation that the IRS currently uses to determine which Social Security benefits are taxable.

Those who have primarily made nondeductible contributions in the past may be good candidates for a Roth conversion, because they won't owe taxes on those nondeductible contributions—only investment earnings and deductible contributions will be taxed upon conversion.

Those who have amassed a large estate may want to look at an IRA conversion. Here's why: (a) the Roth doesn't require mandatory distributions, thereby allowing assets to potentially compound and increasing the amount which can be passed to a spouse or heirs; (b) because taxes have already been paid on Roth assets, the overall nest egg which can be passed to heirs will be smaller under the estate tax system, and therefore could help to reduce estate-tax liability.

Of course, the estate tax is another issue that will be changing one way or the other at the beginning of 2013, with the scheduled (and delayed) expiration of the Bush-era tax cuts.

Finally, for those who are unemployed or whose income is currently appreciably lower than it normally is, it might be advantageous to convert at this juncture. Provided that cash is available to pay the tax bill, taxes related to the conversion will be lower than they would be if the taxpayer's income were higher.

Be careful, though—Roth IRA conversions make sense less often than is generally assumed.

What types of people are less likely to benefit from a Roth IRA conversion? Those who don't have the money in other assets to pay the tax associated with the conversion, and those who know they'll be in a significantly lower tax bracket in retirement should think twice about converting.

There are other issues you should consider when deciding if a Roth conversion is right for you.

The longer one lives, the more likely it is that a Roth IRA conversion will make sense, since the retiree will have potentially more years to enjoy the tax-free use of the Roth investment gains and, of course, more years over which to recover the tax paid on the conversion itself.

In all of the above situations, you should be aware that you needn't convert all of your IRA accounts or even all of any single IRA account. Partial conversions are permissible, but you can't pick and choose which IRA assets to convert. For example, although it would be advantageous, one can't convert all of his or her nondeductible IRAs and leave the deductible IRAs intact. Instead, each dollar converted will receive exactly the same tax treatment based on the aggregate breakdown between deductible contributions/investment earnings and nondeductible contributions within the IRA(s).

Minimizing Taxes from a Roth IRA Conversion

Before I discuss potential ways to achieve this outcome, we must first ask the question "What will your income tax rate be in the future and how does it compare with your current rate?"

The **higher** your future tax rate, the more likely it is that a Roth conversion could potentially make sense. So let's take a quick look at some of the issues that may influence future tax rates.

Now, here is a *big* question for all of us:

Will taxes in the future be higher?

The chart in Figure C.1 from Wikipedia 2011 may give us an indication—since the current 35 percent marginal tax rate is as low as it has ever been since the early part of the last century!

You probably won't meet very many people who think that taxes will be getting lower anytime soon!

Historically speaking, tax rates are at extremely low levels now (2012).

We know that the folks in Washington have the power to change the rules, but each taxpayer has a right to use the current rules to try and achieve the best possible outcome—and when it

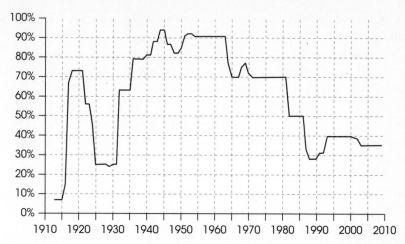

Figure C.1   Federal Top Marginal Tax Bracket Over the Last 100 Years

comes to taxes, that means doing everything you can do legally in order to get the bill down as low as possible!

I believe that taxes as a percentage of gross domestic product (GDP) are destined to rise. But forget about the GDP—taxes as a percentage of your individual income are set to increase. And here is something to remember about THE IRS—if you don't take a stewardship attitude towards reducing your income taxes to the lowest legal minimum, you are allowing more of your assets to become THEIRS!

Budget experts, including the non-partisan Congressional Budget Office, say that the deficit in future years is likely to be quite significant, even if deep spending cuts are enacted. If the spending cuts are not enough, where do you think the Federal Government will turn to stop our country's "wealth leakage"? The only place they can turn to—taxes!

If I take a look at the fiscal condition of Social Security and Medicare, the news is not good. It appears that *federal taxes will potentially need to be raised dramatically* just to cover existing commitments to future recipients of those two programs, assuming that current health trends continue. To emphasize the point, federal income taxes for every taxpayer would have to rise in order to pay all of the benefits promised by these programs under current law over and above the payroll tax.

Raise taxes or break promises—what do you think Washington will do?

Probably both.

So if you believe that taxes are going to rise in the future, should you convert your IRA to a Roth IRA before rates go up?

Clearly, every individual situation is different, but there are many reasons why a Roth Conversion may represent the biggest long-term tax reduction strategy you may ever have the opportunity to utilize.

When it comes to this topic, what are the big issues? Evaluating Roth conversions is really a series of questions:

- Can I convert and How much should I convert?
- When to convert?
- How do I manage the taxes?
- What to invest in with Roth IRA money?

"Can I convert?" and "How much to convert?" are based upon an individual assessment of your financial specifics.

Having worked closely with clients on this topic since 2009, I can assure you that—just like snowflakes—no two individuals are alike.

"When to convert" has an easy answer if all the analysis of your particular situation indicates that conversion is a suitable strategy, then sooner rather than later is a good answer from one important perspective. If you convert, you have a "mulligan" or ability to have a "do-over" all the way to the date you file your return for the year the conversion is made. In other words, once you convert, you can still change your mind within some basic IRS rules. You can re-characterize all or part of the conversion, dialing in your final taxable income to exactly the right dollar amount desired.

This approach also buys you time to see how your investments within the ROTH IRA have performed.

Here is a good example of this approach—For an individual who was invested in U.S. equities, what month during 2009 would have been the best month to convert? The answer, with 20/20 hindsight, is March—when the equity markets were at the lowest point during the market decline. If an individual were to have converted at that time, their IRA would have probably been at its lowest point.

A conversion based on that lowest value would have yielded the lowest tax on the conversion.

Let's discuss a bit further the characteristics of taxes on IRA assets, before we look at ways of managing the taxes resulting from a Roth conversion. The above questions are all important, but before you try to answer any of these, there are two critical concepts to consider and understand.

Concept #1—Tax on an IRA Is Nothing More Than a Debt That Must Be Paid

What does the tax that is embedded within an IRA truly represent? It is a debt owed that must be paid. When you contributed to the IRA, or deferred income into your 401K, the tax you saved that year was not a gift, it was basically a loan.

Debt Free?

Many people approaching or in retirement consider themselves to be debt free. They have no car payments, home mortgage payments, or ongoing credit card debt.

Let's look at a hypothetical example of this—Assume the following:

- IRA balances valued at $500,000
- Real estate valued at $500,000
- Non-IRA assets valued at $500,000
- No mortgage or traditional debt
- Marginal tax bracket at required minimum distributions beginning at age (70½) will be no less than 30 percent, due to other sources of income (Social Security, pensions, investment income)

Are they truly debt free? As this example suggests, you have a total net worth of $1.5M.

$$\$500,000 \text{ IRA} + \$500,000 \text{ Real Estate} + \$500,000$$
$$\text{Non-IRA} = \$1,500,000$$

If you were filling out a balance sheet for a lender, the liabilities section would have nothing but zeroes in it. But is this a true reflection of their financial position? Not really.

Consider the fact that the IRA balances were created from pre-tax contributions and tax-deferred growth over time. Thus, the tax saved each year you contributed is simply deferred. In essence, you have nothing more than a loan from the IRS that will be collected someday! The IRS is quite pleased to sit back and wait for the amount they are owed to grow. Very much like a "balloon payment" that cannot be refinanced away.

In this example, there is an embedded tax on the IRA balance—assuming a 30 percent marginal tax bracket—of approximately $150,000.

So your true net worth is not exactly $1.5M, it is only $1.35M or potentially less, depending on future tax rates.

What happens to this debt if you find yourself in a 40 percent tax bracket as a result of a future tax increases? The debt rises to $200,000!

An optimal outcome would be to find ways to reduce the impact of this tax debt coming due all at once.

Growing IRA Debt?

Money in a traditional IRA will continue to have a built-in embedded tax liability against the balance. As long as it exists, you don't truly control it. If you don't deal with it, it is a debt that will—intentionally or not—pass to your heirs. It is a debt that will increase over time, as a result of the potential growth of the asset. Worst of all, the amount of the debt can be increased at any time by the folks in Washington in the form of tax increases.

Just Pay the Tax?

In the preceding example, doing a Roth Conversion and paying the tax would reduce the total assets by $150,000 but at least you would be truly free of all debt in your retirement account.

But is there a better way to deal with the tax?

Change the Nature of the Debt!

Here is an outside the box idea. With mortgage rates being at historical lows, use a home mortgage—or a home equity line of credit—to free up the dead equity of the home, and use these funds to pay the tax on the IRA conversion.

You just have to decide which is most desirable—having a growing tax debt to the IRS, or a shrinking debt collateralized by other assets, whether that is mortgage on real estate, margin debt on investments, or other means of spreading out the payment of the tax. This allows you to take control of the debt versus letting the IRS and Federal Government dictate what you will owe in the future.

Whether you use an interest-only or an amortized loan on real estate, keep in mind that the IRS is subsidizing the financing of the tax used to unshackle the IRA by converting to a Roth IRA. The subsidy is in the form of mortgage interest deductions against personal income.

But if we just write a check—regardless of the source—and do nothing else, we might miss an opportunity to use the Roth Conversion in conjunction with other strategies to potentially realize a discount on the taxes paid.

Pattern of Debt Over Time

There are two types of debt, an increasing type and decreasing type as shown in Figure C.2.

The decreasing and amortized debt is, in my opinion, the most desirable to have on your balance sheet.

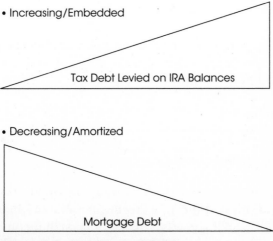

Figure C.2 Two Types of Debt

If you choose to transfer the debt which presently exists against the IRA, to one of the other assets, you have taken control over which debt pattern is potentially impacting your finances.

If a Roth Conversion makes sense for you, what is going to be easier—coming up with $150,000 out of after tax funds such as savings or investments in a single year, or making small payments between $8,000 and $13,000 per year over 15 to 30 years and have the IRS (based on current tax rules) subsidize the payments?

Said another way, you borrow against your home using a 15- or 30-year fixed-rate mortgage, pay the tax with the borrowed funds, and then slowly pay back the borrowed money via installment payments.

By spreading the IRA's embedded tax cost out over a number of years, you take control of your tax outcome so that you can potentially use future tax reduction strategies to offset the future repayment of the tax debt—the debt that you transferred away from the IRA balance.

Unfortunately, when you consider the terms of the IRS loan on the deferred taxes on your retirement account, as described above, it is a very debilitating type of debt. Eliminating, or at least dealing with this debt on your own terms, is something that I believe must be evaluated.

Concept #2—Discounted Roth Conversions!

What other techniques exist to get a 35 percent, 30 percent, or even a 25 percent tax bill on a Roth Conversion potentially reduced to 15 percent or even 10 percent? That would represent a significant victory in protecting your retirement accounts from the ravages of the eventual tax bill.

In order to potentially achieve these lower effective tax rates on conversions, you must understand the concept of discounting asset valuations and how it could apply to potential Roth conversions.

Preliminary Measures

By putting a little thought into the process, you can optimize your tax outcomes, keeping two things in mind:

1. Structure your conversion so that your total taxable income does not exceed the 15 percent marginal tax bracket threshold, which, in 2012, was $70,000 of taxable income.
2. Use available strategies to help offset your taxable income in the same year as the conversion.

Additionally, don't overlook opportunities to defer or delay the actual payment of the tax—effectively amortizing the cost over as many years as you may like. For example, if you have $100,000 of embedded tax within your traditional IRA, and you own your residence free and clear, you may want to do the math regarding taking out a mortgage against your residence, and using the proceeds to pay the tax. Presuming the use of a traditional mortgage with a 30-year amortization, you are locking down this single action of shifting the debt from your IRA to your residence, other real estate, or other assets effectively changes the tax debt on the IRA to a manageable debt on your terms, with the interest being deductible as well (under current tax law).

Effectively, if you are stretching out the payment of the tax, this creates opportunities to recapture or recover the taxes paid (repayment of the debt) over time through earnings on the $150,000 that was not used to pay the tax upfront.

Discounting Methodology

Discounting methodologies, which have historically been used with the transfer of entity interests (e.g., the gift or sale of the limited partner's interest in a Family Limited Partnership, or FLP) during life or at death, adjusts the valuation of the assets or interests based on a lack of control, marketability, and liquidity. These discounts can range from 25 percent to 45 percent, subject to structure and asset characteristics.

In estate planning, this methodology is well established. IRS Revenue Ruling 59-60 lists relevant factors to be considered for valuing closely held corporations for estate and gift tax purposes, which include consideration for rights and privileges of stock ownership, as well as marketability of stock. Further, Revenue Ruling 68-609 approves the application of Rev. Rul. 59-60 factors in determining the fair market value of other business interests *for income and other tax purposes.*

The asset's liquidation value is generally reduced by a discount that properly reflects fair market value (FMV) for federal income tax purposes.

Certain assets, when held in an IRA, can also generate substantial discounts. The result is a reduction of taxable income from a Roth IRA conversion. Correspondingly, the tax on the conversion is reduced, while the long term value of the asset is not diminished.

The application of this within an IRA is summed up in an August 2010 article "How to Enhance Roth Conversions" in *Advisor Today Magazine*, written by Joe Luby:

> "Fair Market Value (FMV) must take into account the nature of the LLC or LLP units, including their illiquidity, lack of marketability and the fact that investors will generally hold minority interests in each fund. Thus a valuation adjustment may apply. In many cases, this adjustment may be from 25 percent to 35 percent from NAV. For example, a private fund with an NAV of $100 may be appraised at $70 for FMV purposes (adjustment discount of 30 percent)."

Please note—professional valuation of IRA assets is essential for this technique. Consult with your CPA, tax attorney, and other financial professionals for details.

Let's look at an example, using two hypothetical brothers. Dave has an IRA valued at $1M, invested in stocks, mutual funds, and cash. The conversion to Roth generates a 1099R for the full fair market value (FMV) from the IRA custodian for $1M (see Figure C.3).

Assuming no other measures are implemented, in his combined 40 percent federal/state tax rate, Dave will owe a tax debt of $400,000 of income tax.

$1,000,000 × 40 percent combined Federal and State = $400,000

If Dave does NOT convert to Roth, and his IRA doubles in value in 10 years, then his tax debt will have grown to 40 percent of $2M, or $800,000.

Additionally, Dave's portfolio is fully correlated to the equities markets, and for someone like Dave who is approaching retirement, tolerance for the level of market volatility will have to be very high.

Absent any planning to the contrary, Dave is not willing to bite the bullet today, so he does nothing. An unfortunate outcome, but considering a $400,000 tax bill, doing nothing is certainly understandable.

Let's take a look at Dave's brother Bob. Bob also has an IRA worth $1M, but he is invested in private and non-traded investments, such as REITs, Real Estate LPs, Equipment Leasing Trusts, Business Development Companies, and other Reg. D Royalty Funds.

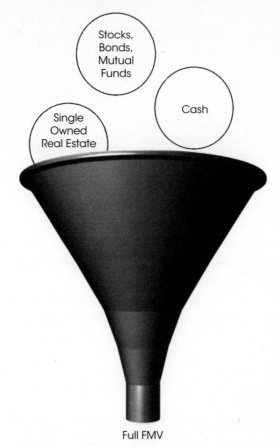

Full FMV

Figure C.3   Full FMV Assets

An independent analysis by a qualified appraiser results in a Fair Market Value Estimate of the IRA at the time of the conversion of $700,000 (Figure C.4).

Thus, the income tax realized in the conversion is $280,000 ($700,000 × 40 percent combined federal and state income tax rate). Because his IRA assets were in illiquid investments, combined with an independent Estimate of Fair Market Value, the resulting tax savings is $120,000 over his brother Dave.

$400,000 (No discount tax bill) − $280,000 (Discounted tax bill) = $120,000 tax saved

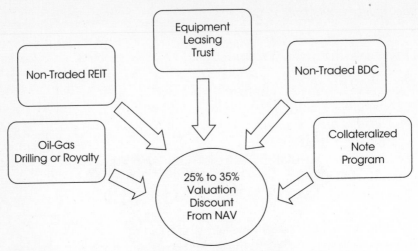

Figure C.4   Assets which May Qualify for IRS Value Discount

Additionally, Bob's assets within the Roth IRA are not correlated to the equities markets and should potentially have lower volatility in daily, weekly, or monthly changes in value that are common with the stock market.

Bob's goal was to sleep well at night and not feel tied to the daily headlines swaying the equity markets and his retirement accounts.

Beyond the Discount—Offsetting the Income from a Roth Conversion

Let's take a look at how additional planning, beyond the discount indicated above, can accomplish a significant reduction in the tax outcome.

After the asset level discount, reducing the IRA valuation down to $700,000, we are still left with a tax bill of $280,000.

Let's evaluate the potential mechanisms in reducing the Roth conversion tax bill further.

- Offsetting the conversion income with Energy IDCs
- Offsetting the conversion income with Accelerated Charitable Contributions
- Offsetting the conversion income with Renewable Energy Tax Credits
- Offsetting the conversion income with participation in a Conservation Easement Partnership

Energy Intangible Drilling Costs (IDCs)

If a client is suitable for oil/gas drilling investments with their associated IDCs, they could consider making an investment using after-tax funds and use the corresponding tax deduction to offset the conversion income of a Roth IRA rollover. IDCs are typically 70 percent to 100 percent of the invested amount.

For instance a client with established suitability has a CD with $50,000 in it and he feels this money would be appropriate in an oil/gas drilling partnership with a corresponding 90 percent IDC deduction. He makes the investment and during the same year converts $45,000 of a separate IRA account to a Roth IRA.

The reportable income increase of $45,000 for the Roth IRA conversion will be offset by the $45,000 IDC deduction of the new oil/gas investment.

$$\$50,000 \text{ oil/gas investment} \times 90 \text{ percent IDC}$$
$$= \$45,000 \text{ self-employment loss(income tax deduction)}$$

Alternative Minimum Tax levels apply and an investor looking to make a Roth conversion should work closely with the financial adviser and CPA to calculate the maximum IDCs they can use without hitting AMT levels. Not all is lost if you exceed your limit to deduct the IDCs. If you go over the amount which can be used in a particular year, the excess carries forward to the next year.

Donor Advised Funds (DAF)

If a client is charitably inclined and annually makes deductible gifts to charity, one potential solution is called a Donor Advised Fund (DAF) which can be used to accelerate his charitable deductions over several years to realize a present-year tax deduction.

A cash charitable deduction is able to reduce AGI by 50 percent, so if a client had $200,000 of income, the most they could place in a DAF in a given year would be $100,000, thus reducing their net income by that amount. They could place more, but the excess would have to carry forward to the next year's tax return.

DAFs are very beneficial, if a client is charitably inclined, to reduce the conversion amount of Roth IRAs.

Renewable Energy Tax Credits

As a means for the government to incentivize private participation in the development of green technologies such as wind, solar, clean coal, and so forth, they issue the companies which are involved in these technologies federal tax credits under IRS Section 45.

These companies have the ability to sell these tax credits to private individuals or corporations at a discount.

For instance, you could invest $65,000 in a green technology company and they would sell you company stock with an associated $100,000 federal tax credit. Effectively you just paid 65 cents on the dollar for tax.

Once you make your investment, you should never expect to see that money again as the start-up costs for these companies usually eats it all up. That being said, if you were going to pay taxes of $100,000 on your income, paying $65,000 for the green credits to satisfy the $100,000 federal tax bill keeps the remaining $35,000 in your pocket.

As an aside, if you buy too many tax credits, they can be carried forward 20 years or can be carried back to the prior year's tax return to reclaim taxes already paid.

Conservation Easements

In the early 1960s and 1970s, around large cities with tremendous development going on, a desire to preserve open space grew to the point where the government began incentivizing large land owners to not develop their land. The government would allow the land owner to give an appraisal of the developed land value after subtracting the value of the raw land to equal a charitable tax deduction.

For example, let's say a parcel of land is worth $1M. If this parcel was fully developed it would appraise for $5M. If the farmer donates the developmental right to the land as a conservation easement, the farmer will be given a charitable tax deduction of the difference between the appraised value and the raw land's value, in this case, $4M.

These tax deductions are only good for 12 years and many of these large land owners did not have enough income to make it worth their time, so they found a way to sell off their land-development rights to what are called Green Preservation Trusts. Treasury Regulation 1.170A-14 spells out how conversation easements can be used or sold.

In the previous example, an investor in a green preservation trust would receive $4 in charitable tax deductions for each $1 donated. Due to the charitable nature of this gift, it is limited to 30 percent of Adjusted Gross Income.

Back to Bob and His $280,000 Tax Bill

Let's go back to our example of Bob with his now reduced tax bill of $280,000. Let's say we combine two of the four additional means of reducing his out-of-pocket expense.

Using a conservation easement trust and noting a maximum of 30 percent AGI charitable reduction limit, Bob with $700,000 of income to report could use up to $210,000 of charitable deductions.

Conservation Easement Trust typically will provide a leverage ration of between 2 to 1 and 5 to 1. That means you invest $1 into one of these trusts and you will receive between $2 and $5 of charitable deductions. For our hypothetical example, let's assume a 4 to 1 ratio, meaning he could place $52,500 into one of these trusts and realize the $210,000 charitable deduction, knocking down his reportable income from $700,000 down to $490,000.

Then, assuming he is in the top 35 percent federal tax bracket on this reportable income. His total tax bill would be $171,500.

Using a Renewable Energy Tax Credit, it would take only $111,475 to offset the $171,500 tax bill.

Summarizing Bob's cost to eliminate his Roth IRA conversion tax bill:

IRA Valuation	Utilized Tax Strategy Discount	Out of Pocket Expense
$1,000,000 − 30% (discount) = $700,000	Illiquid Asset FMV report (30%)	$10,000
$700,000 −$210,000 ($700K × 30%) = $490,000	Conservation Easement Charitable Gift (Max 30% AGI)	$52,500 (assume 4 × 1 conservation easement leverage)
$490,000 × 35% Fed. Tax Bracket $171,500 owed	Renewable Energy Tax Credits Cost 65 cents on the dollar	$111,475 ($111,475 ÷ 65% = $171,500)
$171,500 −$171,500 Tax Credit $0 Tax Bill		Total Out of Pocket Expense: **$173,975**

Bob utilized several strategies for his Roth IRA conversion. The net cost out of Bob's pocket was $173,975 or 17.4 percent of the value of his IRA.

$$\$1,000,000 \times 17.39 \text{ percent} = \$173,975$$

My final recommendation was for Bob to refinance his home which was paid off, and convert this tax bill into an amortizing payment over 30 years.

With interest rates at historic lows, a 4 percent 30-year fixed mortgage of $173,975 would carry an annual payment of $9,972.

Considering he just converted $1M of an IRA into a tax free Roth IRA, his new Roth would only have to earn one percent per year to equal the payment. How much will his Roth IRA grow above the one percent per year depends on the investments, but with a well-diversified *Wealth Code* portfolio, Bob's future could be pretty bright.

Do the Math

Taxes are likely to be considerably higher in the future, which means that a Roth conversion today is more likely to be a good idea. But there's no substitute for a careful evaluation of your situation and consultation with a professional to determine if it makes sense for you. The bottom line is clear—to make the right decision you have to do the math.

What to Invest Roth IRA Balances In?

This is the third and final question. Over the long run, this is more important—from a tax savings standpoint—than any of the other issues I have discussed up to this point. After all, the Roth IRA assets are now under the shelter of tax-free growth, and you sure do not want to leave the funds invested in a low yielding bank environment. In fact, the Roth IRA is where you may want to position your more aggressive investment positions, especially if you are not anticipating needing the money during your lifetime, and it is considered a legacy asset. If you take advantage of the discounted valuation strategy, utilizing market alternative investment strategies which have timeframes ranging from three to 10 years or more, then your course is already set for the next few years.

Beyond this, what to invest in is a question best left to discussions with your investment professional based upon your specific risk tolerances and financial objectives. Many Roth IRA owners will name grandchildren, rather than children, as beneficiaries of Roth IRAs, in order to preserve the tax free treatment of the Roth IRA over another 20 to 30 years of the third generation's lifespan. This additional time frame may allow different types of investments to be considered, thus allowing time to be an ally in growing the legacy asset for future generations.

Appendix D: 1031 Real Estate Exchanges

What Is a Tax-Deferred Exchange?

In a typical transaction, the property owner is taxed on any gain realized from the sale. However, through a Section 1031 Exchange, the tax on the gain is deferred until some future date.

Section 1031 of the Internal Revenue Service Code provides that no gain or loss shall be recognized on the exchange of property held for productive use in a trade or business, or for investment. A tax-deferred exchange is a method by which a property owner trades one or more relinquished properties for one or more replacement properties of like-kind, while deferring the payment of federal income taxes and some state taxes on the transaction.

The theory behind Section 1031 is that when a property owner has reinvested the sale proceeds into another property, the economic gain has not been realized in a way that generates funds to pay any tax. In other words, the taxpayer's investment is still the same, only the form has changed (e.g., vacant land exchanged for apartment building). Therefore, it would be unfair to force the taxpayer to pay tax on a paper gain.

The like-kind exchange under Section 1031 is tax-deferred, not tax-free. When the replacement property is ultimately sold (not as part of another exchange), the original deferred gain, plus any additional gain realized since the purchase of the replacement property, is subject to tax.

What Are the Benefits of Exchanging Versus Selling?

- A Section 1031 exchange is one of the few techniques available to postpone or potentially eliminate taxes due on the sale of qualifying properties.
- By deferring the tax, you have more money available to invest in another property. In effect, you receive an interest-free loan from the federal government in the amount you would have paid in taxes.
- Any gain from depreciation recapture is postponed.
- You can acquire and dispose of properties to reallocate your investment portfolio without paying tax on any gain.

What Are the Different Types of Exchanges?

- Simultaneous Exchange: The exchange of the relinquished property for the replacement property occurs at the same time.
- Delayed Exchange: This is the most common type of exchange. A delayed exchange occurs when there is a time gap between the transfer of the relinquished property and the acquisition of the replacement property. A delayed exchange is subject to strict time limits, which are set forth in the Treasury Regulations.
- Build-to-Suit (Improvement or Construction) Exchange: This technique allows the taxpayer to build on or make improvements to the replacement property using the exchange proceeds.
- Reverse Exchange: A situation where the replacement property is acquired prior to transferring the relinquished property. The IRS has offered a safe harbor for reverse exchanges, as outlined in Rev. Proc. 2000-37, effective September 15, 2000. These transactions are sometimes referred to as parking arrangements and may also be structured in ways that are outside the safe harbor.
- Personal Property Exchange: Exchanges are not limited to real property. Personal property can also be exchanged for other personal property of like-kind or like-class.

What Are the Requirements for a Valid Exchange?

- Qualifying Property—Certain types of property are specifically excluded from Section 1031 treatment: property held primarily for sale; inventories; stocks, bonds or notes; other securities or evidences of indebtedness; interests in a partnership; certificates of trusts or beneficial interest; and chooses in action. In general, if property is not specifically excluded, it can qualify for tax-deferred treatment.
- Proper Purpose—Both the relinquished property and replacement property must be held for productive use in a trade or business or for investment. Property acquired for immediate resale will not qualify. The taxpayer's personal residence will not qualify.
- Like Kind—Replacement property acquired in an exchange must be like-kind to the property being relinquished. All qualifying real property located in the United States is like-kind. Personal property that is relinquished must be either like-kind or like-class to the personal property that is acquired. Property located outside the United States is not like-kind to property located in the United States.
- Exchange Requirement—The relinquished property must be exchanged for other property, rather than sold for cash and the proceeds used to buy the replacement property. Most deferred exchanges are facilitated by Qualified Intermediaries, who assist the taxpayer in meeting the requirements of Section 1031.

What Are the General Guidelines to Follow in Order for a Taxpayer to Defer All the Taxable Gain?

- The value of the replacement property must be equal to or greater than the value of the relinquished property.
- The equity in the replacement property must be equal to or greater than the equity in the relinquished property.
- The debt on the replacement property must be equal to or greater than the debt on the relinquished property.
- All of the net proceeds from the sale of the relinquished property must be used to acquire the replacement property.

When Can I Take Money Out of the Exchange Account?

Once the money is deposited into an exchange account, funds can only be withdrawn in accordance with the regulations. The taxpayer cannot receive any money until the exchange is complete. If you want to receive a portion of the proceeds in cash, this must be done before the funds are deposited with the Qualified Intermediary.

Can the Replacement Property Eventually Be Converted to the Taxpayer's Primary Residence or a Vacation Home?

Yes, but the holding requirements of Section 1031 must be met prior to changing the primary use of the property. Currently, the IRS has no specific regulations on holding periods. However, many experts feel that to be on the safe side, the taxpayer should hold the replacement property for a proper use for a period of at least one year.

If the owner later on wants to take advantage of the homeowner's exemption (currently up to $250,000 or $500,000 for a couple), there is now a five-year holding period requirement.

What Is a Qualified Intermediary?

A Qualified Intermediary (QI) is an independent party who facilitates tax-deferred exchanges pursuant to Section 1031 of the Internal Revenue Code. The QI cannot be the taxpayer or a disqualified person.

- Acting under a written agreement with the taxpayer, the QI acquires the relinquished property and transfers it to the buyer.
- The QI holds the sales proceeds to prevent the taxpayer from having actual or constructive receipt of the funds.
- Finally, the QI acquires the replacement property and transfers it to the taxpayer to complete the exchange within the appropriate time limits.

Why Is a Qualified Intermediary Needed?

The exchange ends the moment the taxpayer has actual or constructive receipt (i.e., direct or indirect use or control) of the proceeds from the sale of the relinquished property. The use of a QI is a safe harbor established by the Treasury Regulations. If the taxpayer meets the requirements of this safe harbor, the IRS will not consider the taxpayer to be in receipt of the funds. The sale proceeds go directly to the QI, who holds them until they are needed to acquire the replacement property. The QI then delivers the funds directly to the closing agent.

Can the Taxpayer Just Sell the Relinquished Property and Put the Money in a Separate Bank Account, Only to Be Used for the Purchase of the Replacement Property?

The IRS regulations are very clear. The taxpayer may not receive the proceeds or take constructive receipt of the funds in any way, without disqualifying the exchange.

If the Taxpayer Has Already Signed a Contract to Sell the Relinquished Property, Is It Too Late to Start a Tax-Deferred Exchange?

No, as long as the taxpayer has not transferred title or the benefits and burdens of the relinquished property, he or she can still set up a tax-deferred exchange. Once the closing occurs, it is too late to take advantage of a Section 1031 tax-deferred exchange, even if the taxpayer has not cashed the proceeds check.

Does the Qualified Intermediary Actually Take Title to the Properties?

No, not in most situations. The IRS regulations allow the properties to be deeded directly between the parties, just as in a normal sale transaction. The taxpayer's interests in the property purchase and sale contracts are assigned to the QI. The QI then instructs the property owner to deed the property directly to the appropriate party (for the relinquished property, its buyer, and for the replacement property, taxpayer).

What Are the Time Restrictions on Completing a Section 1031 Exchange?

A taxpayer has 45 days after the date that the relinquished property is transferred to properly identify potential replacement properties. The exchange must be completed by the date that is 180 days after the transfer of the relinquished property, or the due date of the taxpayer's federal tax return for the year in which the relinquished property was transferred, whichever is earlier. Thus, for a calendar year taxpayer, the exchange period may be cut short for any exchange that begins after October 17. However, the taxpayer can get the full 180 days by obtaining an extension of the due date for filing the tax return.

What if the Taxpayer Cannot Identify Any Replacement Property Within 45 Days or Close on a Replacement Property Before the End of the Exchange Period?

Unfortunately, there are no extensions available. If the taxpayer does not meet the time limits, the exchange will fail, and the taxpayer will have to pay any taxes arising from the sale of the relinquished property, *unless the IRS has expressly granted extensions in specified disaster area(s).*

Is There Any Limit to the Number of Properties That Can Be Identified?

There are three rules that limit the number of properties that can be identified. The taxpayer must meet the requirements of at least one of these rules:

- Three-Property Rule: The taxpayer may identify up to three potential replacement properties, without regard to their value; or
- 200 percent Rule: Any number of properties may be identified, but their total value cannot exceed twice the value of the relinquished property, or
- 95 percent Rule: The taxpayer may identify as many properties as he wants, but before the end of the exchange period,

the taxpayer must acquire replacement properties with an aggregate fair market value equal to at least 95 percent of the aggregate fair market value of all the identified properties.

What Are the Requirements to Properly Identify Replacement Property?

Potential replacement property must be identified in writing, signed by the taxpayer, and delivered to a party to the exchange who is not considered a disqualified person. A disqualified person is anyone who has a relationship with the taxpayer that is so close that the person is presumed to be under the control of the taxpayer. Examples include blood relatives, and any person who is or has been the taxpayer's attorney, accountant, investment banker, or real estate agent within the two years prior to the closing of the relinquished property. The identification cannot be made orally.

Are Section 1031 Exchanges Limited Only to Real Estate?

No. Any property that is held for productive use in a trade or business, or for investment, may qualify for tax-deferred treatment under Section 1031. In fact, many exchanges are multi-asset exchanges, involving both real property and personal property.

What Is a Multi-Asset Exchange?

A multi-asset exchange involves both real and personal property. For example, the sale of a hotel will typically include the underlying land and buildings, as well as the furnishings and equipment. If the taxpayer wants to exchange the hotel for a similar property, he would exchange the land and buildings as one part of the exchange. The furnishings and equipment would be separated into groups of like-kind or like-class property, with the groups of relinquished property being exchanged for groups of replacement property.

Although the definition of like-kind is much narrower for personal property and business equipment, careful planning will allow the taxpayer to enjoy the benefits of an exchange for the entire relinquished property, not just for the real estate portion.

What Is a Reverse Exchange?

A reverse exchange, sometimes called a *parking arrangement,* occurs when a taxpayer acquires a Replacement Property before disposing of their Relinquished Property. A pure reverse exchange, where the taxpayer owns both the Relinquished and Replacement properties at the same time, is not allowed. The actual acquisition of the parked property is done by an Exchange Accommodation Titleholder (EAT) or parking entity.

Is a Reverse Exchange Permissible?

Yes. Although the Treasury Regulations still do not apply to reverse exchanges, the IRS issued safe harbor guidelines for reverse exchanges on September 15, 2000, in Revenue Procedure 2000-37. Compliance with the safe harbor creates certain presumptions that will enable the transaction to qualify for Section 1031 tax-deferred exchange treatment.

How Does a Reverse Exchange Work?

In a typical reverse (or parking) exchange, the Exchange Accommodation Titleholder (EAT) takes title to (parks) the replacement property and holds it until the taxpayer is able to sell the relinquished property. The taxpayer then exchanges with the EAT, who now owns the replacement property. An exchange structured within the safe harbor of Rev. Proc. 2000-37 cannot have a parking period that goes beyond 180 days.

What Happens if the Exchange Cannot Be Completed Within 180 Days?

If the reverse exchange period exceeds 180 days, then the exchange is outside the safe harbor of Rev. Proc. 2000-37. With careful planning, it is possible to structure a reverse exchange that will go beyond 180 days, but the taxpayer will lose the presumptions that accompany compliance with the safe harbor.

Can the Proceeds from the Relinquished Property Be Used to Make Improvements to the Replacement Property?

Yes. This is known as a Build-to-Suit or Construction or Improvement Exchange. It is similar in concept to a reverse exchange. The taxpayer is not permitted to build on property she already owns. Therefore, an unrelated party or parking entity must take title to the replacement property, make the improvements, and convey title to the taxpayer before the end of the exchange period.

What Is the Difference Between Realized Gain and Recognized Gain?

Realized gain is the increase in the taxpayer's economic position as a result of the exchange. In a sale, tax is paid on the realized gain. Recognized gain is the taxable gain. Recognized gain is the lesser of realized gain or the net boot received.

What Is Boot?

Boot is any property received by the taxpayer in the exchange that is not like-kind to the relinquished property. Boot is characterized as either cash boot or mortgage boot. Realized Gain is recognized to the extent of net boot received.

What Is Mortgage Boot?

Mortgage boot consists of liabilities assumed or given up by the taxpayer. The taxpayer pays mortgage boot when he assumes or places debt on the replacement property. The taxpayer receives mortgage boot when he is relieved of debt on the replacement property. If the taxpayer does not acquire debt that is equal to or greater than the debt that was paid off, they are considered to be relieved of debt. The debt relief portion is taxable, unless offset when netted against other boot in the transaction.

What Is Cash Boot?

Cash boot is any boot received by the taxpayer, other than mortgage boot. Cash boot may be in the form of money or other property.

What Are the Boot Netting Rules?
- Cash boot paid offsets cash boot received
- Cash boot paid offsets mortgage boot received (debt relief)
- Mortgage boot paid (debt assumed) offsets mortgage boot received
- Mortgage boot paid does not offset cash boot received

What if I Bought the Property as a Single Person, and I Would Like to Acquire the Replacement Property Together with My Spouse?

The most conservative way is to stay consistent and complete the exchange the same way it was started and to add the spouse after the completion of the exchange. An exception can be made if there is a lender requirement that the spouse has to be added in order to qualify for a loan. If an exchange is planned well ahead of time, another solution would be to add the spouse to the title of the currently held property. Timing should be discussed with the CPA.

I Closed Escrow on My First Replacement Property Within the 45-Day Identification Period. Can I Now Identify Three More Properties Within My 45-Day Identification Period?

If you are using the three-property rule, the completed acquisition counts as one and you may identify only up to two additional properties.

How Do I Identify Two Different Properties (or Percentages of Ownership Through a DST) Covered by One Purchase Contract?

If the properties could be sold separately at a later date, they should be identified as two properties.

About the Author

Jason Vanclef was born in Eugene, Oregon, and grew up in Palo Alto, California. He attended Cal Poly, San Luis Obispo, earning a B.S. in Biological Chemistry. Over the years, Jason has felt that this degree taught him to think "outside the box" versus traditional degrees in Business or Finance. After 5 years as a Homicide/Narcotic Senior Criminalist with the California Sheriff's Department, Jason created Vanclef Financial Group, Inc., a Los Angeles based comprehensive financial services practice, offering planning services to a wide range of individuals and small businesses. For over a decade, he has developed extensive experience in asset preservation, retirement and estate planning strategies. Jason has mentored and coached hundreds of financial advisers on his contrarian and somewhat unique viewpoint about the necessary addition of tangible assets to a financial portfolio. To bring his fascinating investment philosophy to a wider audience in 2010, Jason hosted The Wealth Code Radio Show Sunday mornings on KABC 790AM talk radio Los Angeles. Jason has also been featured in June 2012 Forbes Advisor Spotlight, and various TV, Radio, and Print appearances from Time, Fox, CNBC, The Balancing Act, Sirius Satellite Radio and so forth.

Jason is a Series 24 (General Securities Principal), Series 7 (General Securities Representative) and Series 66 (Investment Advisor Representative) licensed financial representative, and also has his California Life Insurance license. Additional certifications include Certified Estate Planner (CEP) and Registered Financial Consultant (RFC) professional designations. Jason and wife Tami have two sons, Grant and Cole, and make their home in the community of San Luis Obispo, California.

Index